Drake Travis knows how to create faith in people. As he pours out his heart in his book, *Healing Power*, Drake inspires the readers and sets a new fire in them. Drawing on many years of experience, Drake Travis calls the church to greater works. It is obvious that he desires the body of Christ to be powerful and victorious.

—HAROLD R. EBERLE
PRESIDENT, WORLDCAST MINISTRIES AND PUBLISHING

Real people, real testimonies. A must-read for those wanting to see healing ministry return to the local church.

—PAUL STADLER, DIRECTOR
HEALING ROOMS OF YAKIMA, WASHINGTON

I was so stirred by the biblical data and authentic stories of divine healing that after reading this book, I pledged in my heart to not only win all the souls I can to Jesus, but to be deliberate in consistently offering the gift of healing in my evangelistic crusades throughout the world. I have occasionally offered to pray for the ill in my ministry; however, I will offer to do so at each of my engagements from here on.

Healing Power: Voice Activated deftly links the Great Commission with Christ's mandate to heal the sick and cast out demons. But Drake also argues rightly that to experience miracles, signs, and wonders, the heart must be right with God and childlike in faith.

Simply put, Drake Travis is right. He argues from the Bible and through authentic testimonies that divine healing is alive and well. It did not die with the Apostles in A.D. 100. This is a great read. I like his in-depth perspective and theological analysis of healing followed by practical application. It sounds just like the epistles of the New Testament. I will add that the way Drake dealt with the matter of Paul's "thorn in the flesh" is the best I've ever read on the topic.

This book is energizing for anyone who prays for the sick—even people who are struggling and discouraged in this area of their faith. It will clearly shed new light upon those who have been willfully ignorant about the signs and wonders that are still possible and happening in the modern world.

There have been many books written about healing. This one, however, is much more; it's deeper, it's helpful, it's exciting, it enhanced my view. I honestly had never read anything like this.

—REV. MATTHEW J. WELDE
INTERNATIONAL EVANGELIST
BOARD MEMBER, THE U.S. CENTER FOR WORLD MISSION

HEALING
POWER VOICE
ACTIVATED

DRAKE TRAVIS

CREATION
HOUSE
A STRANG COMPANY

HEALING POWER, VOICE ACTIVATED by Drake Travis
Published by Creation House
A Strang Company
600 Rinehart Road
Lake Mary, Florida 32746
www.strangbookgroup.com

Unless otherwise noted, all Scripture quotations are from the Holy Bible, New
International Version of the Bible. Copyright © 1973, 1978, 1984, International
Bible Society. Used by permission.

Scripture quotations marked KJV are from the King James Version of the Bible.

Design Director: Bill Johnson
Cover design by Amanda Potter

Library of Congress Control Number: 2009924880
International Standard Book Number: 978-1-59979-765-6

09 10 11 12 13—9 8 7 6 5 4 3 2 1
Printed in the United States of America

I AM GRATEFUL TO:

- My aunt Ruthie Travis, who counseled me, "Drake, you must write."

- Harold Eberle, Paul Stadler, Garrett Grobler, Karen Hull, and Brian T. Wilson. I thank you again for assisting.

- My late friend, Mario R. Liberatore (1958–2005), a fellow pilgrim who helped in countless ways. I asked him to go a mile with me and he went fifty. And then he "went on ahead."

- Dr. Keith Bailey, whose grasp of this healing topic, immense knowledge of theology, and willing, helpful spirit are a true blessing.

- Larry Fookes, your mentoring and friendship is better than a personal GPS.

- Rick and Terry Welch, your encouragement has always been wind in my sails.

- Urb and Liz Travis, dad and mom, who helped in reading through the drafts, again. Where would I be without you? I mean, really?

- Larry and Diep Miller, this faith thing…you don't just talk about it, you live it. Thank you.

- The warm hearts and families at Connections Church in Yakima, Washington. You live the joy of the Lord with your welcome and love.

- The dear folks at Wiley Heights Covenant Church in Washington. You must be the happiest Swedes outside Minnesota!

- My children: Brooke, Valentina, Michael, Darek, Luba, Marshall, Hannah, Daniela, Josiah, and Matthew. I am sorry that each of you has been orphaned in your own way. I am sorry that parents have died for most of you. I am sorry that some of you were forced to spend dismal years in a communist orphanage. Yet I am grateful to be the one that you call "Daddy."

- My wife, Serena Nevaeh Travis. Day after day you thrill my heart with your love, cheer, beauty, affection, competence, humility, laughter, and fascinating spirit. You make me look at life anew and ask of God, "All this, and heaven, too?" Thank you again, dear.

CONTENTS

FOREWORD

H EALING POWER: VOICE Activated is a fine book that hits the soul like a burst of wind. Drake comes across very enthusiastically about the fact that healing is done at God's will, by His voice, and that we indeed are the ones who are called to speak for God and heal in God's name as we walk through a hurting world.

Drake speaks from firsthand experience, which is very persuasive. He isn't writing theoretically from a pedestal about what ought to happen. He walks us right through the venues where healing is taking place in our day.

His use of Scripture is excellent and well applied. I appreciate his weaving together of accurate scholarship through the draft and stories, and he does so in a relaxed manner. His contemporary style makes for easy reading that I think people will find enjoyable.

I feel a kinship with this topic since I myself have experienced miraculous healings on several occasions. I claim no special powers but have simply anointed and prayed for people, as is taught in James 5. Through obedience to the Scriptures, I have seen amazing miracles in my over fifty years of ministry in Vietnam, Guam, Hong Kong, and in the USA.

I also feel kinship with the Travis family, having been raised on the same mission field as the author's father from the 1930s through the 1950s. I was the youngest of seven children; Drake's father was the youngest of five children. We were both blessed to have missionary fathers who always prayed first for their children before taking us to the hospital. None of us were disinclined to hospitals; it's just that we were healed prior to arriving so we never saw the inside of one!

I can tell you that healing ministry is not a newly discovered aspect of ministry for this author. It intrigues me that the beliefs, theology, and amazing stories in the book you are about to read are simply a continuum of Drake Travis' grandparents' lives and deeds—a couple who began ministering in Southeast Asia in the 1920s.

In the course of time, it was almost comical for me to be "over" Drake's grandparents when I was appointed as superintendent of the evangelical mission in Vietnam. I was in my early forties at the time and they were in their early eighties with forty more years of ministry experience than me! During winter 1975, as the fall of Saigon was looming, they sailed from Vietnam to the USA for the last time. Within weeks I departed Vietnam myself. The final day in Vietnam was the most frenetic and painfully impassioned day I have ever known. It was spent atop the US Embassy loading people onto helicopters. Perhaps you have seen the photos from April 30, 1975.

I say all that to express that I know this family. I knew this family two generations prior to Drake. I know the Travis family's passion to see people saved into Christ's kingdom and healed in body and soul.

After leaving Vietnam and two other mission fields, I went to work as the president of Evangelism Explosion (EE) in Coral Ridge, Florida. Dr. James Kennedy and I teamed up for twelve years as I headed the EE ministry until Dr. Kennedy's death in 2007.

Since I have been involved in evangelism all my life, I appreciate the emphasis the author gives to evangelism and healing as partners, not as ministry matters that are in isolation of one another or in competition with each other. Too often evangelism is thought to be a gift for the zealous only, and healing is often labeled as the calling upon the fanatical or the wild prophet types. Neither is so. Healing and evangelism are wedded assignments given us by the Holy Spirit. Jesus usually did them together. Drake reminds us of this obvious fact, which some have forgotten. The subject is too overlooked by conservative Christians, so the book meets a great need in those circles.

To sum up my feelings and thoughts: this is a very good book. It's a fine read that you will find to be a blessing and an inspiration. May God use this message to touch and change many hearts and minds. May it touch you also as you read this, and may it spur you to touch many others with our healing and saving Christ.

—DR. TOM STEBBINS
MISSIONARY AND FORMER
EXECUTIVE VICE PRESIDENT OF EVANGELISM EXPLOSION

PREFACE

A Chat with a Friend

I was eight years old when the seeds of this book were first planted in my heart. It was breakfast time in the late 1960s. Father was reading from the Gospels as he had read to us every morning. That morning's story was about the paralyzed man being let down through a hole in the roof—as told in Luke 5. The hope of the four men, who were unable to reach Jesus through the crowd, was that this would get His attention. They knew Jesus could heal their friend. So their thinking was that the daring stunt of tearing a hole in the roof of a stranger's home was worth the risk.

The plan worked. Jesus declared the man to be forgiven of his sins and He spoke healing to him. He could walk again. The reaction to Jesus doing a healing was the usual: the regular people rejoiced and the religious leaders grumbled.

"What a clever story," I thought to myself while chomping my breakfast. Personally I had asked Jesus into my own heart at five so I had been a Christian for three years. But hey, I was in grammar school. Who, at that age, is counting anything besides the days until vacations, birthday parties, and holidays? I knew that these stories about Jesus and His healing power were real. But then again, so was Jack and the Beanstalk, Santa Claus, Peter Pan... The fantastic was all very real to me, and healing stories were part of it all. I did not have any special abilities to understand Jesus at eight years old. Truth, fiction, fact, reality, perception, dreams, the latent, the apparent, the mystical—it was all a happy mental mush to me as a third grader.

But that morning as father was finishing this story, and I was finishing my cereal, things ended a bit differently. He completed the story and... was silent for a moment. It was odd. He never did that. The breakfast Bible story time had always ended abruptly, then we went straight to prayer, then cleared the table, then brushed teeth, grabbed our books, said goodbyes, did our hugs, and then biked to our Christian school a mile away. It was like clockwork and we were accustomed to this. But that morning my mind took a turn and it has never turned back.

The silence following the story gripped me. It felt like the pause button had been pressed on life itself. To me the quiet was just as piercing as the story. Father said, "Kids..." And finishing the last of my breakfast, milk running down my chin, I froze and gulped. Staring us straight in the eye, he continued, "Kids, this story is real." That incident that morning was virtually the most memorable moment of my entire childhood. It even outshined days at Disneyland. I had forgotten about it for many years, but the longer I live, the louder and clearer that moment, that story, that sentence, and that memory becomes.

Staring us straight in the eye, he continued, "Kids, this story is real."

Somewhere in the research, layout, and writing of this book I realized that all the healings I was studying either built up to or flowed from this watershed healing of the paralytic being let down through the roof. All the healings in the Old Testament are readying us for that great statement of Jesus: that He grants forgiveness; that He proves it through healing; and that it is Jesus who is the One who does the healing. Subsequently every healing in the Bible (and history) can be perceived in light of this healing in Mark 2:1.

It was also somewhere during the writing of this book that I first remembered hearing this paralytic-lowered-through-the-roof story decades prior. The salient memory came back and I realized it was God all along who was planning for me to write this book so many years later. That first hint, which was dropped in my life as a third grader, steered me for life.

I say that to tell you that God has plans for you, too. As you read this, it is my prayer that you fully realize God has tipped over a barrel full of gifts marked for you to use for His kingdom and glory. His gifts are *not* out of reach. They are as accessible as He is. Call His name and learn. Taste and see.

Use them and be blessed. Bless innumerable people with what you have been given already. Open them and enjoy your life!

Just a word about my style: some of the healings that are looked at in depth are analyzed from multiple angles in different settings. In realizing this as you read, one may ponder along the way whether my major in college was redundancy. It was not. What may seem to be repetitive is simply reiteration from another slant for the purpose of embellishment; for bringing full light onto a healing incident. Jesus' healings are worth it. This is especially evident when there is a pivotal healing that casts a long shadow over one or many other aspects of healing ministry. Seriously, I do not mean to be redundant. If things like this bother anyone, perhaps that person should tear Mark and Luke out of their Bibles, yes? For more than 90 percent of those two Gospels is redundant, seen elsewhere in the other Gospels. The prophets say hundreds and hundreds of times, "Follow and worship God, don't sin, and be blessed. Follow God, don't sin, or be cursed." And do we get it? Does the world get it? In reading the prophets, many react, "I read this already. It all sounds the same. OK, OK, I get it!" Really? As our culture lurches toward greater evil, it does not heed the warnings of God. What is God to do? Say it again? Perhaps He should. Repetition enables learning, so I employ it to a point.

As for the gender-sensitive, politically correct (politically concocted) culture that we are forced to tolerate today, I must speak for myself here. I do not play along with that game. My wife has my feminine side. I do not have a feminine side that I am trying to get in touch with. That is her job and she does that better than any feminist or metro-man could ever hope to. So in my writing I simply refer to the masculine. For example, "Jesus heals a man to bless him and change his life." That refers to everyone, every gender, not just *that* man. I do not liable-qualify everything with mouthfuls of possessive pronouns in hopes of not offending the forever irritable. For example, I don't blather on, "When Jesus heals a man or woman or boy or girl, He does so to bless him or her so that he or she can live his or her life to testify that sheesh or himsher that he or she is…" Enough already! My high school English teacher, who for thirty-five-plus years was rated as one of the most effective teachers in the entire state of California, instructed us that speaking in the masculine includes everyone. That is what *she* taught us. And that is good enough for me.

Also, all pronouns that refer to divinity are capitalized; any reference to the Trinity, God, Father, Jesus, Holy Spirit, or any reference to any facet of *Him* is capitalized. I think it makes for a clearer read. When the rules of grammar allow it, I prefer to capitalize the word *Cross*, for it is the capital issue of history. In my opinion it is proper for a Judeo-Christian to refer to ultimate reality in such a manner.

I hope you perceive and experience this book as a chat with a friend. I do not lecture on and on about what *you* need to do, telling you that *you* need to pray, *you* need to have faith, *you* need to get a move on, *you* need to heal, *you* need to be bold, you, you, you... No. I speak in terms of "us," what *we* can do in Jesus' name. If Christ is your Savior, then I am your brother. Do not think otherwise. I walk this pilgrimage with you. I am a student of our Savior, also. I am writing and talking *with* you in the following pages, not *at* you. I am cheering you on and you have my brotherly love in your pilgrimage. So as you read, let's walk this road together. Do not think of me as some expert with a colossal ministry operating from a marble tower.

[A fascinating journey awaits all who join in.

Enough about my mannerisms. Let's be done with the lesser things. Reach out for God's healing hand and take a walk with His Son. A fascinating journey awaits all who join in. And to those who ask Jesus to increase their faith and climb to a new level with Him, nothing will ever look the same again. For being used of God to heal people in the family of God and to build up, strengthen, and grow the family of God is what our lives with our Father is all about. I pray you are blessed and filled with His Holy Spirit. There is a River of Life flowing over the earth today. Jump in.

one

ENTERING the MARVELOUS REALM of DIVINE HEALING

S IX PALLBEARERS SOLEMNLY carried the casket while mourners had gathered to remember the life of young Charles. Despite many warnings from his grandmother to repent, Charles refused to live a wholesome life. Though she had passed away, Charles was still caught up with a gang. Being entangled in a life of crime, the risk caught up with him and he was shot through the chest and killed in a gunfight. As he felt his life ebb away, Charles describes himself descending down a shaft the size of an elevator and coming to rest at the bottom of a deep, dark, dirt-walled chamber. The top was so far above him by now that the light of day was far from visible. It seemed as though days passed while he sat there alone, numb, cold, and frightened.

Eventually, a hideous, giant man-like creature came into his presence and picked him up growling, "Your time is up. I have come for you." Charles struggled, but fighting this huge being was hopeless as there was no escape. The creature was carrying him down a long hallway that had a dull, orange glow in the distance. Charles noticed that the hallways were lined with windows, like dioramas in a museum. In one window, he caught a glimpse of his grandmother out in a shimmering field. She waved at him as he was carried past. Charles was entranced with the beauty that surrounded his grandmother. Each blade of grass glistened like an entire rainbow of its own. The pond that seemed to be the "Crystal Sea" sparkled like melted diamonds that danced in a light that was warmed without burning and brightened without blinding. The swans moved like angels. The beauty of it all! Charles realized that his grandmother was in heaven and he was not!

What had Grandma said about getting to heaven? She said that Jesus was the only Way. He broke out of his mesmerizing stupor and struggled anew against the creature that had him locked against his huge chest. "Let me go. I don't belong here. I want out of here!" Charles was practically screaming by now.

"Oh no, you had your chance and now you belong to me," was the creature's reply as he marched onward toward the menace of that fiery abyss.

"No! I don't want to be here. I don't want this. I want out. I want Jesus! I want to get to Jesus!" Charles screamed. As he screamed "I want to get to Jesus!" Charles *revived* inside his own coffin and began pounding on the inside of the lid. The visibly shaken pallbearers panicked and dropped the coffin. They scrambled to find a screwdriver and before long had the lid opened.

"I want to get to Jesus!" Charles blurted out again the instant he sat up out of his coffin. The mourners who had gathered were frozen in shock. Some of the mourners scuttled and ran away in sheer fright. The officiating minister at the funeral succumbed to reality. He closed his Bible with the funeral program inside, raised a hand to Charles, and announced his question, "Would you care to share a word with us?" Charles then gave the address to the people. He spoke about what he had witnessed the eight days prior, and how the desperate desire for Jesus had brought him back to life and secured his eternal life. You heard right—Charles preached at his own funeral! Those who stayed listened to Charles as he testified of his experience of the dead coming to life again: his life was being returned to him and his burial was canceled and here he is doing the preaching! All who were at the funeral who had not yet trusted Christ for salvation were saved that day—100 percent of them.

This story is not an allegory. It is true. A colleague of mine knows the pastor.

Think of the science aspect of someone being raised or brought back from the dead. The number is too great to ponder, but it has been estimated that there are fourteen trillion cells in the human body. At the point of death, decay begins immediately in all plasma-based cells; the bones obviously decay slower than the other cells. Doctors insist that the dead immediately be removed from the living, especially in a hospital where there are people needing healing. The power of death is that pervasive, that contagious. To this day, death remains the insurmountable problem. But as demonstrated with

Charles' experience, and the resurrection stories in the Bible, God can reverse death in a moment. And since God is able to this, the real question is what is God *not* able to do?

God's healing touch is exciting, rejuvenating, and refreshing. The word *relief* is most commonly used to describe healing. Such relief means to have life restored. Healing is a reviving promise that God is present and that He cares deeply for our life and soul.

And for those yet searching, God's healing touch can seem like trying to find buried treasure. Will it be found or not? Receiving healing can be like stumbling upon gold that has been tucked away underground by the forces of nature since the beginning of time. Finding His treasure is such a marvel that it literally overwhelms and can completely change the landscape of one's life. And at the same time, some others can spend their entire lives hunting for "treasure" only to come away empty handed. Along with that, they can also feel like their life has been wasted. And then there is the envy directed toward those who appear to just stumble upon the treasure of divine healing. Both scenarios will leave everyone wondering why. Why does one particular person experience the exhilaration of finding the gems of healing, while someone else does not even when they earnestly looked for it?

Alberta has prayed for the gift of healing for well more than fifty years. Almost sixty years, in fact. She claims that God simply never gave her the gift. Conversely there is a certain Todd Bentley who got saved out of a dismal home of drug abuse. He was headed for certain death at a young age. Within a month of salvation he was given the gift of healing. And it is not a restrained endowment either. Straight away his peers were filled with wonder at what God had done in this man's life. His blessing immediately drew a staff to surround and support him. Soon an offering was taken that launched him into ministry. From 1998–2008 he traveled to more than fifty-five countries doing healing crusades and revival services. Only God knows how many have been healed and saved through his ministry that was named FreshFire.

I personally have seen the FreshFire team minister while assisting at two of their crusades. Granted, the style is very different. Some observers would even say "peculiar" to the point of being unnerved. All the same, the results of Todd's ministry were nothing short of spectacular. And why would it not be? He ministered Jesus. Jesus drew enormous crowds and touched tens of thousands regularly. Would not those who serve Jesus operate in a similar manner?

That being said, I need to be frank and state that it remains to be seen what the future holds for Todd. The FreshFire Team has resumed without him following the Lakeland, Florida, Revival of 2008. See their new changes at www.itransform.ca. Todd was thrust from oblivion to ten years of international ministry and needs some intense therapeutic rest and counsel. The FreshFire Team is restructuring and needs our prayers and grace. Whatever comes, Todd has been used of God mightily because he was willing to be. If someone is going to judge Todd, they better ignore most of their Bible because it is the story wherein 80 percent of the characters, including all of our heroes, failed. Yet, still we can be blessed by their Psalms and struggles and stories.

Healing evangelist William Branham worked to exhaustion and died in his early fifties. He could have paced himself and lasted another twenty to thirty years, but what happened is what happened. His untimely death does not cancel the thousands of amazing sermons he delivered, nor does it undo the healings that were administered via the Holy Spirit's using William Branham.

An astonishing story is the ministry of Bill Johnson. Bill is a fourth-generation pastor in the far north of California, who teaches on healing and trains droves of people in healing and prophetic ministry. You will not hear a better English speaker on the topic of healing, by the way. Bill instills such servant-gallantry in his students that they launch into society and touch lives for Christ in ways that surpass the Book of Acts. Their attitude is that the world is God's chapel and healing is not to be confined to a church building. Those who are trained in his ministry actually perform more healings outside the church than inside it.

There are even students and staff at his training school who, when they go into town to practice their healing gift, will wait by the handicapped parking signs at stores and plazas. This way they are sure to meet more people to pray for! It is just like Jesus going to the Pool of Bethesda in John

5. The handicapped and infirmed would wait there. So if one wanted to heal the sick, here they were. In America today, if one wants to minister to the handicapped, it's rather smart to set up and wait by a handicapped parking spot. It is a sure bet that the needy will be found. Bill Johnson's students figure if we just wait there, they will come. When we have such boldness and are certain God is going to move, then we act like it. I personally had never heard of such boldness prior to Bill's telling us this live at a conference.

Randy Clark is another man with a vigorous healing ministry. He holds training conferences and leads mission trips and crusades that the interested can join him on. Randy was the minister who humbly went to Toronto Airport Vineyard church years ago to have meetings for a few days. When revival fell, the meetings were extended for weeks on end. People came, met the Spirit anew, were touched, blessed, filled, changed, and commissioned. People have left there renewed and gone on to literally flip whole countries upside down with the healing power of the gospel.

Yes, there is healing going on in our world. One missionary writes me, "Healing is happening in Africa—just come on down and be a part of it all!" The dead are being raised. Food is being multiplied. This may sound too fantastic to be true, but when one meets numerous people who are giving parallel testimonies, even the skeptical must deduce that it is not possible for so many people to be making up stories in unison.

At the same time, people today (usually Westerners) can view healing ministry as a phantom blessing. They think it floats up here or there, or that it is some sort of a four-leaf clover that is a rare and fortunate find. They think that receiving or ministering healing is guesswork, like finding buried treasure as mentioned above. In God's realm however, healing is not so. Healing is a normal blessing. It is as normal for God to pour Himself out and touch both His children *and* those He is calling to Himself as it is for people to breathe, fish to swim, and flowers to bloom. Healing is what God does. He blesses, restores, and builds. Those who are His, who are owned by Him, are living and ministering at their best when they *expect* to do what God does. It is pure excitement to live on the edge of the Holy Spirit's agenda, constantly eager, waiting, and wondering what God is going to do next.

[The book you are reading is an invitation to immersion into a whole new way of living.

Part of the scheme here, by way of introduction, is to make it clear from the start that this is not a quickie healing book. The purpose herein is not to give the "three easy steps" to becoming a healer in your town. No, I am not teaching a three-hour course that will have anyone become a healing superman just by "stepping into a spiritual phone booth" somewhere, or anything of the like. The book you are reading is an invitation to immersion into a whole new way of living. You are being invited to change the way you think about your life, calling, future, abilities, and God's grace. All of this is waiting to be poured upon you with even more bounty than you can dream. It is inspiration and a reference meant to give a sky-high perspective along with resources to put people on a path to a much more vibrant life and ministry than what is currently being experienced. The goal is to prompt change that will put souls onto an apostolic and prophetic pilgrimage.

Apostolic means to be the first wave to go into an area or to practice a certain flagship ministry. This is originally what is meant by the apostles being the *first* ones that Jesus sent out. And *prophetic* means to be one who speaks for God. There are other books listed in the back so as to open the mind to whole new worlds where the power of God is flowing. They are to further urge you to jump into the stream where Living Water is flowing. There are Web sites to browse that regularly inform of healing schools starting, conferences being held, or crusades that are being planned. All of these are presented in the recommended reading list in the back of this book.

The first step in thinking anew about healing is to enter the realm of God's thoughts about healing. I will say it again: to God, with Whom nothing is impossible, healing is normal. Sadly, there are so many millions of people (perhaps billions is more precise) who think that normal life is "over here," while miraculous living in God's blessing is "way over there." Too many think that there is a mysterious barrier between what they experience regularly and what their soul longs for. Do we realize that God views much of our resolve to live in monotonous drudgery as abnormal? When we resign to such a "normal" life of boredom, God sees that as reticent cowardice, even disobedience, not "pious and faithful."

> ...to God, with Whom nothing is impossible, healing is normal.

And yet, think about "normal." What is normal? Universally, people view *their* personal history and experience as normal. But in reality, our familiar perspectives are jaded, for ultimately nothing is "normal." For example, an Eskimo near the Arctic Circle has a certain view of normal life. An oilrig worker in Texas will have another. So too does a Dutch fisherman, a Southern Baptist elder in Georgia, a Pentecostal in West Virginia, a shipping tycoon in Greece, and a homeless man in South America. All will give an extremely varied opinion on what they assume "normal" to be.

Normal is whatever one has become accustomed to. So the goal herein is to encourage us to leave our mental comfort zone (our "thought ruts!") to launch into the realm where God operates—to where He operates phenomenally, regularly, and effortlessly. It is a spiritual world that has more to do with real life than does the physical world! It is a place where God longs to bring us and turn us into vivacious saints that dream with God, become like His Son, and operate entirely in the Holy Spirit. It is here that we do what He does. Once a person gets a taste of being on assignment with the Holy Spirit, of being on a mission that bursts through what was once thought impossible, there is no going back to the hum drum of what has become cemented as "normal" in the minds of most. It is a thrill to let God raise our definition of the word *normal* to what the angels, not men, view to be normal.

God...is not impressed with the false piety
that shuns His kind and gracious gifts.

When our souls abide in the earthly definition of "normal," it is a disappointment to God. We are exercising no faith and God is not pleased. What follows is that our lives become an immense disappointment to us as well. To illustrate, can we imagine the heartache that parents would have if their children did not awake one Christmas morning at the crack of dawn? The stockings had been hung by the chimney with care and gifts were neatly wrapped and arranged around the tree to be hip deep next to their little ones. Then comes Christmas morning and the kids opt to sleep in! Say what? The parents go and wake the kids wondering if the kids have the flu or something. Finally the children rouse with much prodding. The children whine, groggy from sleep as they are walked to the Christmas tree. They prefer to be in bed. Amid this strange scenario the parents exchange a glance that asks in quiet desperation, "What happened to these kids during the night?" Finally the kids are walked to the tree and their pile of gifts. The parents squeal "Merry Christmas," and the kid's response is one big mope. One of them offers, "Can we skip the gifts this year? Can't we just have a normal morning? Isn't it more important to be spiritual than to desire gifts?" The parents' hearts would sink like stones in a pond.

Can we imagine how our resolve to live "normal" and to thus shun God's gifts must grieve Him? God has blessings to bestow upon His children and He is not impressed with the false piety that shuns His kind, gracious, and exciting gifts. And healing is one of His gifts to us.

It is important that as followers of Christ we become convinced that God has *always* sustained and healed His children. There is a continuum of healing that flows from God's hand. He healed in the Old Testament era. He healed in Jesus' day. God healed through the disciples and apostles of the early church and in the early centuries of the young church. God has healed through the ages. He heals in modern times and God is still healing people today. He is healing tens and hundreds of thousands of people—today! And curiously He does the same for those outside the Covenant, those hearts He also is aiming to reach with His loving hand.

Divine healing, according to Scripture, began in Abraham's day (Genesis 20:17). God has been actively involved in touching lives in a healing manner since around 2,000 B.C. The Bible tells us this. It happened for two millennia in this era as God graciously supplied for His children (and to pagans on occasion) from these ancient days up to and through Jesus' ministry.

Jesus' arrival simply opened the spectrum to reveal the sheer magnitude of what it was like to be actually and physically touched by God. Colossians 1:19 forever answers the question of what God is. God says, "I AM. If you want to know what I AM is like, look at my Son Jesus" (author's paraphrase). And Jesus in the Gospels is healing people nearly 40 percent of the time (don't jump to chapter three yet). It is true, almost two-fifth's of activity in the four Gospel texts are Jesus doing healing.

Healing people is quite important to the Judeo-Christian God. It is so important that Jesus models this healing for His followers and then sends the disciples on healing and exorcism internships. He wants to mentor others into healing ministry. He does that because He wants healing to continue.

We see the disciples astonished at first by their own ability to heal people in Jesus' name (Luke 9 and 10). But by the time they are operating in ministry after Jesus' departure, they are healing with the same calm and assertive nature with which Jesus healed. They are healing in the power of the Holy Spirit. They heal from the same Source that Jesus did, so they have the same poise that Jesus had. Consequently the disciples' healing ministry has the same effect that Jesus' healing ministry had—the disturbed suffering are drawn to them and comforted, while society's power brokers, the pagan entrepreneurs and the religious scrutinizers, want the disciples hushed and quashed in a hurry.

Healing ministry is seen in operation throughout the centuries. The Catholic Church, the monolithic institution of Christianity from circa A.D. 300–1500, has been quite interested in healing ministry. So much so that today many

Catholics have an easier time believing in miracles than many Evangelicals do. Divine healing happened during the Reformation (which began in A.D. 1519) and has continued onward. Since I do not mean to create an encyclopedia of healing throughout history, for the sake of brevity, it is expedient to simply refer those interested to Eddie Hyatt's work listed in Recommended Reading in the back of this book, *2000 Years of Charismatic Christianity.* The works of J.S. Baxter and Morton Kelsey are listed there as well. There and in many other tomes, healing ministry has been referenced at length and verified voluminously as a regular occurrence since the time of Christ.

It is noteworthy that healing ministry, for the purpose of advancing the kingdom of God, went into overdrive during the 1800s. These are the healings that have occurred in what is called the modern era (see chapter 5). Still there were some who argued that such miracles did not need to happen anymore because they were not necessary. The argument was that the advances in industry and medicine replaced the need for healing prayer. But actually the opposite is true. Medicine has only delayed the suffering and the inevitability of death's sting. Medicine has eradicated neither. In many cases, medicine has merely transferred some of the suffering from the body to the mind. The incidence and the need for intervening acts of the Holy Spirit have only multiplied in modern times. And it is intriguing that the surge in healing is a phenomenon that has paralleled missionary advances across the world. The Book of Acts was reoccurring, with apostolic preaching and miracles to match it as the gospel was reaching new people that strangely had been delayed in receiving the gospel for eighteen or nineteen centuries. Historically, as the need had fully ripened, missionaries had been raised up, and the financing was available via industrial advances, the gospel went forth and the healing power of the Holy Spirit accompanied the work of evangelism to confirm the message and convert souls.

A plurality of this part of the book, chapter 5, is devoted to A.B. Simpson. He is the one who founded the Christian and Missionary Alliance (C&MA). If one were to count the most influential Christians in history on one hand, it can be strongly argued that Simpson is among them. His work in healing, his writings on the subject, the missions he launched, the schools he inspired to open, and the other denominations that spun off of his movement and were influenced to endeavor into healing ministry cannot be overemphasized. Simpson was instrumentally involved in taking divine healing off the shelf labeled "vague blessings" and putting it on the working agenda of Christianity and missions once again. Incidentally most of the denominations that branched off of the C&MA have turned out to be more devoted to healing ministry than Simpson's followers who remained in the C&MA. This is a good pattern, for Jesus stated that His followers would do greater things than He did. Interestingly a notable amount of the denominations that were influenced by Simpson have created a "branch of the evangelical tree" that casts a larger shadow in the evangelical world than the C&MA does.[2] Notwithstanding, A.B. Simpson inspired much in the Christian movement that still ripples across the globe. Therefore much of chapter 5 is devoted to this man.

Chapters 6 and 7 contain a plethora of testimonies regarding the immense healing ministry happening in today's generation. This is included simply to build faith into all who endeavor to join the Holy Spirit in doing greater works for His kingdom. The goal here is to read of this modern-day spiritual outpouring and spur all people to realize that if healing happened in that person's life or in that particular town or in that country, then it can happen in *their* life and in *their* town and in *their* country.

> For those who want to be involved in God's work, the exciting part of healing is that, for the most part, it is voice-activated.

These healings happen; these phenomenal works of God occur by the Spirit's prompting. God in Christ blesses His children as He sees best and the moving of His hand is employed to create His glory on earth. For those who want to be involved in God's work, the exciting part about healing is that, for the most part, it is voice-activated. This is not a strange or new concept. The first verb in the Bible is *created*. The second verb is *said*. What resulted from "God said..." is that Creation happened. Plainly put, God's creation was voice-activated. He spoke and planets came into being. They took their place. The sun and stars ignited. Oceans divided and land gathered into its place—all because God spoke.

This being the Trinity at work, we see Jesus doing hints of the same type of deeds in the Gospels. Jesus shows mastery over gravity and nature as He walks across the Sea of Galilee and calms storms. Essentially, He voice-commands clouds and wind and His voice halts storm activity. He is cancelling the source for wind by speaking to it! On a related note, meteorologists to this day have no scientific explanation for what causes or cancels a low-pressure system, the source of wind that brings rain. Whether the world will admit it or not, God is the only explanation of a storm and God is the only Entity who can stop a storm. He has control over what He has created, thus Jesus' voice has control of storms.

We read of Jesus demonstrating voice commands over physical bodies. He heals through a variety of methods, but Jesus speaking healing is the method He employs the most. At Jesus' command healing takes place. When He speaks cells restructure, bones repair, diseases wither and melt into oblivion, health is restored, limbs straighten and strengthen, mobility is granted or returned, senses like sight and hearing and speaking are restored, and the dead live again—all at the sound of Jesus' voice.

And peoples' participation in these healings must not be overlooked. Ponder it, even as patients and victims, the people who are coming to Jesus are teaming with Him to be healed. These healings occur as *their faith* meets with Jesus' authority, power, and compassion to heal. The elements are needed by both parties. Everyone who was healed by Jesus believed He could heal...or they would not have come to Him or been sent or brought to Him. Not one person who doubted Jesus' ability to heal was healed. Not one person who was healed by Him came to Him with a cynical attitude. He did not challenge or dare people to be healed, nor was He challenged by people to heal. No one dared Him to get Him to act on their behalf. It was fruitless to come to Jesus with the attitude of testing Him in order to get Him to heal.

One example is Herod who wanted to see a healing for amusement. So

Herod did not experience or witness healing. Jesus knew Herod's heart of trickery. The result is that Herod did not even get Jesus to say a word to him. No, Jesus did not heal anyone else who was intending to try and test Him back then. He does not today, either. Jesus' healing ability is activated by the concerned and the suffering who in faith believe He meets their need. There has to be faith on the part of the human.

The people who heal today do so in the same manner that Jesus did. They speak for Jesus—they speak Jesus. They speak in Jesus' power and authority. All authority has been given to Jesus and He lives in those who invite Him to. People's faith to move into the miraculous and speak for Jesus meets the faith of those who long for healing and believe God will touch them. The healing is voice-activated, in faith, through the Holy Spirit. This is how the disciples, stirred by faith, employed the healing power that Jesus gave them. It was prompted by the Spirit and voice-activated by the disciples. Jesus usually healed the same way. Healing is a continuation of the creation; it is re-creation. Those who are in Christ are a new creation. God created the world, the solar system, and the universe the same way that He healed. He used His voice.

> These healings occur as their faith meets with Jesus' authority...

Healing that is true and constructive and blessed and does not come with spiritual baggage, but leaves people better than they were, happens within the providence of the Judeo-Christian God. With Jesus there is no fear, no scar, and no bill. All other sources of miraculous healing are false. Granted, they may be *real*, but they are not true. I will speak at greater length in chapter 5 about what divine healing is versus what it is not, but for now, I will describe it by saying that it happens by the virtuous power of the God found in the Holy Bible. It does not occur through some Hindu mantra, not shamanization, some particular humming pattern, breathing technique, meditation, a certain stance or Lotus position, or anything that is conjured up by this world or any pagan man-made religion. I mention this because the scriptures warn that in the last day there will be those who proclaim healing, but it will not be for the purpose of bringing people to Jesus. It will be for funneling them into pagan beliefs and eventually into outer darkness and condemnation. There are books available on the market today that are about healing that is not natural, not medical, and is not sourced in God's providence. Such healing that is not rooted in Jesus, powered by the Holy Spirit, and glorifying to God is dangerous and is to be avoided like the plague.

The fact that healing is voice-activated is not a new concept. This book may be among the first to articulate it this way, but it is not a new strand of theology or ministry. And as for ministering healing in today's culture, "voice-activated" healing is a perspective that serves as an inroad to those who are skeptical.

This can help boost faith today because people in industrialized nations have multiple commodities that operate on human voice-activation. People's computer software, video machine remotes, and cell phones can be programmed to be voice-activated; as can security sensitive entry systems and the dashboard on upscale new cars. The list of items that use voice-activated technology continues to grow.

We are so accustomed to voice-activation that we forget about its reality. (It is the same way with fish that are ignorant of the fact that they are wet.) We are able to do this these days because God does this. He has been voice activating for thousands of years on this earth. He is the One who granted this idea of voice-activation. Steve Green sings a song about creation being a symphony of praise. It is not a new concept to God. It is creation responding to His work. Are not reliable friends voice-activated? Can we not ask friends to assist us or speak to us and they do? Is not family or any helper or coworker voice-activated? Is not anyone on earth who has decent courtesy voice-activated?

Creation being voice-activated by God is also sustained and repaired and renewed by God. Are we not part of creation under God? And is God at work in us or is He not? Are we surrendered to Him? Do we have faith for Him to act benevolently and restoratively along with the faith and vision that He has instilled in us? All these things are available for the asking; hence they are voice-activated.

It is in order to address a factor about healing that remains a giant, white elephant in the room (and in our churches). I speak about it because there is something we *can* do about it. In America and much of the western world, healing is not happening like it is happening in the developing world and in the primitive world. How can the Holy Spirit be operating so freely in places where the gospel is breaking forth and evangelism is so feverishly exercised? And how is it that healing, one of God's dearest gifts, could be such an issue of argument and derision in other places? Numerous Christian leaders living in America ponder when and why healing became so divisive. Why is such an astonishing gift something that triggers such argument? Why is the Spirit's powerful evangelistic and encouraging gift of healing a frustration for many people? This is not God's plan. It is sad, but healing ministry can throw Christians into a tailspin of competition and jealousy. I personally think heaven weeps over Christians so pathetically missing this blessing and misinterpreting God's hand at work in healing ministry. Many people do not know what to do. Pastors needlessly feel helpless when people are not healed. The victims who remain ill can feel worse from the falsely imposed sense of dejection. And what is to be done then? Sometimes the ill are told they need to pray harder. They hear that they need more faith before they can get better. Many adhere to a false belief that God ceased his miraculous work with the apostles in the Book of Acts. These beliefs are not biblical, but they persist. There are ministers who think they are biblical in believing that Paul's healing the citizens of the island in Acts 28 is the final work of healing. And they think that everything that happened or happens subsequently is sinister magic and is to be suspect. These resolutions and arguments are convoluted and go against Scripture. It is terribly unfortunate that entire churches and even whole denominations embrace this neutralizing and diffident theology. Such congregations of reductionist creeds are serious and intricate, but they also are a resignation to dull prayers and stale ecclesiology that narrate personal theological boredom versus calling on the Holy Spirit to act.

Contemporary thinking on Christ's healing ministry sometimes reveals a curious incongruity. Many of the anti-healing leaders and theologians who call themselves "conservative, committed, and biblical" are the same ones who expend great energy to vigorously defend the gospel accounts of Christ's healing ministry. But the error is that these healings are never related to the present-day healing ministry of Christ. His healings are seen as historical, but practical only to the extent that they verify Christ's deity. They believe that the healing ministry ended by 100 A.D. What gets distilled is that large bodies of believers (who do not believe in miracles!) capitulate to the curtailing creed that the only role of the Holy Spirit is for bringing about conversions.

> Many of the anti-healing theologians who call themselves "biblical" expend great energy defending Christ's healing ministry.

To illuminate the error of this belief, let us first draw a parallel by envisioning a hospital. And since Jesus is much of the inspiration behind the medical field, it helps to envision a Christian hospital. This exercise becomes effective in our minds because part of the church's role is to be a hospital unto a sick world. It is where God does all and does all things well. The Head of this entire endeavor is Jesus; He is "The Great Physician." Jesus is the head surgeon. He is the main teaching doctor. He invented each of the devices in the hospital. He understands absolutely every system in the human body. He has mastery over every disease. He knows the lab, the Emergency Room techniques and atmosphere, the Intensive Care Unit, the pediatrics ward. He calmly executes each brain surgery and soothes even the most tormented person back to peace and rest. Skin issues, cancer, ophthalmology, orthopedics—everything is healed perfectly by Jesus. Sometimes He does so instantly, sometimes He operates in time and uses the pilgrimage to strengthen and further infiltrate peoples' souls. Why wouldn't Jesus be the Master in this and every setting? Would He not understand what He has created?

If this sounds far-fetched then it would be wise to again read over Colossians

1:16–17, that "...all things were created by him and for him...and in him all things hold together." If we do not believe this, and it is not true, then Jesus is not who the Bible says He is.

Let's all step back and ask what we are doing following Jesus to begin with. I am positing this as an aside because if someone believes that Jesus does not heal today, then that person is theologically meandering down an unsafe road—contrary to what they may think. They are in a place that seems to be logically taking them to a dangerous realm where God is not God; for He is helpless, or stubborn, or just mean. Whatever the theological rut someone is in to believe against Christian healing, something is desperately wrong with their thinking.

Still there are those who doggedly affirm that the Holy Spirit is only here for assisting us in interpreting the Bible and for converting the soul; helping the new believers "get on board." (Stay with me, we have not left the hospital yet.) Do we realize the diminution of which this creed is guilty? For these folks, the Great Physician, Jesus, has been reduced to being a part-time tutor at a second rate school and He moonlights as a midwife and volunteer assistant at the hospital's nursery. That's all Jesus does anymore, so they would have us believe.

That is about it for those who think that miracles and the age of miracles died with the apostles at the end of the first century. Apparently Christians are supposed to heal themselves and leave Jesus out of the picture.

> Why has the Great Physician been reduced to a midwife?

May I ask, has Jesus also stopped being a lifeguard for the drowning as well? A retired missionary spoke with chagrin about what had happened to his mission denomination over the years. He assessed, "We once trusted the Holy Spirit for so many things in ministry. He's merely a birth coach or a midwife anymore for our denomination. We were so vibrant when I started in this mission as a youth. But today, once someone has come to Christ we basically tell Jesus, "We'll take it from here. Step aside please, and thank you very much." This is the abysmal state at many churches today, these "hospitals of Christendom" and the churches of the western world. If things continue, they will be reduced further to simply being libraries, civic centers, or museums of what God did in the past. Many of the historical denominational churches in Europe come to mind.

The question is, if we care only for "newborns" in the faith—and that is all we need the Holy Spirit for—and we are not caring about people who are suffering, then what *do* we care about? The problem is that when we tell Jesus' Holy Spirit not to get in our way as we "do church," people—leadership especially—become more controlling instead of more loving and more shepherding. What people are left with is a shrink-wrapped Jesus so monitored by human directives and paranoia that the Holy Spirit cannot enter and bless and heal lives. Herein religious leaders' greatest fear is not the Lord, it is losing control of the sheep. And people wonder why healings stop in settings like this. It is actually quite obvious. When people tell the Holy Spirit not to bother them in their lives and ministry, He doesn't.

It is also a sad commentary to witness the decline in spiritual fervor of such groups knowing that they once were more vibrant in their service. For example, research within the C&MA denomination reveals a significant shift away from healing ministry; the third sector of their "fourfold gospel." This was not the founder's plan. I think I have liberty to address this matter. My family has been in the C&MA since World War I days. My paternal grandparents served as missionaries with them for more than fifty years. There were C&MA pastors in my extended family. I was ordained in the C&MA in 1994. That was after writing a book on C&MA ministry and graduating from two of their schools, plus serving in limited capacity on many of their mission field posts. Many within the C&MA talk with transparent vexation about the denomination not being what it once was: a flagship mission that led the way into new territory.

A. B. Simpson's stalwart character and heart for healing ministry led the way in igniting healing ministry across America. Simpson and the C&MA were instrumental in inspiring whole denominations with healing ministries. They expanded internationally in courageous mission endeavors. Simpson conducted a magnificent healing service each week in New York City, plus he founded and funded a prominent healing home. But neither the healing service nor the healing home was sustained after he passed on. Healing ministry began the long process of coasting to a near halt in the U.S. For reasons that are assessed in part below, healing ministry began to wane in the C&MA immediately following Simpson's death. The healing home was officially and permanently closed within two years of his death. Many appraise that healing has eroded from the C&MA's greater agenda.

An extensive survey was done over a five-year period. Two hundred randomly selected missionaries and pastors in current staff and leadership positions plus all of the theological educators revealed that 90 percent of Alliance leaders/ministers do not practice a healing ministry.[1] (By the way, there are stories included in chapter 5 from churches among the 10 percent who do.) A mere 25 percent of the C&MA theological educators at their five North American institutions have the vital goal of imparting the doctrine of divine healing to their students. Twenty-two of the thirty-seven theological educators use a curriculum void of instruction in divine healing. About two-thirds of the two hundred surveyed have read very few books on divine healing (as they put it). Every two years there is a healing service at the C&MA National Council, but it is more of a "heritage day" that seems to pay homage to what Simpson was doing from 1881 to 1919 than an actual healing service. I have been in electrifying healing meetings. The C&MA biennial healing service is not one.

C&MA journalist Bob Niklaus, who has written copiously of the history of the movement, gives three reasons why healing ministry has steadily declined in the C&MA. He says that Simpson's view of divine healing ran much deeper than most every other person's experience. Simpson perceived healing to be a consequence of abiding in Christ. This constant inflow of the Holy Spirit pushes out the old life. Simpson's view became difficult to maintain after he died in 1919. Second, most people have a "body parts" idea about healing. They want their arm, wrist, ear, or lymph glands fixed. That is all. These are not the desires that sustain a movement, but only meet an immediate need. Third, there evolved in the C&MA a desire to disassociate themselves from Charismatics and Pentecostalism of any sort. In the 1940s the C&MA ceased writing its own curriculum and began purchasing from Scripture Press. Thus teaching on divine healing disappeared from the regular teaching curriculum. It had been roughly twenty-five years since Simpson's death and the C&MA was veering away from their founder's objective to heal.[2]

What does this result in? I was preaching on divine healing in a C&MA church in the late 1980s. Simpson had died several miles from this location seventy years prior. The church was a twenty-minute drive from the place where the C&MA was founded and the dynamic Friday healing services that Simpson had conducted. In a sense this area was the pituitary gland of the healing ministry that was launching into much of the navigable world circa four generations back. But as my message on healing ended, I realized I was much farther than fifteen miles and four generations away. The people looked at me as if I had just given a message on the UFO's that were in my shoe closet. They had no idea of the healing I was talking about. It felt grim.

The point is that if someone is looking for an example to follow into divine healing ministry there is hardly a finer model than what Simpson lived and taught. Whereas Simpson is a sterling example of what ministry can be, most of the leaders in the movement he founded have let the fire of healing ministry go out. Just because something has been founded does not mean it has been maintained. The Holy Spirit is needed in a fresh, daily way. He is needed in every person, every family, every village, every church, every city, state, and nation on earth.

A hindrance to healing ministry is the reticent attitude many Christians have toward spiritual warfare. This tends to erode interest in healing ministry. Regardless of what people are comfortable with, deliverance from demonic influence is related to the practice of divine healing. That does not mean all illness has its origin in the demonic; it simply means that deliverance from demonization in its various forms is an *aspect* of healing. Some people fear this encounter with the powers of darkness and therefore steer clear of healing ministry. Others abandon it altogether.

Many dismiss the matter of healing because of an unhappy experience with the practice of healing or the teaching related to it. Some have attempted to believe for healing and they have perceived that effort to be a failure. Perhaps they prayed for a loved one who did not recover. The error in this response is generated by self-pity and results in a blatant disregard for scriptures. I apologize if I am not being gentle enough here, but that is what is going on. Promises and instruction for the ministry of healing are undeniable in the Word of God. The Acts and Epistles call for the eternal continuation of divine healing ministry through the church in the name of Christ Jesus our Lord.

People have many reasons why they have ceased involvement in healing ministry. None of the excuses impress God. He said to heal the sick. We are to heal the sick. We may think we cannot or that we are disqualified because of a broken life, broken heart, or broken soul. We are wrong in this thinking. This brokenness provides the fractures and fissures through which the Spirit of God can pour His healing oil *through* us. This truth is relieving.

It really comes down to this: those who desire the Holy Spirit, God's will, and Jesus' fellowship more than food, sleep, riches, or human approval—more than anything that this world affords—are the souls who receive Him fully. These are the souls who become filled with Him and model their lives after their Savior Jesus Christ. They desire the Holy Spirit to use them so fervently that when they are seeking Him with all their heart they feel like they are being held underwater—they are that desperate—and they are the ones who find Him. These prayers that pursue God like a heat-seeking missile are the prayers that open doors across the universe and crash through hell's gates to free people.

The Lord never turns away anyone who desperately wants Him. Those who desire to abide in Him and be used by the Holy Spirit are the ones who find satisfaction with God and in their lives. It is a joy that is finer than the richest of food or any treasure. Nothing on earth is greater. Just one drop of pure fellowship in Jesus is so life changing that anything this world has to offer in exchange is total boredom at best. When we surrender to Jesus and take on His yoke, we find rest for our weary souls and contentment that the world knows nothing about. And in the Holy Spirit, there is fellowship that is sweeter than honey. In serving and trusting Him fully, there is found a wealth and strength that staggers the mind, for all the power of heaven stands behind us through the end of time. And by the way, with Jesus upon us, we heal others as He did. Healing moves from being miraculous to being normal.

CHAPTER 1 ENDNOTES

1. Surveys were administered by the author in 1989, 1994, and 1995.

2. Content taken from the author's interview of journalist Bob Niklaus at the C&MA National Office, April 1998.

"So Moses made a bronze snake and put it up on a pole. Then when anyone was bitten by a snake and looked at the bronze snake, he lived" (Num. 21:9). Artwork by Gustave Doré.

two

HEALING in the OLD TESTAMENT

THE TRUTH OF physical healing as an act of God in response to faith, prayer, and need is found all through Scripture. The theology and the principle of divine healing are first set forth in the Old Testament. God made it clear to those whom He had called to be His people that He would meet their needs. He would be their doctor, their surgeon, their "mid-wife" if you will, their physical therapist, nurse, pharmacist, and geriatric specialist—all in One.

A persistent theme in Scripture is laid out from the beginning. In Genesis for example, the obsession of Abraham's family, who is to bless the earth, is that they were to have three things. First, they would have a land God would give them. Second, they would have "seed" or children; families that, again, God would give them. Third, they would have God's blessing. Genesis 12:1–3, God's promise to bless Abraham, sums up much of this. I have met Bible scholars who state that this passage of Scripture is the most important verse in the Bible. It certainly sheds light on much of world history. These were the three themes for the Hebrews from their beginning: land, seed, and blessing. Of these three, the second pertained directly to their physical bodies. God promised that they would have children. Children were thus a great issue of joy to the early Hebrews. They still are today. Conversely, the absence of such children/descendants was an issue of tremendous anxiety. That has not changed, either.

The Book of Genesis chronicles the Hebrew beginnings. These years are marked by the Patriarchs and their wives who consequently all struggle in their odyssey to have children. Abraham and Sarah, Isaac and Rebekah (plus Leah), Jacob and Rachel—each of them go through personal crises in their need and quest to procreate. In the middle of all this there are five healings in Genesis. They are the first five healings in the whole Bible. Each of them is the distinct blessing of having the problem of infertility healed. This healing was the direct intervention of God. And this healing even pertained to those outside God's initial calling.

People who claim to follow the God of Abraham ought to take note that the first divine healing in Judeo-Christian history is graced upon nonbelievers (Genesis 20:17). God healed the infertility that had stricken Abimelech's entire household since Abraham's wife had been returned to Abraham. I personally see this as a sign for the ensuing four millennia and beyond. God was not only going to use divine healing to bless his chosen ones. He was going to use it to reach those outside the covenant; healing would be used for evangelism. This is insinuated from the first healing. With Genesis being humanity's introduction to how God functions, and children are the tangent obsession at this point in history, God is there to touch upon this need. God is the one who gives children. God is the one who can withhold children. God was training His young nation that He was the One to approach to have their needs met. God never changed this theme for His people: "You have needs? Come to me." God's distinctive involvement in His children's physical care is a theme laid out from the start.

THE OLD TESTAMENT CONCEPT OF MAN

The Old Testament concept of man came from God by revelation. To the Hebrew, man was a whole harmonious unit. This perception clearly contrasts with Greek thought on the nature of man. The Greeks saw man comprised of many parts frequently at war with each other, the body being one of them. In Greek thinking, man's body was perceived as evil; evil that must be subdued. Where the Greeks perceived that man *had* a body, to the Hebrews, man *is* a body. And to the Hebrew, the body was not evil. The body was thought of as a receiver or receptacle of God. They perceived that God employed their bodies to talk to man. The body was an "earpiece," so to speak. God desired to reside in the body. God communicated with man by way of his body.

The body was thought of as a receptacle of
God....an "earpiece," so to speak.

The Hebrew was constantly conscious of the one true God and the Law He had given them. God's Law dealt with every aspect of life. This consciousness of the Law carried into every activity, occupation, business deal, relationship, meal, health condition, thought, act of worship, and emotion. Under God, life was interrelated like a networked computer system is today. Such a relationship called for total dedication to God in obedience and worship.

The Old Testament/Hebrew concept of wholeness was God-centered. This way of living safeguarded the Hebrew against the spiritual, physical, and emotional imbalances that bedevil people in the modern day. The Word of God provided a complete program of guidance in the best interest of the whole man. This blessing extended throughout families and to all Hebrew society.

THE HEBREW IDEA OF HEALTH

The biblical concept of *wholeness* included health. The Hebrew cherished health as a blessing from God. Good health was equated with having one's entire life in order. When one's heart, soul, mind, and body were functioning harmoniously well, that person was considered to be blessed by God.

Conversely, in the Old Testament era, sickness was not seen as a great perplexity, but as part of God's intervention in life. It was sent as correction. Some received this correction. Others refused it to the end. God's ultimate goal was therapeutic; heal the relationship, heal the body. There was no question as to whether one should call on God in time of illness. Sickness was a call to prayer and spiritual renewal.

In fact, it was sin to not call on God in times of physical need. In 2 Kings 1, Ahaziah died because he did not call on God when he was injured. He called on the god of Ekron and God struck him for it. Similarly there was King Asa. Second Chronicles 16 tells of his grim conclusion. Verse 12 reads, "Asa was afflicted with a disease in his feet. Though this disease was severe, even in his illness he did not seek help from the LORD, but only from the physicians." Studying this man in 1 Kings 15 and 2 Chronicles 14–16, the scriptures assert that he is fully committed to the LORD. But even in his commitment there are things he will not do: he does not remove the high places, he will not rely on God when in the heat of conflict, and he will not come to God when he is in physical pain. Though he is committed, he is not humbly surrendered. To him it is worse to be in God's loving care than to have severe foot pain. So he suffers and dies with this pain. This stubborn commitment of Asa's remains prevalent and universal to this day.

Wholeness was the root idea and comprehensive plan of holiness according to the Book of Leviticus. Gordon Wenham, in his commentary *The Book of Leviticus*, explains the Hebrew concept of "wholeness."[1] He draws from the studies of Mary Douglas, a social anthropologist, who offers a sound interpretation of the *kosher* system and how it contributed to wholeness.

The *kosher* system was in compliance with the laws of separation found in Leviticus. It gave thorough instruction for diet, relationships on all levels, health care, hygiene, housekeeping, and many other guidelines for everyday living. The *kosher* system applied not only to wholeness, which indicates completeness, but also to holiness, which refers to purity and consecration unto God. This purity concept pertained to bacteria and mold as well, and it referred to one's spiritual state. They were to be purified from the world and separated or consecrated unto God. Separation unto God was basic to a life of completeness, balance, and worship. Therefore, anything presented in the temple had to be without flaw, perfect, and whole. Anyone approaching the temple to make an offering had to be clean.

The *kosher* theme of separation from a pagan and defiled world affected every area of life. To combine certain things was perversion. The mixing of things that should not be mixed symbolized confusion, even lunacy. There was to be no mixing of the holy and the unholy. In terms of religion, they had one God and no other. In marriage, adultery was forbidden; it was mixing, symbolic of madness. They had one God, one spouse, one home, one calling. In agriculture only one type of grain was to be planted in a field. Much of the world was eating filthy, parasite-filled meats and food. The Hebrews were to abstain from such foods. Relationships were to be forthright and honest, be they social or business. God's Word condemned deceptive dealing in one's public or private life. The Hebrews were to separate themselves from anything that hinted of duplicity. Such things were considered diabolical.

Leviticus also lays out the dietary plan for wholeness. Meat from land, air, or sea creatures could be eaten (since the flood of Noah's day). The regulations were as follows: a land animal must chew the cud and have a split hoof to be *kosher*. Only flying creatures that had two wings and two feet were *kosher*. Only creatures of the sea that had fins and scales were *kosher*. Any creature with mixed characteristics was not to be eaten. For example, pigs, camels, most insects, and eels (the list is extensive) were unclean. Pigs have split hooves but do not chew cud. Camels chew cud but do not have split hooves. Most insects have multiple legs, and eels have a fin, but no scales. According to Douglas, these were forbidden because they symbolize mixing and not wholeness. Carnivorous scavengers and things that flew in swarms versus patterns (e.g. geese fly in patterns) were creatures of confusion, squalor, and madness, therefore unclean. Carnivorous animals, especially scavengers that ate carrion (today it is called "road kill") were creatures filled with bacteria and parasites. They were *unkosher*, not fit for human consumption, and not even to be touched in many cases.

> Leviticus…is God calling to us…I want you clean so we can be together.

The food laws had a greater purpose than intestinal hygiene. Through the *kosher* laws, the Israelites were ever distinguishing clean from unclean. It kept the subject of holiness and integrity foremost in their hearts and thinking. Imagine every bite of food or transaction or conversation or thought or journey compelling you to ask yourself, "Is this holy? Is this healthy? Does this bring me closer to my God? Will this next decision hamper my communication with God? Will this meal or dish help me or hurt me? Will I be stronger or weaker because of eating this? Will this next step I am about to take please the Lord or grieve Him?"

By the way, people today could stand to ponder this line of thinking. There is more for us to learn from Leviticus than popular culture realizes. Most of us know what it is like to commit to reading through the Bible in a year. It is rather exciting for a few weeks. Then sometime in early February, there we are in Leviticus! Oh dear. If the book is not understood for what God is trying to portray, Leviticus can seem dreadfully laborious. But it becomes a thrilling book the moment someone reading Leviticus realizes that it is God calling to us: "I am clean. I want you clean. This is so we can be together because I *want* us together." He wants His children with Him that badly. Once one sees this, Leviticus is a joy.

We are just like God in this way. We want things we come in contact with to be clean. We want to be seated at a table in a restaurant that does not have the last customer's gravy still on the table. After that we demand that the silverware given us be shiny clean. We detest close conversations with people who have halitosis. We hold babies at arms length when they have soiled diapers. We do not like people's homes to smell like a kennel or a compost heap.

Our sentiments are stronger regarding our own homes. Just the same we croon over an iridescent car that is washed, waxed, and shined inside and out; newly vacuumed and smelling like it is right from the factory. We all prefer our laundry to be cleaned, pressed, and neatly in order versus piled up and smelling like a locker room. We want our hair, skin, and teeth to be clean. So does God. There is something to be said about how nice it feels to take a hot shower and Jacuzzi after getting home from a grubby ten-day camping trip where facilities were not available. It is a joy to be clean again.

It may sound overzealous to make the same statement about reading and understanding Leviticus, but it is true. To truly delve into this book and realize God's detailed concern for His children's godliness is a humbling and indeed moving experience. To meditate on God's comprehensive care for our well-being can be overwhelming if we let it sink in.

The main lesson from Leviticus was that wholeness was an important aspect of true holiness. The Hebrews were to experience this *shalom* wholeness in their faith, their homes, their bodies, their relationships, and in society. They were to avoid anything contrary to wholeness. The wholeness presented in Leviticus included God's gift of health. To enjoy this health, Israel must remain true to God in covenant with Him. And all pilgrims know, walking with God the Creator, resembling Him in holiness and wholeness, relating to Life at its source, is exhilarating.

HEALING AS PART OF THE COVENANT

Among the benefits for those following the stipulations of the covenant was health and strength. The Lord promised this to the Israelites. The price of this vitality was to carefully obey the Law as given through Moses. Health and fellowship would then result, just as surely as pain and suffering would result from disobedience. These were their two options.

1. Obedience vs. Disobedience

Shortly after Israel crossed the Red Sea, the Lord gave the promise of healing to His people (Exodus 15:26–27). God said that if they obeyed His commandments they would be exempt from the diseases that plagued the Egyptians, "From this point on, Israel was to understand that their physical well being was dependent upon abiding in the redemptive covenant."[2] God alone was their Healer. This was "a matter not of feeling or religious inclination, but a fact."[3] The contract for the future was very clear. The blessing of healing was associated with obedience to God's Word.

Remember these Israelites are a people numbering in the millions who had known nothing but Egypt for more than four hundred years. They were isolated by Egyptian culture, religion, calendars, practices, medicine—the whole sorry gamut. Egyptian medicine was "hit or miss" at best. Some aspects were rather creepy; others outright cultic. Sorcery and magic were used. Potions and concoctions were given to people and smeared on wounds that would make anyone wretch with nausea were it to be done today. There were even pastes applied to wounds in the second millennium b.c. that were made of smashed bugs. Ancient Egyptians believed it healed!

And though this is revolting to us today, it had been normal thinking back then. This young nation of Israel was ignorant of health and the myriad details that must be tended to in order to maintain health. They also had no idea who this real God of Moses was. There was no Bible written yet. Moses wrote the first five books over the next forty years. Just after they had crossed the Red Sea, they were hungry, thirsty, bewildered, and feeling quite lost and exposed, no doubt. They had been harassed in slavery back in Egypt, but they had never felt quite like this before. God's timing of assuring them the way He did in promising to be their healer (Exodus 15:26) was nothing short of relief delivered at the perfect time. His insisting they be in Covenant with Him was essential.

In Deuteronomy 28, Moses explained the conditions of covenant blessing to Israel. On the one hand, God assured consummate blessing for obedience. Their status, children, livestock, food, travels, weather, and even political situations would be maintained in blessing. Life could not have been better as they obeyed.

The ways of the LORD stood ominously before them: obey God or wither and die.

On the other hand, disobedience would bring on a nightmare of disaster. Sickness would be among the curses sent upon the disobedient. Wasting, painful diseases, fever, inflammation, blight, boils, tumors, festering sores, madness, blindness, and insanity would plague them. These "plagues" would be a judgment of God according to the prophets. Prophets writing during the years of national rebellion refer to the threat of "plague" thirty-six times. In short, the avenue of obedience to the Lord would be marked by health and wholeness. Peter Craigie sums up Deuteronomy 28: "The whole future of Israel depended on faithful obedience to the law of God. Thus the long and solemn sermon on the curses of God provides a final incentive for wholehearted commitment in renewing the covenant."[4] The ways of the Lord stood ominously before them: obey God, or wither and die. The future could not be more clearly contrasted. They had the future resting on their obedience or vice versa.

Lest we become critical of a people and a situation that we are analyzing from more than 3,400 years away, remember that doctors today tell us that 85 percent of people who are in hospitals are there because of poor choices based on bad judgment, negligent behavior, horrendous diet, and calendar-induced stress from bad priorities—basically self-inflicted problems and illnesses.

Neither at the beginning nor at any point in their journey were the Israelites perfectly obedient. Neither are we. Many times they were miles from perfect. God sometimes used sickness as a corrective measure with them, "The purpose of inflicting the sickness was to get at the underlying spiritual condition."[5] And God has always had effective instruments of discipline.

One instance where sickness is seen (from a human standpoint) as God's judgment is in 1 Kings 17:7. Elijah visits the widow at Zarephath. After several unfortunate incidents her son dies. She interprets the death as punishment for her sin. Elijah arrives, and she says, "What do you have against me, man of God? Did you come to remind me of my sin and kill my son?" (17:18). Some may assess her statement as fatalistic. It could be that she simply knew consequences from Genesis 2:17: you sin, you die.

This covenant that was given final verification in Deuteronomy 28 was reaffirmed by Solomon in his prayer of dedication for the Temple (2 Chronicles 6:14-42). Roughly five hundred years after Moses, Solomon petitioned God to hear the prayer of those afflicted by diseases and to heal them, "The sufferer could only look to God, the Physician of his people, for healing and recovery."[6]

2. Healing as Part of Redemption

The Old Testament treats physical healing as an integral part of God's redemption, "Since God was the physician of his people, it followed that healing constituted a manifest token of his forgiveness."[7]

One might note that when healing was a manifestation of forgiveness, some ritual was required in order for the supplicant to experience healing.

One example is in Numbers 21:4–9. The Israelites had received deadly snake-bites because of their complaining. To be forgiven of their complaining they were required to look at a bronze snake that Moses was instructed to put on a pole. Healing was simultaneous with the activity. Notice God required them to look *upward*.

Similar situations are recorded in Numbers 16:47 and 2 Kings 20:7. In the former, Aaron offers incense and a plague is halted immediately. In the latter, figs are applied to Hezekiah's boil and he recovers. This is how God involved people in the process of forgiveness and healing. Wherein God played the main part in these healings, man had a corresponding part to play as well. They were not what we would call "hammock healings," in which God does all the work while we take it easy.

Healing provided a powerful reason to rejoice and praise God. It also renewed a person's commitment to the covenant. There were times when even those who were not Hebrew and not part of the covenant would praise God in the highest for divine healing. One impressive example is Nebuchadnezzar of Babylon. He is struck with insanity because of his pride. At the moment of his healing, he replies:

> Then I praised the Most High; I honored and glorified him who lives forever. His dominion is an eternal dominion; his kingdom endures from generation to generation. All the peoples of the earth are regarded as nothing. He does as he pleases with the powers of heaven and the peoples of the earth. No one can hold back his hand or say to him: "What have you done?" . . . Now I, Nebuchadnezzar, praise and exalt and glorify the King of heaven, because everything he does is right and all his ways are just. And those who walk in pride he is able to humble.
>
> —DANIEL 4:34–37

It was the common assumption that forgiveness and healing went together. Just as forgiveness caused a renewal of relationship with God, so did its tangent reality, the healing of the physical body. R.K. Harrison has stated that "because sickness was a spiritual matter, in the last analysis, healing could only properly be expected to follow a revival or revitalizing of the relationship between the individual and God."[8] As surely as God used sickness to bring attention to sin, He used healing to restore joy. God is often very specific to mark the road of godly fellowship with joy. Just the same He marks the road away from Him with desolation, isolation, and pain.

GOD THE UNCHANGING HEALER

The biblical fact of God's immutability also covers the biblical fact that God heals His people. God states that He is the Healer of His people in Exodus 15. He does not withdraw this statement. Therefore "God as Healer" must be perceived as an established institution that He keeps, not a theological phase that He passes through. There are some theological schools, many of which could be categorized "dispensational," that believe God healed *for a while*. For them it is as if God spoke His healing promise to Moses and the Israelites, but then flipped an hourglass and as much as said, "Your healing is temporary. It's for the period between Moses and the Apostles. After they leave earth, I'll have a cosmic mood swing and you are on your own. But, relax. You'll be fine. Someday you will think of band-aids and have surgeons and lots of electronic tools to x-ray yourselves. So, stay calm, people." I do not mean to be comical here. Indeed, it is disturbing how many people, mostly Westerners, embrace this despondent theology about healing.

The Old Testament describes God as Healer, and as such He is supreme and immutable as He is in all of His attributes. The Old Testament is not old in this sense. Jesus was clear in that He came to fulfill the Old Testament law, not eclipse it. So the healing that God declares in this era of history is not temporary. It is the beginning of an eternal installment.

1. Yahweh–Rapha (Exodus 15:26)

After crossing the Red Sea God gave His word to the Israelites. He told them not to fear disease, but to keep the covenant because, "I am your healer [(your) rapha]." In other words, God was telling them that He could and would fix any problem they had, so they had to remain in relationship with Him. He was their completely capable Great Physician. This declaration testified to a definite office He held and a power He dispatched.

This is significant because it is not an action that God is doing for merely a season. The statement, "I am the LORD, who heals you..." is not a temporary blessing but a proclamation of lasting theological import. It is an eternal statement from God who is eternal. He does not say He is the God who heals you during a short window of time.

2. God's Immutability

Malachi 3:6 says, "I the LORD do not change." God is perfect; He does not need to change, learn, or grow. I have an old friend who strangely thinks that God is always learning, changing, and growing. If that were true, the question would be, what books is He reading? Who wrote those books? If any of this prattle *were* true, then God is studying under someone who is smarter than He is. And God in the ultimate sense is Someone else. Thus, where is the end of this peculiar thinking?

God is who He told us He is. His power does not grow. He was not less in the past. His power does not decline. He was not more in the past. He does not lose His attributes. He is an unchanging God and He heals his people. Yet "it is strange how many people think of God as the 'I was'"[9] It was not so in the days of the Old Testament. No one thought that God used to do great things "back in the Bible days" the way many do now. Those who knew God took Him at His word to be their Healer. They were taught this from their distinctive beginning through the time of Malachi and into the inter-testamental period.

To their knowledge it was God's plan to heal them. Psalm 33:11 says, "...the plans of the LORD stand firm forever, the purposes of his heart through all generations." The psalmist, no doubt, knew God as the Healer. Psalm 102:27 reads, "But you remain the same, and your years will never end." The prophet Malachi, whose work closes out the Old Testament, gave the final promises for better days: "But for you who revere my name, the sun of righteousness will rise with healing in its wings. And you will go out and leap like calves released from the stall" (Mal. 4:2).

Despite the fact that the Old Testament reiterates that God is a healing God, there are present-day theologies that void out God as the Healer (*Yahweh-Rapha*). Modern existentialism, for one, eradicates this promise that God made nearly 3,500 years ago. Oswald J. Smith asks, "If He is not *Jehovah-Rapha*, then how can I be sure that He is still *Jehovah-Tsidkenu* [the Lord our righteousness] or *Jehovah-Jireh* [the Lord who sees]? When did He change?"[10] The crystal clear logic of the question insists that He never did and never will change. If God has stopped healing, then who is He? Did He stop saving, too? Has He stopped providing? Does He still rule the weather or has He handed that detail over to Baal? Nonsense! Healing, along with the other attributes of God, is a sealed and ever functional doctrine.

BIBLICAL HEALING IN THE OLD TESTAMENT ERA

There are many references to and incidents of divine healing in the Old Testament text. Healing is displayed in propositional statements and promises. From about 2,000 B.C. in Abraham's day (early in Genesis) to the prophets, the Bible gives the glorious record of God healing His people. This is usually accompanied by spiritual healing as well. Keith Bailey asserts that, "The truth of divine healing is a part of the theology of the Old Testament. The historical, the poetic, and the prophetic books all teach healing for the saints."[11] And keep in mind, biblically speaking, "saints" are not people who are way off in some spiritual land living on a level that is higher than the rest of us. A saint is anyone who wholeheartedly follows God.

THE MAIN REFERENCES ABOUT HEALING

Sometimes oblivious Christians can forget and think that healing began with the earthly ministry of Christ. But even a casual reading of the Old Testament shows that the experience of divine healing among God's people began in Old Testament times during Genesis.

1. God Himself as Healer: the "I" Proclamations

The initial reference to God Himself as a Healer is found in Exodus 15:26. It reads, "I am the LORD, who heals you." As mentioned prior, God heals five times in Genesis, but this event in Exodus is His first statement about being their Healer. It is a revelation.

The Israelites had witnessed the entire nation of Egypt inflicted with calamity and diseases prior to leaving. They had been rescued through a chasm of seawater during the greatest event of the ancient world. They had seen their nemesis the Egyptian army flooded over and obliterated. Now on the opposite side of the Red Sea, their dramatic escape accomplished, Egypt's army was found to be gone and though they were awestruck and overjoyed, they stood in need of some assurance. Would God strike again? Was He a caring God? Was He kind? Would He love and provide for them? If they made one mistake, would He flood them, too? Or starve them? And by the way, where were they now? And what do they do now? We would do well to remember that the Israelites did not know the answers to any of these questions.

Within three days of the Exodus, the comfort they needed was delivered. God promised them that the horrible diseases they had seen in Egypt would not come upon them. God Himself told them He was their Healer and they could rely on Him. This was not only an action He would perform, but an office He upheld. In other words, He and no one else was their Physician. "Being [Yahweh], or their reconciled God, He, of necessity, is also their Healer."[12] God knew what to do with their pains and their concerns and He told them so. It was the first of a long series of lessons that would last well over a millennium.

This instruction was that His people were to come to Him for everything, to view all of life in reference to Him. Shortly after this event, Moses was commanded to tell them, "Worship the LORD your God, and his blessing will be on your food and water. I will take away sickness from among you, and none will miscarry or be barren in your land. I will give you a full life span" (Exod. 23:25–26).

In following God there was provision, health, and security for the young, old, and unborn. The care they would receive at God's hand was neonatal, geriatric, and everything in between. Life could be almost free from stress provided they stay in touch with the God who was communicating this to them.

In Deuteronomy 32:39 Moses is preaching in his farewell address to all Israel, preparing them to enter the land of promise. This is at the end of their forty years in the wilderness. On behalf of God he says, "I put to death and I bring to life, I have wounded and I will heal." This is within his final reminder before he views the land, blesses the tribes, and dies. They must never forget that God does and will heal. He promised them that He was their healer within days of their arrival in the desert. He was telling them the same thing again at their finale in the desert.

Hundreds of years later, in Isaiah 42, God speaks of His servant whom He upholds, has chosen, delights in, will put His Spirit on, and who will bring justice to the nations (42:1). This same servant opens the eyes of the blind (42:7). In Isaiah 57:18–19 God makes a promise to the contrite in heart:

> "I have seen his ways, but I will heal him; I will guide him and restore comfort to him, creating praise on the lips of the mourners in Israel. Peace, peace, to those far and near," says the LORD. "And I will heal them."

Jeremiah 30:16 speaks to a broken nation when God tells His people that the captivity, oppression, and pain will end. He assures, "I will restore you to health and heal your wounds" (30:17). In Jeremiah 33 the Lord speaks about Judah and Israel being restored. In 33:6 He says, "Nevertheless, I will bring health and healing to it; I will heal my people and will let them enjoy abundant peace and security." God is going to put them together again; individually and corporately.

Hosea 11:3 reads, "It was I who taught Ephraim to walk, taking them by the arms; but they did not realize it was I who healed them." God's healing was a faded memory by Hosea's day. It had been about seven hundred years since they were given the initial promise from God who heals them. God promised He would be their Doctor in residence. He was even closer and better than a doctor on call 24/7. But they had forgotten. When the reading of the Word stops, the memory also stops.

They had forgotten this in Hosea's day and it appears we have forgotten in our day. John Wycliffe (A.D. 1320–1384) translated the Bible into English more than seven hundred years ago and the whole English-speaking world was impacted. But the current spiritual atmosphere in Britain, the core of the English-speaking world, resembles Hosea's day. And today, church attendance in the U.K., according to surveys, appears to be at about 3 percent.

It is curiously similar to the ignorance in Hosea's day. It has cycled around again as Bible reading and spiritual concerns rooted in the Judeo-Christian faith seem to have bottomed out in Britain.

In each of the above passages, except Exodus 23, the Hebrew word *rapha* or its root is used. *Rapha* basically means to sew together what has been torn apart. God is the self-proclaimed Healer who puts things back together.

2. The Classic Passages of Psalm 103 and Isaiah 53

Psalm 103 shines as a psalm that testifies to God's wide-ranging care and goodness. It is the first of a group of five praise psalms that were used in worship services of thanksgiving. The setting is that of a singer who would voice the sentiments of an entire congregation.

For some, the crippling handicap of sin had earlier manifested itself in illness. Now, thank God, it had been removed by healing, which was the outward sign of His [God's] gracious forgiveness. He had proved their champion, rescuing them from Sheol's premature clutches.[13]

Psalm 103:2 gives the reminder to not forget the manifold benefits of the Lord. These benefits are spelled out in verses 3–6. He forgives all sins, heals all diseases, redeems life from the pit, crowns His own with love and compassion, satisfies desires with good things, renews youth like the eagles, and works righteousness and justice for all the oppressed. The seven verbs listed above are ample reason to take special note of them, meditate on the breadth of His care, and praise the Lord. According to Psalm 103, "The blessing of healing includes recovery from disease, deliverance from the grave, and renewal of physical vigor."[14] Such joy we are given. What else could be needed to enjoy an abundant life in God?

Verse 3 upholds the Old Testament belief that forgiveness of sin and healing of disease are wedded blessings. These two blessings are grammatically paralleled in the Hebrew text. In this passage it does not say that He heals certain diseases, or diseases up to a point. He does not heal diseases until He runs out of pixie dust. He heals "all your diseases" (103:3). This is King David asserting around 1,000 B.C. that any healing that took place anywhere, from the time of Adam to the time of Malachi and beyond was the work of the Lord.

]

He forgives, heals, redeems, crowns, satisfies, renews, and works righteousness…praise Him!

Isaiah 53 is one of the most powerful healing passages in the Old Testament. It speaks of the essence of One who is to be a Savior: His work, His suffering, and the meaning of it all.

> Surely he took up our infirmities and carried our sorrows, yet we considered him stricken by God, smitten by him, and afflicted. But he was pierced for our transgressions, he was crushed for our iniquities; the punishment that brought us peace was upon him, and by his wounds we are healed.
>
> —ISAIAH 53:4–5

"Our infirmities" refers to being frail physically; "our sorrows" refers to being frail emotionally. A.B. Simpson comments that the same Hebrew word used here for infirmities is translated as "sickness" roughly one hundred other times in the Old Testament in the King James Version. *Infirmities* also refers to disease. Any worthy translation of this first phrase in verse 4 denotes it as any sort of ailment. "Although the figure of sicknesses used here refers to sin itself, the verse also includes the thought of the removal of the consequences of sin. Disease is the inseparable companion of sin."[15] These ailments He "takes up" and the "sorrows" He carries are what precipitates from the ailments and life's compounding hardship apart from God's blessing. One catches the implication that Isaiah is setting forth. Pain is not only suffering, but the fact that disease often lingers to bring on an anguish and sorrow all its own, resulting in heartbreak and the eventual crushing of the person's spirit. One example I encountered was a twentieth century polio victim who said that the worst part about living with braces and crutches is the depression.

The suffering servant lifts all this. "It should be noted that the consequences of sin and not sin itself are mentioned. Nevertheless, when it is said that He

41

bore our sicknesses, what is meant is…that He bore the sin that is the cause of the evil consequences."[16] Informal English uses phrases such as "down with the flu" or "under the weather" to mean one is being held down by sickness. Isaiah employs the same word usage in announcing that this is lifted away. The two verbs for "taking up" and "carrying" in Hebrew are *nasa* and *sabal*. "The former implies not only the taking of it, but bearing of it away; and the latter emphasizes the weight of the load."[17] Isaiah speaks of the perfect, the necessary, and the comprehensive remedy. This remedy removes the illness and the spirit that was withered because of illness is completely restored.

Nasa and *sabal* are not only words of healing and restoration, they are sacrificial terms. They are notable strands in the tapestry of the worship culture. They speak of one being used to carry something for another. Note the motif of elevation. For example, Othniel in Judges 3:7–11, is a deliverer who is "raised up for them" (v. 9). He returned the nation to a state of peace. Moses ministered healing when he made a bronze snake and "put it *up* on a pole" (Num. 21:8–9). Jesus alluded to this same lifting process from the Book of Numbers when He is conversing with Nicodemus in John 3:14. The lifting of Himself would be similar to the lifting of the serpent after the Exodus. Note that in a burnt offering sacrifice the smoke rises up to the Lord and is pleasing to Him. And it is the result of lifting up Jesus as a sacrifice that would be the ultimate and final healing unto eternal life for all who believe.

The lifting and carrying away of our sickness and sorrow is not some vague hope. Isaiah 53:4 begins, "Surely he took up." The Hebrew word for "surely" is *akhen*. The *Brown-Driver-Briggs Hebrew-English Lexicon* defines *akhen* as "surely, truly; an adverb with strong assertive force."[18] They continue, "… expressing the reality, in opposition to what had been wrongly imagined."[19] This word that translates as "surely" in English is in effect the strongest word in the Hebrew language. And A.B. Simpson adds, "The only 'surely' in the chapter is the promise of healing, the very strongest possible statement of complete redemption from pain and sickness by His life and death."[20]

Simpson also says in *The Lord for the Body*, "It is an underlining of the passage intended to mark it as very important…not only important but absolutely true."[21] What is stressed is the certainty of substitution. One is suffering so others do not have to. Isaiah is prophesying about the reality and propensity of Jesus seven hundred years prior to the Incarnation.

From the grammar it is not possible to conclude that this substitutional sacrifice applies only to sin and not to sickness. All believers agree that God forgives and removes sin. But some think that this scriptural reference to alleviating human pain is to be spiritualized. However, a careful look at the passage shows that to spiritualize healing does not agree with Old Testament theology and further ignores the laws of grammar. And theology is simply applying the laws of grammar to divinely inspired literature and letting the text speak for itself.

Isaiah describes the full benefits of the suffering Servant's death. As mentioned above, all agree that substitution for sin has been made. Isaiah 53:12 reads, "For he bore the sin of many." This is clear theologically. But looking further, Isaiah employs the same word used for the sacrifice for sin to describe what is done to infirmities, sicknesses, and diseases. It is not honest scholarship to dismiss the grammar here. To argue against what Isaiah emphasizes here is reckless heresy. One is left only to conclude that He lifted away both sin and sicknesses. To say "By his stripes we are healed" just means spiritual healing is tautology [senseless repetition].[22] Along with the spiritual healing of Isaiah 53, physical healing is clearly offered in verses 4 and 5. Do we dare reference God's gracious gifts to us and then dismiss them through spiritualizing these gifts into oblivion?

THE OLD TESTAMENT CONCEPT OF HEALTH (A LEXICAL SURVEY OF THE WORD *HEAL*)

To "see it like a Hebrew" one must look more closely at the Hebrew words for such related terms as *healing* and *health*—how and where they are used as God originally defined it for the Israelites. This is easy to overlook in modern times. We are quite far removed from the setting wherein the events took place and the cultural literature from which they derived.

For instance, in English there are minimal words for "heal." There is *therapy*. There is also *cure*, and *restoration*, but restoration is more linked to a building being updated than a body being healed. The Hebrews have eleven words for the term *heal* and its related processes. Think about why Eskimos have eighty-plus terms for the word *white*. It is because their world is very white and they see hues within the whiteness that others living south of them do not see. White is a very rich color to them. I hear the same about Navajo Indians and their use of the word *brown*. They are in the American southwest and their world is sandy brown. Therefore they see many dimensions to the color *brown*. They define this world through many terms that people outside their culture and language have not thought of defining.

With a realization like this, and the fact that there are over triple as many words for "healing" in Hebrew as there are in English, it only warrants further exploration of these Hebrew words: *rapha, marpe, te-alah, arukhah, kehah, subh, alah, qum, hayah, hadash, halaph*. These Hebrew words paint a clearer portrait of God our Healer. And any linguist, anthropologist, or educated person will tell you that to understand a people one must understand their language. The words they use and their usage of their language reveal what is valued by them. Again, learning the Hebrew words for "heal" helps us "see it like a Hebrew."

1. The Hebrew Definitions of Healing

I apologize if the following pages are overwhelming to some. If that is the case, please feel free to jump to the "Shalom" section later in the chapter.

A. Rapha

In the Hebrew text of the Old Testament, *rapha* is the word most commonly used to denote healing. *Rapha* is defined in *The New Brown-Driver-Briggs Hebrew and English Lexicon* as "heal," "mend," "repair," "pacify," "stitch together."[23] Several different forms and stems of *rapha* are employed.

The verb *rapha* initially refers to the healing or general correction of a physical situation. It means to restore something (assumed to be physical) that is in a state of disrepair. This always refers to something tangible, even though it may have direct spiritual or emotional ramifications. *Rapha* means to restore something to its original state. But *Brown-Driver-Briggs* includes "pacify" within its definition. Most humans understand the pacifying effect of having a situation returned to normal. Anxiety then dissipates and peace returns.

There are many settings in the Old Testament where *rapha* refers to the repair of bodily ailments. One is found in Numbers 12:13. Here Moses cries out to God on behalf of Miriam who had become white with leprosy; "God please heal her!" He wanted her to be as she had been before. We all know Miriam had her attitude problems that needed "pruning." Just the same, we understand the frantic nature of Moses' plea. Moses wanted her leprosy gone. It's a prayer for *rapha*. In 2 Kings 20, Hezekiah is at the point of death when God promises that He will heal him (20:5). And Naaman is restored from leprosy in 2 Kings 5. These healings are *rapha*.

The Old Testament teaches that God works *rapha* on the national level as well. God performs *rapha* in three intersecting ways: first, by forgiving sin and reversing its effects; second, by curing disease as just discussed; and third, by restoring the nation in demise.

There are at least six key verses that refer to the healing (*rapha*) of sin on the national level. Second Chronicles 7:14 states that if they will turn from their wicked ways, God will heal their land. According to 2 Chronicles 30:20, Hezekiah prayed and the people were healed (made ceremonially clean) for the Passover. Isaiah 57:17–19 promises healing of sinful greed and the punishment it brings. Jeremiah speaks of Israel cured (*rapha*) of backsliding (Jeremiah 3:22). He also predicted that God would heal wicked Judah (Jeremiah 36:6). God will heal Israel's waywardness according to Hosea 14:4.

Rapha was needed to restore the nation of Israel. Jerusalem had been terrorized and crushed in judgment (Jeremiah 8:15). The people were longing for peace and a time of healing—"healing for the wound of my people" (Jer. 8:22). Jeremiah 30:16–17 refers to plundering enemies coming to loot and destroy. "'*But* (italics mine) I will restore…and heal your wounds,' declares the LORD."

Rapha is also used to fix anything in a condition of disrepair. In 1 Kings 18:30 Elijah repairs (*rapha*) the altar of the Lord, "which was in ruins." The New International Version of the Bible translates the verb here "he repaired." The altar in ruins testified to Israel's state of spiritual decline. So *rapha* means to put back together that which has fallen apart or disintegrated. For it is God's nature to work *rapha* in people's bodies as well as for the nations; healing sin, disease, and ruin.

The Hebrew word *rapha* also applies via prayer to the distressed individual. For instance, Jeremiah was oppressed, scorned, and rejected by his contemporaries. Crushed in spirit and in despair he says to God, "Heal me, O LORD, and I will be healed" (Jer. 17:14). The psalmist, in 41:4, weighed down with sin and being slandered by his enemies, says, "O LORD, have mercy on me; heal me." Psalm 147:3 also helps us understand this definition of *rapha*. It reads, "He heals the brokenhearted and binds up their wounds." God takes people with all their emotional and psychological distresses and puts them back together again.

There is a series of derivations from *rapha* that have the connotation of nursing back to health. In this case *rapha* applies to man's participation in the healing process. In Hebrew grammar this happens to be the reflexive stem.

In 2 Kings 8:29 (and 2 Chronicles 22:6) "King Joram returned to the city of Jezreel to *recover* from the wounds." In this passage *rapha* means "convalescence." *Rapha* in the Hithpael (H-stem) carries the meaning of a "remedy." This is found in Ezekiel 30:21 where a broken arm did not heal because it was not bound or put in a splint. The New International Version actually translates *rapha* as "remedy" in Jeremiah 30:13 and 46:11. It signifies a healing medicine of some sort.

The purpose of healing (*rapha*) is so that life may continue in a healthy and productive manner. When *rapha* occurs, the ensuing power of death itself is halted. This is seen in 2 Kings 2:21–22 where water from a well is making the land unproductive and causing death. Elijah puts salt in the well and the well is "healed," no longer causing death to plants and people. Again in Ezekiel 47:8–9, water is healed so that fish can live, "This water flows there and makes the salt water fresh."

The final derivative of the word *rapha* is *raphoat*. It is related to *rapha*. Adding the suffix changes the verb to a noun. *Raphaot* means what is healed or in a state of heath. It relates in a similar way that the meaning of the

English word *health* is similar to the English *heal*. A simple "th" is added to turn the verb *heal* into the noun *health*.

B. Marpe

Another Hebrew healing word is *marpe*. *Brown-Driver-Briggs* defines it as "healing," "cure" and "health."[24] It is distinctive in that it deals more with the state of healing than with the process. *Brown-Driver-Briggs* listed three areas of healing covered by *marpe*. (These are similar to *rapha*.) First, *Marpe* is used for the healing of national woes. Second, it can indicate health and profit for a person. Third, *marpe* is used for the healing of disease in one's physical frame.[25]

Jeremiah used this word in 14:19 in relationship to Israel's problems. It reads, "We hoped for peace but no good has come, for a time of healing but there is only terror." Here *marpe* refers to a curative for catastrophic situations. In Jeremiah 14:19, with Judah predicted to fall victim to both sword and famine, Jeremiah asks God, "Why have you afflicted us so that we cannot be healed?"

In Proverbs the writer uses *marpe* to express health and prosperity (Prov. 4:22; 12:18; 13:17; 16:24). These passages are about wholeness. They say, "[Listening to wisdom is] health to a man's whole body," "The tongue of the wise brings healing," "A trustworthy envoy brings healing," and "pleasant words are...healing to the bones."

Marpe also speaks to the state of those who seek healing. It is found in Malachi 4:2 wherein healing is promised to those who fear the name of the Lord. In Proverbs 14:30 *laiv marpe* is translated, "a heart at peace." Peace of heart is conducive to good health. In Ecclesiastes 10:4 *marpe* is translated "calmness" and, like peace, it aids healing. Doctors assert that stress and anxiety destroy health, will kill anyone, and greatly impedes the healing process.

C. Te-alah

Another word for "healing" in the Old Testament is *te-alah*, which has the general meaning of new flesh over a wound. It is used exclusively for healing. In the context of Jeremiah 30:13 there is much talk about wounds, injuries, and pain. The Lord says, "There is...no healing for you." In both references they are simply left to bleed. That is, open wounds will *remain* open wounds.

Te-alah is also the word for "conduit" or "watercourse." This is a graphic metaphor of a trench of some sort. And with this same term meaning "healing," it is then considered to express healing for a trench-like incision in the flesh. *Te-alah* is actually to dress a wound, and by doing so to stop the flow of blood.

D. Arukhah

The word *arukhah* (accent on third syllable) refers to the healing of a wound, the new flesh that grows at the wounded spot. As for health, it carries the sense of healing as a restoration.

Isaiah 58:8 promises, "Your healing (*arukhah*) will quickly appear." But, God laid down prerequisite conditions for receiving the promise of healing. They were to act justly, clothe the naked, and cease from turning away their own flesh and blood. In 2 Chronicles 24:13, *arukhah* is translated "repairs." The Temple, in need of reinforcement and restoration, is being repaired. *Arukhah* is translated "restore" in Jeremiah 30:17. The Lord will "restore" them to health. Jeremiah 33:6 was mentioned before because the word *rapha* is found within it, but *arukhah* is used in this same verse as well. Jeremiah 33:6 uses *arukhah* along with *marpe* and *rapha* in this verse about healing. Being one of the most healing-laden verses in all Scripture, it reads "I will bring health (*arukhah*) and healing (*marpe*) to it; I will heal (*rapha*) my people and will let them enjoy abundant peace and security." The context shows that the wound, too, is sin and it must be remedied before people can return to God and enjoy His peace. Jeremiah brings both spiritual and physical healing together in this verse.

E. Kehah

Next there is *kehah* (kay-HAH). It means "alleviation." It is a healing in the sense of the lessening or dimming of disease. Its single reference in the Old Testament is in Nahum 3:19. Nineveh is to receive terrible punishment for her endless cruelty. They are told "Nothing can heal [*kehah*] your wound; your injury is fatal." In other words, the injury will persist until it has finished them. This will be a forceful punishment. This singular reference and definition tells of the import of pain and disease as it was perceived in that day. Since a wound/injury worked against a person, a healing—*kehah*—worked against the wound or injury for alleviation of the grief. (Although Ninevah had no hope of *kehah*.)

F. Subh

The word *subh* (pronounced "shoove," rhymes with "groove") is a Hebrew word for healing that means "restore." *Subh* refers specifically to the process of bringing back. *Brown-Driver-Briggs* defines *subh* as "to return."[26] In the area of health it means a returning from bad to good health. For example, Job 33:25 discusses one's flesh being restored as in the days of youth.

In the quest for healing, repentance was required. Isaiah speaks of the reconciliation and healing that results from returning (*subh*) to God. Often translated "return," *subh* expresses healing in spiritual relationships. Hosea 6:1 says, "Come, let us return to the LORD." Returning is part of the healing process. Hosea 14:2 urges Israel to return to the LORD for forgiveness and healing. In 1 Kings 8, Solomon is praying for the people, that Israel might return to the LORD for healing and restoration (see 8:33). Returning is a pivotal factor in the theology of healing.

Restoration leads to refreshment. It is in this sense that Psalm 23:3 uses *subh*. David says, "…he restores my soul." (He returns David's soul to where it should be.) Meditating on the use word *subh* here is a definite eye-opener. For our soul to be restored as David uses *subh* here is like having arresting stress cut away. He is meaning a stress that has so wrapped us like cords winding around our body as tightly as a cocoon from ankles to neck causing life to grind to a halt. I had a friend who worked on Wall Street. He said at times the stress was nearly paralyzing. He told me once, "It's not that stress might kill you…stress *will* kill you." When David says that God restores his soul, he is saying that God cuts this stress away. Those choking cords are gone now and he can rest.

Proverbs 25:13 says, "He refreshes the spirit." We can see how God returns (*subh*) people to spiritual health. In Isaiah 58:12 those who are rebuilding the walls are called "Restorer [*subh* is a participial noun] of Streets with Dwellings." Daniel prophesied to restore (*subh*) Jerusalem (Daniel 9:25).

G. Alah

Alah, which literally means "to bring up" in terms of new flesh, is ordinarily a sacrificial form, but it also applied to physical healing.

The psalmist has seen many troubles, but displays his confidence in 71:20: "From the depths of the earth you will again bring me up." Jeremiah 30:17 assured, "I will restore (*alah*) you to health." God lifted Israel back up to where He wished they would stay. And here again in Jeremiah 33:6, Jeremiah writes, "I will bring health (*alah*) and healing" (*Alah* is a participle in this verse.) Lamentations 5:21 reads, "Renew our days as of old." *Renew* is a stem of *alah*. It is a prayer that the nation be brought back up to where it once was or to where it needs to be.

H. Qum

The word *qum* (pronounced "koom," rhymes with "loom") means "to arise" or "stand." It refers to rising from the dead. An example is found in 2 Kings 13:21, where the dead man is thrown into Elisha's tomb, "When the body touched Elisha's bones, the man came to life and stood up (*qum*) on his feet." Isaiah 26:19 promises, "But your dead will live; their bodies will rise (*qum*)."

> David says that God restores his soul, he is saying that God cuts stress away.

I. Hayah

Old Testament healing includes ideas like "restore to life," "revive," "quicken," "refresh" and "preserve." The corresponding word in Hebrew is *hayah*. An example of *hayah* is found in 1 Samuel 2:6: "The LORD brings death and makes alive." The same thought is found in Deuteronomy 32:39, "I put to death and I bring to life." King Hezekiah thanked God when his life was spared. He rejoices before God in Isaiah 38:16 and prays, "You restored me to health and let me live." *Hayah* is employed to describe the incident where Elisha revived the young boy to life again (2 Kings 4).

Isaiah 57:15 testifies to God's power to revive (*hayah*): "I live...with him who is contrite and lowly in spirit, to revive the spirit of the lowly and to revive the heart of the contrite." Psalm 119 speaks repeatedly of how God's Word revives. In this chapter the Word of God has the power of *hayah*, translated to mean "the preservation of life" (see vv. 25, 37, 40, 50, 88, 93, 107, 149, 154, 156, 159). *Brown-Driver-Briggs* also gives *hayah* the meaning "to be quickened," meaning revived from sickness, discouragement, faintness, or death.[27]

J. Hadash

The words *hadash* and *halaph* are translated "heal" in the New International Version. Both words literally mean "to renew." First, for *hadash*, it is used in 2 Chronicles 15:8 when Asa repaired (*hadash*) the altar of the Lord. Nine chapters later in 24:4 Joash is gathering money to repair (*hadash*) the Temple. This same concept is in Isaiah 61:4: "They will renew the ruined cities." In Psalm 51:12 (51:10 in the New International Version) David prays that God would renew a steadfast spirit within him. This would give David a chance for a new start. Later in Psalm 103:5 the benefits of the Lord are summarized with the renewing of youth like the eagle's. Psalm 104:30 praises God's Spirit who makes all creation and renews (*hadash*) the face of the earth. This *hadash* is a sweeping work, making new temples, altars, cities, man's spirit, man's youth and vitality, and ultimately the face of the whole earth.

K. Halaph

Halaph is used in Isaiah 40:31 which reads, "Those who hope in the LORD will renew (*halaph*) their strength." The King James Version, from which the popular song is written, reads, "But they that wait upon the LORD shall renew their strength." The body is strengthened when they seek the Lord. Isaiah 41:1 commands, "Let the nations renew their strength!" Renewal comes with placing one's hope in the Lord.

God has displayed His omnipotent power to heal the sick in the Old Testament. The Hebrew words *rapha, marpe, te-alah, arukhah, kehah, subh, alah, qum, hayah, hadash,* and *halaph* paint the portrait of God our Healer. Check "Hebrew Words for Healing" at the end of this chapter for a concise summary of these powerful words. There is also a compelling pictorial representation of all eleven words on "The Shalom Path" shown at the very end of this chapter. To simply realize the power of these words is evidence enough to convince anyone that our God is a healing God and He has been from the beginning.

2. *Shalom*: The Hebrew Concept of Health

The entire purpose of God healing His people is to bring them to a state of *shalom*. All the words analyzed above are the process. What follows is an analysis of *shalom*. Wherein healing is needed for the journey, *shalom* is the destination. When God makes sick people well He also gives them rest. We all know about the proverbial grumpy relative who is only doleful and agreeable when sick. Then after they recover, they go back to being grumpy. While families may joke about this trait or "wellness barometer," it is not the mark of true restoration to *shalom*. God wants to do more; He wants to truly bring people all the way home to a relationship with Himself.

In some instances, God disrupted people's lives to bring them back from the road of ruin and to put them at peace again. *Shalom* has been described as "a state of well-being in which nothing essential is lacking."[28] This *shalom* means one has ample resources and the heart/soul/mind/body are in harmony. Surely God is present in that situation.

Shalom is an abstract noun. Its general definition, according to *Brown-Driver-Briggs*, is "completeness," "soundness," "welfare" and "peace."[29] *Brown-Driver-Briggs* goes on to define the word with six subdivisions to more fully explain its meaning.

As prior mentioned, first, *shalom* means "completeness" similar to the peace and rest we experience when a task has just been completed and completed well. Second, *shalom* means "safety" and "soundness." David laments in Psalm 38:3, "My bones have no soundness because of my sin." His body, because of his spirit, was apparently becoming scarecrow-like and David knows why. Job 5:24 translates *shalom* as "secure" when Eliphaz replies, "You will know that your tent is secure." One can see the illustration given: ropes are tight, stakes are driven deep, poles high and in place. Scripturally speaking, man lives secure in *shalom* when he is safe and sound and everything is in place.

Third, *shalom* means "welfare," "health," "prosperity." This third aspect is twofold. First, it is a statement regarding general welfare. It signifies whether one is "OK" or not. *Shalom* is found twice in Genesis 43:27. The New International Version reads: "He asked them how they were, and then he said, 'How is your aged father you told me about?'" In Jeremiah 38:4 "the good of these people" is their peace; their *shalom*. In this definition, *shalom* is equivalent to the American English greeting, "How are you doing?" or "Are you well?"

This aspect also hints more directly of physical health and wellness. For example, in Genesis 29:6 Jacob asks of Laban, "Is he well?" i.e., is he "in *shalom?*" In 2 Samuel 18:28 is the greeting, "All is well!" The context of 2 Kings 4:26 is the Shunammite's son being restored to life. Gehazi used *shalom* four times as he inquired about the whole family.

Fourth, *shalom* means "peace," "quiet," "tranquility," or "contentment." This is a peace that is both national and personal. Isaiah 32:17 says, "The fruit of righteousness will be peace." What follows is quietness and confidence. Psalm 4:8 says, "I will lie down and sleep in peace." It is a peace that allows one to depart from this life in tranquility. God assures Abram in Genesis 15:15, "You, however, will go to your fathers in peace and be buried at a good old age." In 1 Kings 2:6 the wicked are to be without peace at death. Isaiah 32:18 prophesies, "My people will live in peaceful dwelling places, in secure homes, in undisturbed places of rest." Peace, security, and quiet contentment—it is all *shalom*.

Fifth, *shalom* is peace in terms of friendship. It is peace among humans. Genesis 26:29 and 31 tell of the peace established between Isaac and Abimelech. Psalm 35:20 talks about those who live quietly in the land. There is harmony with the neighbors. Those who promote peace have joy according to Proverbs 12:20. *Shalom* in terms of man-to-man relationships is the harmony necessary in society.

This fifth definition of *shalom* also describes peace between God and man. In Numbers 25:12 the Lord is making a covenant of peace with the Israelites. Isaiah 53:5 says, "The punishment that brought us peace was upon him, and by his wounds we are healed." Since the penalty of sin is paid by the suffering servant, man's relationship with God is restored. The result: man is offered peace and healing. In Isaiah 54:10 the Lord assures of His love and covenant of peace: or *shalom*. This *shalom* is referred to again in Malachi 2:5–6.

Finally, *shalom* is peace from war. Leviticus 25:6 promises that there will be peace in the land if they are obedient. The Old Testament discusses a time when peace will be ultimate. Isaiah 9:6 says that the child born is the Prince of Peace. As He comes to rule His ever-increasing government, peace will be universal. This will be *shalom* without end or borders. Micah 5:4–5 gives a very similar prophesy foretelling Jesus' majestic reign.

In summary, the lexical study shows that healing in the Old Testament era is extended to groups as well as individuals. God restored those in distress and, in the process, He blessed them. Healing was for the body, heart, and soul. The soul means the mind, will, and emotions. The mind governs people's thoughts, the will governs decisions, and the emotions of the heart govern people's feelings. These factors run people's lives and God gives *shalom* in every one of these areas.

> The goal of healing is to bring man to a state of *shalom*.

While sin was the root problem that needed curing, the forgiveness of sin normally precipitated physical healing. This healing applied to broken bodies, broken spirits, broken hearts, even broken altars, dwellings, and cities. Healing is also a restoration or returning to a right state. God's action of restoring a body is fourfold. He restores by 1) bringing back, 2) filling or bringing up, 3) raising, and 4) infusing or putting life into. Restoration to health is the work of God even when medical means are used and the victim of illness is given the best of nursing care. Healing happens through renewal. To be renewed is to be repaired, to start over, to sprout new life.

While the above are facets of biblical healing, the goal of healing is to bring man to a state of *shalom*. God desires peaceful fellowship with His children. This is best facilitated while they are experiencing *shalom*. *Shalom* was health, fertility, longevity, prosperity, and peace. It was completeness and security. These were all promised by God in the covenant blessing and were the natural consequences of remaining in the covenant. The entire context of God's Old Testament blessing and security is summed up in Psalm 128:5–6:

> May the LORD bless you from Zion all the days of your life; may you see the prosperity of Jerusalem, and may you live to see your children's children.

Peace be upon Israel.

This is *shalom*. The Hebrew concept of *shalom* should not be equated with the popular "health and wealth" gospel of modern times. It runs so much deeper than earthly comforts that can easily lull us away from God. It cannot be inferred that having *shalom* means possessing the material benefits that some people today feel are necessary or they are not going be happy. *Shalom* does mean that health and/or healing are part of man's total well-being.

Shalom is just like the other Hebrew words that we need to see like a Hebrew, not a Westerner. To think that God has to have us rich is an irresponsible deletion of Luke 6:20 where Jesus preaches, "Blessed are the poor, for theirs is the kingdom of Heaven" (author's paraphrase). There is more about this concept in the conclusion of this book.

The promises, the commands, the prophecies, and the instructions regarding divine healing in the Old Testament reveal four basic principles of healing: 1) Jehovah is the Healer; 2) healing is generally reserved for those in covenant relationship to Him (though healing does happen outside the covenant as an evangelistic testimony); 3) healing is embraced through believing prayer; and 4) healing is secured by the blood atonement. These principles are more fully developed in the New Testament by the accounts of Jesus' healing ministry and the healing ministry of the early church as described in Acts. The New Testament epistles, though briefly, address the theology and practice of healing. What God unveils in the Old Testament of His healing grace is merely a foreshadow of the splendor of healing revealed in Christ Jesus' earthly ministry and redemptive work that still goes on today through His followers.

CHAPTER 2 ENDNOTES

1. Wenham, Gordon J., *The Book of Leviticus* (Grand Rapids, MI: Eerdmans, 1979), 23–24.

2. Keith M. Bailey, *Divine Healing: The Children's Bread* (Harrisburg, PA: Christian Publications, Inc., 1977), 67.

3. Ibid., 84.

4. Peter C. Craigie, *The Book of Deuteronomy*, N.I.C.O.T. R.K. Harrison, ed. (Grand Rapids, MI: Eerdman's, 1976), 341.

5. Bailey, 70.

6. George Arthur Buttrick, ed. *The Interpreter's Dictionary of the Bible* (Nashville, TN: Abingdon Press, 1962), s.v. "Healing, Health," by R.K. Harrison, 546.

7. Ibid., 542.

8. Ibid., 546.

9. O.J. Smith, *The Great Physician* (New York: Christian Alliance Publishing, 1927), 30.

10. Ibid., 31.

11. Bailey, 95.

12. J.H. Oerter, *Divine Healing in the Light of Scriptures* (Brooklyn, NY: Christian Alliance Publishing, 1900), 35. In this quote I have inserted the name "Yahweh" in place of "Jehovah."

13. Leslie C. Allen, *Psalms 101-150*, "Word Biblical Commentary," vol. 21 (Waco, TX: Word, 1983), 22.

14. Bailey, 78.

15. Edward J. Young, *The Book of Isaiah*, vol. III, N.I.C.O.T. R.K. Harrison, ed. (Grand Rapids, MI: Eerdmans, 1972), 345.

16. Ibid., 346.

17. T.J. McCrossan, *Bodily Healing and the Atonement* (Seattle, WA: T.J. McCrossan, 1930), 20; reprint, Tulsa OK: Faith Library, 1982.

18. *Brown-Driver-Briggs Hebrew-English Lexicon* (Peabody, MA: Hendrickson Publishers, 1996).

19. Ibid.

20. A.B. Simpson, *The Gospel of Healing* (Camp Hill, PA: Christian Publications, Inc., 1986), 23.

21. A.B. Simpson, *The Lord for the Body* (Harrisburg, PA: Christian Publications, Inc., 1959), 82.

22. Ibid., 81.

23. *Brown-Driver-Briggs Hebrew-English Lexicon.*

24. Ibid.

25. Ibid.

26. Ibid.
27. Ibid.
28. H.C. Leupold, *Exposition of Genesis*, Vol. 2 (Grand Rapids, MI: Baker Book House, 1942), 78; quoted in Keith M. Bailey, Divine Healings: The Children's Bread (Harrisburg, PA: Christian Publications, 1977), 64.
29. *Brown-Driver-Briggs Hebrew-English Lexicon.*

HEBREW WORDS FOR *HEALING*

Rapha—heal, sew together, mend, remedy; refers to general correction.

Marpe—cure, healing, health (almost equivalent to *rapha*).

Te-alah—the physical process of the healing of new flesh over a wound; stopping the flow of blood.

Arukhah—the growth of new flesh at the wounded spot; refers to extending out.

Kehah—alleviation; refers to taking away or removing (such as a malady).

Subh—restore, return (from bad to good again); refers to bringing back.

Alah—go up, bring up; refers to filling up.

Qum—arise, stand.

Hayah—revive, "quicken"; refers to putting (life) in.

Hadash—renew, repair, make anew, start over.

Halaph—renew, sprout anew.

SELECTED HEALING-RELATED PASSAGES IN THE OLD TESTAMENT

Genesis 20:17: God heals Abimelech. His wife and slave girls' wombs "opened" again.

Genesis 21:1–2: Sarah becomes pregnant at around ninety-one-years-old.

Genesis 25:21: The barren Rebekah becomes pregnant.

Genesis 29:30–31: Leah's womb is opened.

Genesis 30:22–23: Rachel's womb opened and she bears Joseph.

Exodus 4:6–7: Moses' hand made leprous and restored.

Exodus 15:22–26: Water is cured and God makes the great statement.

Exodus 23:25–26: They will be exempt from many illnesses if they worship the Lord.

Numbers 12:9–16: Miriam's leprosy is healed.

Numbers 16:46–50: The plague is stopped.

Numbers 21:4–9: Israelites are healed from snakebites.

Deuteronomy 28:15–68: Failed health is a major part of the threat regarding disobedience.

Deuteronomy 32:39: "I have wounded and I will heal."

1 Samuel 6:3: The Philistines are offered healing if they return the ark.

1 King 13:1–6: Jeroboam's hand withered and restored.

1 Kings 17:8–24: Widow's son raised from dead.

2 Kings 2:19–22: Well water at Jericho healed.

2 Kings 4:8–36: Shunammite family blessed with a son (vv. 15–17), raised from dead (vv. 32–35).

2 Kings 5:1–19: Naaman cleansed of leprosy.

2 King 6:8–23: Eyesight blinded and restored to Arameans.

2 Kings 13:21: Dead man comes to life in Elisha's tomb.

2 Kings 20:1–11: God promises and Hezekiah is healed.

2 Chronicles 7:14: Conditions for forgiveness and healing of the land are stated.

2 Chronicles 30:20: God heals at Hezekiah's petition.

Job 5:18: "He injures, but his hands also heal."

Psalm 30:2: "I called to you for help and you healed me."

Psalm 103:2–3: "Praise the LORD...heals all your diseases."

Psalm 105:37: "...and from among their tribes no one faltered."

Psalm 107:20: "He sent forth his word and healed them."

Proverbs 12:18: "...the tongue of the wise brings healing."

Proverbs 13:17: "... a trustworthy envoy brings healing."

Proverbs 15:4: "The tongue that brings healing is a tree of life."

Proverbs 16:24: "Pleasant words are...healing to the bones."

Isaiah 19:22: After striking he will heal them; (Egypt).

Isaiah 33:24: No one in Zion will say "I am ill."

Isaiah 35:5–6: Blind, deaf, lame, and mute are cured.

Isaiah 42:1, 7: God's servant will open blind eyes.

Isaiah 53:5: "...by *his* wounds we are healed." (emphasis added)

Isaiah 57:18–19: "I will heal him...I will heal them."

Isaiah 58:8: "...your healing will quickly appear."

Jeremiah 30:17: "I will restore you to health and heal your wounds."

Jeremiah 33:6: "I will heal my people."

Ezekiel 47:12: "...their leaves (will be) for healing."

Daniel 3:19–27: Fire does not burn Shadrach and friends.

Daniel 4:34: Nebuchadnezzar's sanity is restored.

Hosea 6:1: "...the LORD...he will heal us."

Hosea 11:3: "...it was I who healed them."

Hosea 14:4: "I will heal their waywardness."

Jonah 2:10: Jonah is preserved.

Malachi 4:2: "...the sun of righteousness will rise with healing in its wings."

THE SHALOM PATH

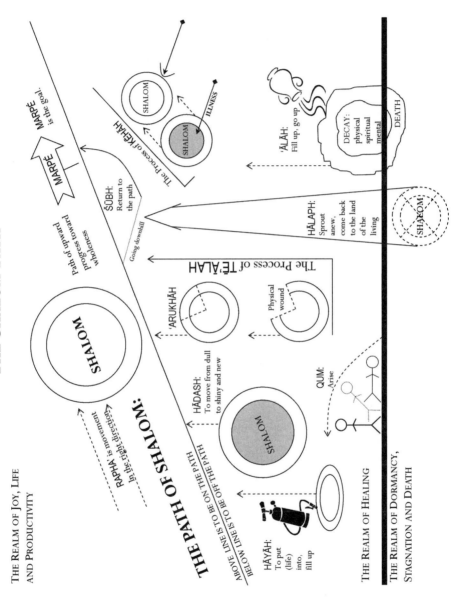

THE REALM OF JOY, LIFE AND PRODUCTIVITY

MARPĒ
MARPĒ is the goal.

Path of upward progress toward wholeness

SHALOM

RAPHA' is movement In the right direction

ŠÛBH: Return to the path

Going downhill

The Process of RĒFÂH

SHALOM

SHALOM

ILLNESS

THE PATH OF SHALOM:

ABOVE LINE IS TO BE ON THE PATH
BELOW LINE IS TO BE OFF THE PATH

ḤĀDASH: To move from dull to shiny and new

The Process of TE'ALAH

'ARUKHÂH

Physical wound

'ÂLÂH: Fill up, go up

DECAY: physical spiritual mental

DEATH

ḤĀLAPH: Sprout anew, come back to the land of the living

SHALOM

SHALOM

QUM: Arise

ḤĀYÂH: To put (life) into, fill up

THE REALM OF HEALING

THE REALM OF DORMANCY, STAGNATION AND DEATH

Jesus healing the sick. Artwork by Gustave Doré.

three

HEALING in the TIME of JESUS

THE UNCHANGING GOD of the Bible, whose healing hand worked for thousands of years in the Old Testament era, is also healing in the New Testament era. Galatians 4:4 says that Jesus came to earth "when the time had fully come." Why didn't Jesus come to start healing and saving shortly after the Fall from Eden's paradise? He could have saved a world of grief and suffering had He done so.

Adam and Eve ate forbidden fruit from the tree of knowledge of good and evil, so apparently, even if subconsciously, they wanted to know everything. So God turned them loose to do so. What is happening for the next four thousand years is man trying to save his condition. It is sad to think of men frustrated agriculturally, fighting weeds and thorns, to grow food that once was freely given. Life is now telling them, "Well, you had to know everything, so study agriculture." The same is true for weather and sociology as the environment and people become more hostile against safe, peaceful living. Here, life is declaring through the pain, "Study weather, study the human heart and mind, study good and evil. You needed to know everything. Learn it."

Next, what about the pain in their body? Offspring, one of life's greatest joys, will now be received only through excruciating labor and birth pains. And as such, mankind was invited to study obstetrics.

There is a telling verse at the end of Genesis 4. It reads: "At that time men began to call on the name of the LORD" (v. 26). It had been 235 years since leaving Eden (see opening verses of Genesis 5) when men began to call on God for help. Reading back, what is the mark of Genesis 4 from the time they left Eden to the time they began calling on God? Murder and its repercussions. Murder, the height of human anger, horror, and pain, had become man's reaction of choice. Afflicted men opted to inflict death upon others. The implications here echo all the way to the Resurrection of Christ. God could have solved this problem right after our leaving Eden. But remember the theological contrast needs to be illustrated fully or God's salvation and healing will have no significance. Life and its agonizing pain are now screaming at humanity—Adam and all his descendants. They have pains and fears *and* they are killing each other! Again God opts not to give a quick fix but lets them spend a few millennia trying to solve it themselves; remember they who had to know everything. To ponder this, the cries of history almost become audible, "God, my body hurts!" And life responds, "Dissect it, learn it, fix it. This was *your* idea. God had handled all this for you. But then again, through your disobedience you had to take over—because you had to know everything."

So after four thousand years man had tried everything on his own by then. Salvation from a divine source was due. A divine incarnation was desperately needed. Religion was a tangled worldwide illustrative mess via man doing creative guesswork. It was not working. Jesus clarified the path of man's quest for God. Weather was a nemesis. Jesus showed his mastery over it through calming storms. Gravity was no issue. He could walk on water. The age old hunt for food (What's for dinner? Is there enough food for the winter?) is shown to be trivial as Jesus simply created food in His hands for thousands of people. Jesus understood societal and religious, and personal and psychological and social problems. He knew peoples' problems and what to do with them even before they shared about it (John 4:7–26). And as for the pain in people's bodies, Jesus healed it. All of it. He knows exactly what to do. It was His prerogative and power to do physical healing. Truly, the Savior had landed in Jesus.

The Gospels and Acts detail the healing ministry of Christ and His followers. The four Gospels record forty-one separate healing incidents demonstrating Jesus' divine authority and power. An impressive amount of the gospel narrative is devoted to healing. "Of the 1,257 narrative verses in the Gospels, 484 verses—38.5 percent!—are devoted to describing Jesus' healing miracles."[1] If one adds the verses that include the immediate reactions of the crowd, the percentage of these healing-related verses exceeds 40 percent.

It is evident that Matthew, Mark, Luke, and John (referred to as "the Evangelists" hereafter), regarded healing as indispensable to the mission of Christ. And they are determined to portray His healing mission to others. They want people to know about Jesus' healing ministry for all history. The Evangelists repeatedly tell of Jesus either healing the sick or teaching a lesson through healing. Much of Jesus' teaching is His preaching after He had the attention of the crowd following a healing. They reported extensive details that revealed both Jesus' human and divine nature. The healings bear witness to His power, His authority, and His compassionate heart that understood human emotions. His gentle touch seen in His handling of the ill, the suffering, the frightened, and the grieving is still comforting to people twenty centuries later.

Even the apostle John, who devotes the least amount of his gospel to physical healing, maintains healing as a priority.[2] Healing was an important element in Jesus' mission of redemption. Therefore, healing in the New Testament must be viewed in light of redemption. As Michael Harper asserts, "Supremely the New Testament is about redemption or deliverance. It tells the story of how God sent his own Son on a mission of restoration, to make good the damage done since man's fall from grace."[3]

Jesus ministered from town to town where His healings, signs, wonders, and powerful preaching attracted large audiences. Through word and deed Jesus taught these audiences the good news of redemption as He healed them. The lesson was comprehensive, for in Hebrew thinking (as was alluded to in chapter 2), to be healed was to be forgiven. Forgiveness before God meant spiritual restoration. And the spiritual restoration resulted in physical restoration.

A classic example is the healing of the paralytic let down through the roof (Matthew 9:2–8; Mark 2:3–12; and Luke 5:18–26). Jesus was in a house that was completely full. The power of the Lord was present to heal the sick (Luke 5:17). Some men brought a paralyzed friend to be healed, but there was no way to enter the building or get through the crowd to reach Jesus. The men were so determined that they hauled their friend with his mat up on the roof and dug a hole through it (Mark 2:4)! This was an extremely aggressive move. Think of it: Jesus, God in the flesh, is inside the house. The Spirit is moving and people are being healed. All were marveling at the sheer power of this man's therapeutic touch. And these men show up and punch a hole in the house! Would they be commended for their determination or rebuked as vandals? Perhaps they might be arrested for destruction of property!

The Pharisees might have arrested them, until Jesus' declaration totally changed the subject for the Pharisees. Because as they had lowered their friend through their newly created hole in the roof, Jesus sensed their faith in His power and declared the man to be forgiven. For the Pharisees, this declaration cast a shadow over any other concerns. The Pharisees were filled with contempt. (Keep in mind that when leaders are determined to be *in control* of a religious setting or atmosphere, they are not blessed by healing, restoration, or joy.) And though they had not said a word, Jesus knew they hotly objected to His indirect claim of deity. His rhetorical question, "Which is easier: to say, 'Your sins are forgiven,' or to say, 'Get up and walk'?" (Luke 5:23) has no answer because neither is easier nor more difficult for the Son of God. Of course the Pharisees were not sure of who He was yet.

Looking straight at the Pharisees, He declared why He was about to perform this healing—that they may know that He had authority on earth to forgive sins. Then, in the same breath, He turned to the paralytic and told him, "Get up, take your mat and go home" (Luke 5:24). The man did so.

By simultaneously granting forgiveness of sin and physical restoration to this man who had been lowered through the roof, Jesus sent a definitive message that echoes through the remainder of His ministry and throughout history. He healed in order to confirm His authority to forgive sins. If He could so easily, confidently, and calmly heal *and* forgive, does this not insist that He was the *Source* of both? Good heavens, what is going on and who in fact is this man?! After the healing of the man lowered through the roof, the houseful of people were not sure. It was too large a lesson to ingest or assess so soon. They could only stand there in awe and praise God.

THE NATURE OF HEALING

Healing is essential to the nature of Jesus. Healing, being an extension of God's character, is also an extension of Jesus' character. In his book, *The Healings of Jesus*, Michael Harper explains that the time of Jesus' ministry was to be a time of healing. This is God's plan because God is Healer. Therefore, when Jesus extended His hand of healing, He was acting out of His compassionate character toward those who were hurting. It was God in the flesh giving people a new lease on life by restoring them in body and spirit—by the thousands!

The Gospels show that Jesus was more than a healer. He was and is the ultimate Source of healing. With simplicity and quiet confidence, He healed people as easily as He breathed the air. Jesus did not strain to conjure up healing power. He was, and is, the Wellspring of healing. People flocked to Him for healing in the same way thirsty people congregate at a cool spring or water fountain in the heat of summer.

Jesus' healings are power in motion. Luke mentions four such incidents of unusual power being available for healing: Luke 4:14, 5:17, 8:46, and 9:1–2. Sometimes when Jesus was in a crowd, they needed only to touch Him and they were healed (Mark 6:56). At those times one needed only to draw near to Jesus and receive. The account in Luke 8:46, where the woman was healed of chronic bleeding by touching the hem of Jesus' garment, is the best known of these incidents. Without making herself known to Jesus, she touched His garment and was immediately healed. Just then Jesus paused to remark that power had left Him. It had been "siphoned" from Him, so to speak. He felt the touch of this particular person. He felt the power leave. The comical factor here is that He is in the middle of a crowd so thick that it is a practical "rugby game" in progress. Rock concertgoers would say Jesus was in a "mosh pit." I do not mean to be funny, but He was near to being crushed by the crowd. Amid this, the woman who touched His robe, believing she would be healed, extracts healing power from Him and she is restored. It worked because she believed it would work. Jesus' power is that prevalent. It works even when He is focused elsewhere.

Jesus' healing power was inexhaustible. It was never rationed because His "tank was running low." He was never "running on empty," as the contemporary phrase goes. There was no need for Him to use some technique in order to gain more power. He never paused to stretch out or breathe deeply. He had power. He *was* power. Keith Bailey says, "No limitations were placed on His healing ministry on earth."[4] To affirm the immensity of Jesus' healing power, the Synoptic writers (meaning Matthew, Mark, and Luke—for their accounts of Jesus are similar—hereafter referred to as "Synoptic") give roughly ten references to Jesus healing great multitudes. (See Jesus' Healings Chart at the end of this chapter, # 3, 4, 8, 13, 23, 25, 27, 28, and 36 on the chart.) These crowds may have varied from five hundred to twenty thousand or more. The size of the crowd never taxed or weakened His power to heal. For brevity, the Gospels describe these scenes in three verses or less, simply mentioning that Jesus cured "multitudes" of people. Some have proposed that there were days when Jesus healed even tens of thousands. All things considered, this becomes difficult to argue against. Eventually the whole eastern coastal area of the Mediterranean Sea knew what Jesus was doing.

Jesus' healing was not only bountiful, it was free. Jesus liberally granted healing to anyone who would come to Him. He did not lecture people to diet or caution them as to what would have prevented their condition. He did not harangue, belittle or bill them for His services. The price of healing today can have a way of transferring agony from the body to the wallet!

Most people know at least one family that has been hit with a catastrophe. The physical aspect of a medical tragedy is bad enough; an auto accident, or cancer or such. The curing of it is good but sometimes the hospital bills, doctor bills, surgeons' bills, and therapist bills can strangle a family for years to come. It was not so with Jesus, ever. When He freed people from their physical anguish they were totally set free to live again. Nothing lingered. There was no need for follow-up or a second opinion.

Jesus' healings were liberation. This liberation was symbolic of the imminent salvation through the resurrected Christ. While speaking in the local synagogue, Jesus identified Himself as the Messiah. He referred to Isaiah's prophecy for Israel about the Spirit's authority being on His ministry.

> The Spirit of the Sovereign LORD is on me, because the LORD has anointed me to preach good news to the poor. He has sent me to bind up the brokenhearted to proclaim freedom for the captives and release from darkness for the prisoners, to proclaim the year of the LORD's favor.
>
> —ISAIAH 61:1–2

Jesus' inauguration message fulfilled prophecy and made it clear that He had come to liberate those bound in spirit and body (similar to Isaiah 42:7, 49:8–9, 58:6; and Psalm 102:20 and 103:6).

The liberation of people from illness, sin, destruction, and hell was the major theme of Jesus' work. He came to liberate people from oppression, blindness, pain, ostracism and demonization. "This is precisely how Jesus conceived His mission: the time of the Messiah would be a time of healing, of liberation, of salvation."[5] The Cross made ultimate liberation irreversible. In actuality, Jesus entered the huge prison of sin called earth and walked the corridors to unlock each cell. And to those who felt further trapped and needed more, to those who called and pleaded for Him to free them, Jesus "kicked the door in." He freed people!

To disclose the reality of liberation, Jesus healed the sick. (Remember, for the Hebrew, to be set free in body was to be set free.) Though healing was not in itself intrinsic and absolute liberation, healing did *proclaim* liberation. Man was again free to be what he was originally intended to be: fully alive and living in joyful communion with God.

Being set free is good news. Francis MacNutt says that to deny healing is to change the gospel from "Good News into Good Advice which lacks the power to transform man into a new creation."[6] If this healing power were not so, then Jesus is not the Savior. He is reduced to being a part-time counselor—one whose effectiveness is held in great question at that.

The Gospels clearly display that Jesus liberated people from demonic oppression. Twelve different examples of Jesus' healing people from insanity and demon possession are found in the Gospels (see Jesus' Works of Healing, # 1, 3, 4, 8, 9, 14, 17, 21, 22, 31, 32, and 37). Thus liberation meant freedom from depression, emotional and mental chaos, hopelessness, and grief. Harper states: "The New Testament shows us how Jesus liberated men and women from all that oppressed them. It was especially seen in terms of freedom from sickness [and] satanic powers."[7] Those who reached out to Jesus were healed and freed to fully live again.

Healing of the body is never purely physical, and the salvation of the soul is never purely spiritual...

Luke used the Greek verb *sozo* (pronounced "SODE-zo") to denote both healing and salvation. The fact that this word is used interchangeably indicates divine healing is a redemptive act of God. Luke uses *sozo* eight times. In 6:9 it refers to "saving life"; in 8:36, releasing a demoniac; in 8:48, halting of chronic bleeding; in 8:50, returning life to a dead girl; in 17:19, the cleansing of lepers; in 23:35, 37, and 39 it depicts "rescue" by those taunting Jesus to save Himself. Some may separate the healing and saving process, but in Jesus' operational ministry they were not separate. From Luke's applied usage of *sozo* it can be further learned that the two processes are not meant to be separated. Jesus did not separate the two. In *Health and Healing*, John Wilkinson, a top-notch British scholar, speaks with insight about the usage of this word *sozo*: "It is clear that its wide application in the Gospels indicates that the Christian concept of healing and the Christian concept of salvation overlap to a degree which varies in different situations, but are never completely separable. Healing of the body is never purely physical, and the salvation of the soul is never purely spiritual, but both are combined in the deliverance of the whole man, a deliverance which is foreshadowed and illustrated in the healing miracles of Jesus in the Gospels."[8]

To digest and understand Wilkinson's words above is to take a giant step toward understanding Jesus' healing ministry. And though while not equivocal, healing and salvation cannot be detached from each other. Both are elements of liberation. Therefore to be physically healed by Jesus is symbolic of the coming salvation through the resurrected Christ.

Through healing, Jesus manifested God's love for humanity. Undoubtedly, it is Calvary that proves the depth of His love. Healing is an overflow of Calvary's love. "The one thing that God seems to want to show people by these healings is that He is real, that He loves ordinary people, and that He wants them to draw near to Him."[9]

God is love; therefore His nature is love. Because He is love He heals not only out of His power, but also out of His compassion. Divine healing demonstrates what God wishes to do for all His children: give them relief, rest, peace, and a life filled with wonder spent walking with Him. Jesus worked on behalf of God and functioned as the Healer, thereby relaying God's message of love perfectly.

JESUS' PATTERN OF HEALING

A pattern of ministry emerges from extensively studying Jesus' healings. There are four questions that can be raised about His mission to heal. Why did Jesus heal? What did He heal? How did He heal? How much did He heal?

Why Jesus Healed

In searching the scriptures, I find six key reasons why Jesus healed the sick. While this is not the last word on Jesus' motive and compulsion for healing, it does cover the prominent reasons for His healing action.

1. As the Son of God

Jesus healed, most believe, because He was the Son of God. "Bible scholars seem to take a common position that healing was exclusively a credential of deity—a validation that Jesus was the very Son of God."[10] Jesus' healings constituted a proof of His deity. The Evangelists, having realized the effect of healing, stressed it in the Gospels. Matthew, Mark, and John were with Him during his ministry of healing and salvation. They watched it happen. And since throughout biblical history God had healed His children, it can only follow that Jesus would heal as God His Father had healed. To borrow a phrase from the vocational world, we could say Jesus follows in His Father's footsteps; "like Father—like Son."

2. As Servant of the Father

Jesus healed as an act of obedience. Jesus was not a man on a personal glory crusade, but a man commissioned by His Father and in subjection to

Him. Jesus knew that His role was that of a servant. He was a man serving His Father. He understood that He had been sent on a mission of love to the needy.

> The Spirit of the Lord is on me, because he has anointed me...He has sent me to proclaim freedom...and recovery of sight for the blind.
>
> —LUKE 4:18

Jesus clearly perceives and shows Himself as anointed and sent. So when Jesus helped man in his need, He served God. And "in taking up the cause of the helpless Jesus proves himself to be the Servant of God."[11]

After healing the man at The Pool of Bethesda in John chapter 5, Jesus gave an explanation of His work. In verse 30 He claims, "By myself I can do nothing...for I seek not to please myself but him who sent me." Jesus did not accept glory for His work. He is not seen basking in the laurels that can be laid upon a healer. When He is healing people, He is doing this to serve His Father and His neighbor as the Son of Man. (Mark prefers "Son of Man" when referring to Jesus.) Of a truth, Jesus is blessing God and serving Him by helping and healing God's children. Ministers today would do well to remember that they are doing both or they are doing neither—serving God and serving their neighbor. To merely do either one is a disservice to both. Jesus' anointed calling was to bring glory to His Father who sent Him. Jesus, in His healing of people, served His Father.

3. As the Prophet of God

Healing was yet another confirmation that Jesus was a prophet. The Pharisees had been taught through their Jewish literature studies that prophets were to be tested by the integrity of their prophecies. Jesus' life certainly fulfilled manifold prophecies. And with certain people, healing even added to the import of their prophetic ministry. While some of the greatest prophets did no miracles, Elijah and Elisha were superlative in their exercise of supernatural powers. This verified their prophetic ministry. So too were the prophetic healings that Jesus did. They verified (prophesied) that He worked for God and spoke for God.

The healings of Christ were a fulfillment of prophecy. In Matthew 8:16–17, Jesus healed every demon-possessed and sick person brought to Him. Evangelist Matthew explains, "This was to fulfill what was spoken through the prophet Isaiah: 'He took up our infirmities and carried our diseases.'"

> We are to serve God and our neighbor: to merely do either one is a disservice to both.

His healings are also a fulfillment of Isaiah 61:1, which He quoted in Nazareth. Israel had been waiting—from Moses to David and into the exile—for the prophet who would be Messiah. The people of His day were fairly certain of what a prophet should be. Their heritage was built upon powerful men of God who did divine acts and miracles. So revered are the prophets who do miracles that Elijah and Elisha had status that elevated them to a plain that was higher than other prophets who simply preached and wrote. Jesus is doing miracles of healing and, in the limited view of His contemporaries, this puts Jesus *up there* with Elijah.

Though some of the greatest prophets of Israel did no miracles, the link between Elijah, Elisha, and Jesus is an intriguing match. Stronstad traces the prophetic similarities of Elijah, Elisha, and Jesus.[12]

	ELIJAH	ELISHA	JESUS
CONTROL NATURE	1 Kings 17:1 2 Kings 2:8	2 Kings 2:14 2 Kings 2:19ff	Luke 8:2ff
RAISE THE DEAD	1 Kings 17:17ff	2 Kings 4:34ff	Luke 7:14ff
MULTIPLY FOOD	1 Kings 17:16 2 Kings 4:42ff	2 Kings 4:3ff	Luke 9:12ff
HEAL LEPROSY	2 Kings 5:8ff		Luke 5:12ff

Jesus was given great credence through His performing the same type of miracles as Elijah and Elisha. Notice that when Jesus is on the Cross and He calls out "My God, my God why have you forsaken me?" the bystanders think Jesus is calling to Elijah. Though they miss the moment, to their credit, in minds of the Jewish leaders, Elijah is one of the "big leaguers." They were forgetting that Jesus had accomplished many times over what Elijah and Elisha combined had accomplished.

There are prophetic reasons that Jesus healed, in addition to fulfillment of prophecy and confirmation of His message. From a social standpoint, healing advanced Jesus' mission of restoration and redemption. For one, it feverishly spread the news about Him to people everywhere. The Gospels say that people remained for hours marveling over Jesus' mighty deeds. This gave tremendous credibility to this preaching. Healing was like an alluring flame, drawing people to Christ Jesus' ministry.

His healings, resurrections, miraculous feedings, and other wonders always drew a massive crowd to hear Him preach. The whole scenario added tremendous force to His prophetic preaching about the kingdom. Consequently, Jesus continued healing until His final days.

4. Because of His Compassion

Jesus healed people because He loved and cared for them. The scriptures record six different times when He was moved with compassion to relieve the suffering and grieving all around Him. (See Jesus' Works of Healing, # 5, 18, 24, 26, 30 and 41.) This compassion is the overflow of His heart; it is Jesus coming forth. His compassion is a fascinating and therapeutic salve.

Compassion drove Him to heal pathetic lepers who were being eaten up by their disease. Jesus was so deeply pained upon encountering the blind that He healed them. Crowds of people with ailments often filled Him with pity. The death of Lazarus and his family's sorrow drove Jesus to sobbing and tears of grief. The popular verse "Jesus wept" doesn't do the setting justice via the English language. It is very clear as originally written that "wept" means Jesus sobbed heavily as He empathized with Lazarus' relatives in their mourning. Bailey calls Jesus' acts of compassion "an index to the very heart of God."[13]

In Walter Bauer's *Greek-English Lexicon*, "compassion" is defined "have pity; feel sympathy with or for someone in a literal and inward way; have one's heart go out to another; have compassion for someone."[14] Jesus' compassion to heal is a testimony to the tenderness and reality of the human element combined with His divine nature.

Among all the reasons Jesus healed, it is Jesus' compassion that puts Him among the crowd as "one who is touched by the feelings of infirmity." This becomes a necessary witness to who Jesus was. It intensifies the fullness of his humanity. The richness of His soul blossoms from such narrative.

The verses about Jesus' compassion describe the warmth of His personality. They illustrate that He is especially drawn to people who need the relief found in a divine yet human touch. His hands were warm and gentle. His eyes reflected His compassion for those in grief. His compassion attested to His love and perfect awareness of human frailty. He was acquainted with grief, familiar with suffering, and felt kinship with those who were travailing. "This evidence...of mercy indicates that the healing ministry of Christ cannot be treated solely as proof of deity or of the supernatural. It must be treated also as an expression of the mercy, compassion and goodness of His pure and perfect heart."[15] Without compassion Jesus would not have shown the meaning of true human kindness.

5. To Advance the Kingdom of God

Jesus preached and healed the sick to announce the kingdom of God. Jesus encountered the destroyer and loosed his captives. People were being rescued from the kingdom of sin, sickness, and death. The gates of hell were assaulted, its code cracked by Christ, and the oppressed were set free. In doing this, "Jesus embodied the kingdom of God."[16] His healing ministry advanced the kingdom of God.

There are numerous references to the kingdom of God in the Synoptic Gospels. Scottish scholar I. Howard Marshall lists thirty-six in Matthew, fourteen in Mark, and thirty-two in Luke.[17] Jesus referred to the kingdom of God regularly in His preaching. Many of His sermons begin with, "The kingdom of heaven is..." This is because turning men's hearts and minds toward God's kingdom is among the most important topics of His mission.

Jesus delegated His followers to proclaim the kingdom. In Luke 9:1 and

10:1 He sends out twelve, then seventy-two disciples to heal and deliver people from harassment by demons. When the seventy-two return from their healing and deliverance campaigns, they are thrilled that people had been healed and they said, "Even the demons submit to us in your name" (Luke 10:17). Jesus responds, "I saw Satan fall like lightning from heaven" (v. 18). He then tells His disciples, "I have given you authority...to overcome all the power of the enemy" (v. 19). The authority over the enemy meant the presence of the kingdom of God. In plain terms, the kingdom of God had arrived.

The parallel saying in Matthew 12:22–30 and Luke 11:14–23 helps us understand Jesus' deliverance and healing as signs of the kingdom of God. Here Jesus' authority to heal is being challenged by religious leaders. After Jesus asserts that Satan has no part of Him, He retorts, "If I drive out demons by the Spirit of God then the kingdom of God has come upon you" (Matt. 12:28; Luke says "finger" of God). Jesus claimed that exorcisms announced the presence of the kingdom of God. Though the kingdom of God has always been eternal (it did not commence at some point), it was now being manifested on earth. In Acts 10:38, Peter says "Jesus of Nazareth...went around doing good and healing all who were under the power of the devil." Whereas Satan imprisons and debilitates in his kingdom, Jesus heals and liberates in His kingdom.

Jesus offered a new creation and fullness of life to people while Satan offered only destruction and death (candy-coated, of course). During the time of Christ's ministry, this battle between these powers raged in view of the people. This was part of the attraction of Jesus' ministry. They could actually witness the power of God winning victory over evil.

6. To Defeat Satan

The winning of a war requires several processes. First, enemy territory must be reached and penetrated. Then enemy troops must be defeated and driven back as territory is reclaimed. Prisoners need to be freed and brought home. Lastly the enemy leader must be apprehended and a rightful rule reinstated over the land.

A parallel to war and victory can be seen in the Incarnation, the ministry, the death, and the resurrection of Jesus. His healings and deliverances were battles won in the war to defeat Satan. Jesus was triumphant in each of these battles. Through healing bodies and lives, Jesus reclaimed territory that had been captured by Satan; they got their lives back.

Adam and Eve did not realize the immensity of the nightmare that lay ahead for all humanity as they yielded to the serpent in Genesis 3. As a consequence, man's spiritual, mental, social, and physical harmony was disrupted. And Satan continued to harass man, as is his delight, for several millennia. Jesus then came into this mêlée to confront the condition of human hopelessness and free men from the dominion of Satan. When Jesus healed or delivered someone, it was therefore a direct assault on Satan's kingdom.

Since Lucifer's rebellion, his agenda has been vandalistic and contrary to God's. Jesus' first temptation serves as a reminder to the dissension. Here Satan offers Jesus the kingdoms of the world (Matthew 4:8–10; Luke 4:5–8). How does Jesus proceed? He rejects Satan's offer and embarks on His own mission to advance the kingdom of God. His method would be to set people free from the kingdom of Satan and build His church against which nothing would prevail. First John 3:8 says, "The devil has been sinning from the beginning. The reason the Son of God appeared was to destroy the devil's work." That is why healing is a large part of Jesus' work. Though not every sickness is a direct satanic work, divine healing of a person in the physical is a powerful weapon that counterattacks Satan.

Satan's empire is one ultimately bent on inflicting agony and despair. Being diametrically opposed to God, Satan's attacks are upon creation and man. He attacks creation for it is God's art studio. He attacks man because we, God's children, are a mirror of Himself and therefore His most cherished possession. Satan's desire for man is to be ostracized as he was and to ultimately be banished as he is going to be. To initiate this, Satan provoked a break in man's relationship with the Creator. The wicked environment of Satan is hostile to God and miserable for man. As if this were not enough, Satan sent demons to actually occupy individuals and ruin their lives. This was his foretaste of hell.

Into this scene of wretchedness came the Prince of Peace to proclaim the good news of the kingdom and to demonstrate the power of the kingdom by casting out demons, healing sickness, disease, deformities, handicaps, and raising the dead. Jesus had executed a powerful work. He was reversing the curse and the losses inflicted since Genesis 3. Satan's losses were real, they threw his kingdom into a panic, and Jesus permanently nixed the authority that Satan had on earth. In Matthew 28:18 Jesus tells His disciples after the resurrection that "all authority in heaven and on earth has been given to me. Therefore go and make disciples of all nations." If Jesus has all authority, then Satan has zero. And people were to live like it.

Jesus invaded Satan's empire and counterattacked by forgiving, healing, and doing exorcisms. Jesus dealt with sin and sickness with precision, power, and authority as it had never been dealt with before. He knew that the origin of sickness was rooted in the deceiver. "In the New Testament, sickness is seen as an extension and effect of sin and…therefore evil in origin."[18] Everything about Christ's life and ministry confronted, neutered, and defeated Satan.

WHAT JESUS HEALED

The healing ministry of Jesus Christ was all-inclusive. It covered the entire spectrum of human needs. People's problems that were physically or organically rooted, spiritually rooted, or emotionally rooted, all were put to rest by Jesus' touch and words. Nothing was out of His realm to heal.

1. Sickness, Disease, Deformity, Handicap, Death

Jesus demonstrated His power and authority to heal a wide variety of sicknesses, diseases, deformities, handicaps, heartaches, and spiritual disorders. The record of His physical healings in the Gospels may be arranged in five categories: internal diseases, chronic diseases, sensory diseases, deformities, and various assorted problems.

INTERNAL DISEASES

- fevers
- sickness (mild or deadly)
- hemorrhaging
- dropsy or edema (excessive fluid in the tissues; swelling that is elsewhere called elephantiasis)
- "severe pain"

CHRONIC DISEASES

- man lame thirty-eight years
- scoliosis/bent spine (for eighteen years)
- leprosy (medically categorized today as Hansen's Disease)
- hemorrhaging (twelve years)

(These last two diseases required the victims to be in isolation.)

SENSORY DISEASES

- blindness
- deafness
- mute/dumb
- leprosy (it affected "touch")

DEFORMITIES

- withered hand
- crippled, lame
- paralysis
- scoliosis/bent spine

ASSORTED PROBLEMS

- severed body parts (Malchus' ear)
- neurological disorders and epilepsy
- demonization
- death or the critically ill
- various/all diseases

The list above is certainly not inclusive of every disease that existed in Jesus' day. However, the healing by Jesus recorded in the Gospels is a clear statement of Jesus' total mastery over all human ailments.

2. Sin and Spiritual Sickness

The biblical record unmistakably teaches that the spiritual sickness of sin lies at the root of all human problems. Stated plainly, Jesus came to remedy the sin problem. "Every time Jesus met with evil, spiritual or physical, he treated it as an enemy."[19] It was usually the pain that Jesus relieved. It could be the death of a relative, or a bent spine, or the isolation of being lame. Whatever was hurting people, Jesus cured it in a moment. He did so because evil is sin and sin is lethal. Does this sin usually kill people right away? Adam and Eve sinned even though they were told that if they did so "they would surely die." Did they die that day at high noon? No. Adam lived another 930 years. But this sin started the inescapable conveyor belt toward death for Adam and all his progeny. This conveyor belt could never be turned off or even slowed down.

In my pastoral and mission work of encouraging the saints, discipling believers, reaching the lost, and urging people to forsake sinful ways, some have responded, "Yeah, I started doing such and such. The Bible says not to, but, hey, I do it anyway. Lightning never strikes. I haven't died yet, so it's fine. I'm fine and I don't care." Sin's conveyor belt is slow enough to lull the sinner into thinking he will be fine. It is also fast enough to get the attention of the wise and with the Spirit's help to turn from the path of destruction. The truth is that unconfessed sin from which a person does not repent leads to outer darkness.

So what now? Jesus has and is the remedy. Sin and its effects never puzzled Jesus because He knew its origin. Jesus knows how to kill sin at its root, and that is His plan for our souls. Why? He knew the grave effects of spiritual sickness. "Spiritual sickness...disrupts our emotions, our relationships and even our physical bodies."[20] At times, Jesus would treat the sin and the physical symptom would be healed, as in the case of the paralytic referred to earlier, the one lowered through the roof (Matthew 9:1–8; Mark 2:1–12; Luke 5:17–26). Upon seeing their faith (both Mark and Luke's first usage of the word *faith*) Jesus said to the man, "Your sins are forgiven" (Matthew 9:2). He could have merely repaired the man's defective body parts, but it was time to expose the core of human malady and also His own authority to remedy that condition.

The truth that healing and forgiveness are related was not new; God had revealed it in the Old Testament. But here the people were astounded when Jesus spoke forgiveness. It was harder for them to believe Jesus could forgive than it was to believe that He could heal. They did not yet understand that He was God among them. And though most of the eyewitnesses did not realize it, Jesus' handling of this incident with the paralytic revealed the extent and fullness of Jesus' deity, personhood, power, and authority over sin. In traversing the terrain of the entire Bible, this defining moment is an alpine moment with repercussions that echo throughout history.

It is noteworthy to see where this healing had fallen in the progression of Jesus' earthly ministry. Up until this point, Luke has testified to the breadth of Jesus' miraculous power as one who had performed exorcisms (4:35 and 41), cured a fever (4:39), healed "various diseases" (4:40), exhibited control over nature, animals, and food supply (5:4–7), and cleansed a leper (5:13). By this, Luke establishes the fact that Jesus is powerful and extraordinary before telling the story of the paralytic. In this second reference to "power" being upon Jesus, it was now time to reveal the extent of His power—His authority to forgive sin. And he does so in a simple statement. Could it be that the curse and problem that had haunted earth since Genesis 3 could be solved by this one man? Could it be that His Life and declaration shall pronounce forgiveness as eternal? After four thousand years, is the timeless cure for sin finally upon them? What is brewing here in this Jesus man's life and deeds is so huge and historical that it was difficult to take in at the time.

Jesus is what the world has been waiting for.

So paramount is this healing and its revelation that Matthew, Mark, and Luke place this healing near the beginning of their narratives. This way Jesus' subsequent healings and teaching can be read in light of this revelation. In this they are instructing that sin and sickness are linked together—and Jesus solves both problems. After Jesus declared the man to be forgiven, the angry Pharisees retorted, "Who can forgive sins but God alone?" Jesus cut to the issue by asking, "Which is easier: to say, 'Your sins are forgiven,' or to say, 'Get up and walk'?" (Luke 5:23). The answer is that neither is easier to say. Neither is easier to say because neither is harder to do for Jesus.

Joseph Fitzmyer says, "The physical miracle is the sign of the rescue of the man from the bonds of moral evil."[21] Once these bonds were loosed by forgiveness, the paralysis was healed and he rose from his mat. Being forgiven and healed, his life was now returned to wholeness. "It suggests the extraordinary character of the new dimension in human life that comes with Jesus' power and authority."[22]

The lesson was that Jesus both heals and forgives, and people are to come to Him for both blessings. The future of humanity depends upon it. The revelation of Jesus' virtue and ability in the above story cannot be overstated. The initial hint of a Savior (Genesis 3:15) who would come someday, who would crush evil and sin, and bring restoration was verified in the above healing of the paralytic. In my opinion, the Bible is building up the arrival of Jesus. Jesus' life is to reveal what has just been told in the above story, the how and why of Jesus healing the paralytic. This is the crucial episode in Jesus' ministry. It is the initial event where who He is and why He is here is emblazoned upon literature and into history. Yes, Calvary and the Resurrection are the crowning event of our Savior, but this statement, "Your sins are forgiven" is the critical revelation of Jesus. The remainder of Jesus' deeds and words must be mentally processed and personally embraced in light of Jesus' statements and deeds done for the paralytic. Jesus forgives sin—which kills death. Jesus heals—which grants restoration. He is what the world has been waiting for.

3. Demonization

Jesus also freed those who were bound by demons. He healed the lives of people who were being destroyed by demons. The Gospels record Jesus driving out demons on eleven different occasions. These accounts are important, for they illustrate Jesus' authority and power to expel and overcome the evil one. They also give a message of hope through Christ for He has power to free them from the fear of demons. A good message for humanity is that since Jesus can do this, and He works on *our* behalf, then we can overcome anything.

Demons have a main assignment, and that is to work destruction in humans: in their lives, personalities, souls, bodies, families, homes, cities, and lands. And when given free reign, they do so. The following list covers the characteristics of demons:

- They have intelligence (Acts 16:16–18; 19:15–16).
- They are spirits (Matthew 8:16; 12:43–45; Luke 10:17–20; Revelation 16:14).
- They manifest themselves in different forms (Revelation 9:1–12; 16:13–14).
- They are malevolent (Matthew 12:43–45; Mark 1:27; 3:11; Luke 4:36; Acts 8:7; Revelation 16:13).
- They know their own end (Matthew 8:29; 25:41; James 2:19).
- They have supernatural strength (Matthew 12:29; Mark 5:4; Luke 8:29; Acts 19:13–16).
- They must bow to Jesus' name (Matthew 8:28–34; Mark 5:7; Luke 8:26–33).[23]

This final point must be our first reminder about demons. That being said, we must remember their agenda. For in their obstinate and unrelenting attempt to invade human beings, the demons will initially attack through the mind. The New Testament speaks of vain imaginations. I believe this is where they begin their work. If they began differently they would be too easily exposed as workers of evil. Their strategy is to spiritually assault the mind and then manipulate people physically so that it looks as if the problem is self-inflicted. In this way the devil keeps people preoccupied with the symptoms of his work, which can in turn divert us from dealing with the root. Jesus recognized demonization when He saw it. He would quickly expel the "demons at work" as well as reverse the destruction they had caused.

For example, the most ostentatious display of demonization was in the Gerasene demoniac. The Synoptics all determine to get this story divulged (Matthew 8:28; Mark 5:1–20; Luke 8:26–39). Fitzmyer calls it "fantastic" and "grotesque."[24] The man had been reduced to a worse than animal state. Jesus met him to administer healing and peace and to display authority and power over the demons. This encounter occurred directly after the storm on Galilee as described in all three accounts. "The Jesus who stilled the storm on the lake, and took authority over the elements, also took authority over the storm in this man's life."[25] The man was being subjected to a hurricane of demonic possession.

The satanic team was hard at work in this man. He made the whole area a threat to pass through. He wore no clothes and, obsessed with death, he lived among the tombs in a graveyard on the eastern shore above Galilee. With satanic strength he broke every chain they put him in. He did not sleep. Doctors will tell you that this insomnia will make anyone psychotic. Day and night he roamed the hills crying out and cutting himself. His life was a frenzied, maniacal nightmare of chaotic horror and mutilation. History has hardly ever produced a person who has been in a worse state than this puppet of the devil.

Who are you going to call? We can forget about *Ghostbusters*. Who else is there to summon but Jesus? When Jesus arrives, the powerful encounter takes place. The man is delivered. The demons enter the herd of pigs who then rush down the cliff to their death. When the city dwellers hear about this they come to see what had happened. "When they came to Jesus, they found the man from whom the demons had gone out, sitting at Jesus' feet, dressed and in his right mind" (Luke 8:35). He had been brought back from his demented state to peace, health, and wholeness. In grave irony, some of the locals were afraid and did not like what had happened. Notwithstanding, this marvelous display of Jesus' power and authority was a great victory. Following this Gerasene's cleansing, Jesus tells him to go to his towns east of Galilee (ten Greek cities called the Decapolis) and to tell everyone what God had done in his life.

The point to be remembered from the deliverance of the Gerasene demoniac, the other deliverances, and healings is that Jesus has the power and authority to heal anything Satan inflicts. No matter what level of demonization victims suffer, Jesus can make them whole. Jesus' healing reverses the work of demons and expels them so that those left in their hideous wake may return to a sane, productive, joyful life. Therefore with Jesus there is no reason for anyone anywhere to ever be in fear.

How Jesus Healed

There were two important factors in how Jesus carried out His healing ministry. First, Jesus was empowered by the Holy Spirit for this ministry. Second, Jesus required faith from those who desired healing for themselves and/or for others.

1. Through the Anointing of the Spirit of God

Jesus delivered and healed people through the power of the Holy Spirit. Any conflicting belief is heresy. He was God in the flesh and was capable of doing any of these works in His own power. But for the purpose of His incarnation, Jesus laid aside His power and carried out His ministry as a man filled with the Holy Spirit (Luke 4:18–19). Prior to Jesus' baptism there is no record of Him performing any miracles. The only remarkable event during His first thirty years is the temple incident when He was twelve-years-old. Here He displays precocious knowledge about Yahweh, His Father, and related matters. Any details about Jesus doing supernatural works prior to having the Holy Spirit come upon Him are the deductions of irresponsible "scholarship," possibly even reckless musings.

Jesus' deeds are acts of the Holy Spirit. They are not initiated independently. Of the four Evangelists, Luke illustrates this the most clearly. For him, the activity of the Holy Spirit is perfectly lived out in the ministry of Jesus. There is not a hint of ego operating in Jesus either by word or gesture while He is healing. He is fueled by the Holy Spirit, and is fully human and fully God. Since Jesus' ministry is ordained of God, it is, in essence, His call. Therefore "the gift of the Spirit to Jesus in the inauguration narrative . . . is vocational. This vocational gift is specifically prophetic. Jesus is not only anointed by the Spirit, but He is also Spirit-led, Spirit-filled, and Spirit-empowered."[26]

It was by the Spirit that Jesus commenced the work of the kingdom of God. It was by the Spirit that He healed the sick, blind, and lame, raised the dead, and preached the good news. From His baptism to His ascension, Jesus was completely gifted for His work. Gifted here is meaning *"charis."* That is what the scriptures label it. This is how Jesus operated. The Spirit is His fuel and compass. Looking at the big picture of Jesus' person here, seeing what He both says and does, He is the archetype charismatic Prophet. There is not a more accurate way to state it. And Jesus labored in dependency upon the Holy Spirit throughout the length of His ministry. Are any of us to do differently? Who is our model in life and ministry anyway?

2. Through Elemental Faith

Faith is a requirement for Christ's healing touch to be received. Norman Perrin says, "Many of the most characteristic sayings about faith in the gospels are associated with miracles, especially healing miracles."[27] It is almost as if faith is the spark that starts a fire. Faith is seen nearly to melt Jesus' heart (if such a verb is permissible). When He saw faith in a person He had a practical compulsion to heal them. The Gospel writers specifically note "faith" as the catalyst in at least thirteen of the forty-one recorded miracles. Jesus was stirred to action by faith in such incidents as the paralytic (see #6 in Jesus' Works of Healing), with Jairus and his daughter (#10), the Syro-Phoenician and her daughter (# 14), the blind Bartimaeus (# 18), and the centurion with his servant (# 19). Faith could be expressed on the part of the sick or by someone else who cared for them. It was of no matter. People expressed faith, for instance, by obeying Jesus' commands like "go wash in Siloam" or "stretch out your hand."

Jesus just finished spitting and making mud and smearing it on this man's eyes…on his face, mind you. I do not meet too many people who like to walk across town with mud on their faces. Many ladies pack their faces with mud for cosmetic reasons (don't ask me why), but they do not go to market looking like this. Here is a man who walks across town with mud on his face. And God told him to do this! Blind men normally prefer to hide and huddle in coves and corners and to wearing a covering. What's the deal here? He wants to get well and he is convinced that what Jesus told him to do will work. So he is a spectacle walking across town with mud on his face and He did not seem to care. That is faith!

The man stretching out his withered had a similar assignment (#7). Drop the shame, and do what Jesus says—raise your hand. We all know what people with beautiful muscles or figures or expensive clothes do, don't we? They show them off. On the contrary, people with handicaps, blemishes, or upsetting conditions conceal them. Leg scars are covered with long dresses or pants. Pimples are covered with make up. Withered hands are gloved or kept in pockets. And what does Jesus tell this man to do? He's in the synagogue. The place is crowded. Anyone who would have asked him to stretch out his hand would be harassing him, trying to make sport of him, ridiculing him. But it is different this time and he stretches out his hand. The man showed faith and he is marvelously rewarded.

Lack of faith was the only apparent barrier to Jesus' healing ministry. When He returned to Nazareth after His baptism, His healing power was hindered by unbelief (Matthew 13:58, Mark 6:5–6). Matthew says that He "Did not do," but Mark goes so far as to say He "*could* there do no mighty work" (KJV, emphasis added). These scriptures imply a refusal to violate a theological law. Not that lack of faith nullified the omnipotence of God, but simply that He would not force anyone to have faith in Him. That, for one thing, would not be love. If He did, it would be like a codependent and insecure parent begging a stubborn six-year-old to open a birthday present. This is nonsense. God will not beg to bless anyone. That would be a violation of His character, and He will not be mocked.

It is important to clarify this "faith" concept. Faith is not a coin for healing that will turn God into a therapeutic vending machine. The "name it, claim it" trend implies that man is in charge. The truth is God is in charge, not us.

Some use the "if it be Your will" clause as a disguise for presupposed unbelief. That is a pious slogan that can just as easy be a resignation or a cop-out. That way if nothing happens, the hollow drivel can be masked, "Oh well, it wasn't God's will."

Faith is believing that Jesus is able and willing to heal. Christ's followers are obligated to express faith for healing. If not, then it is Christians who say "no" to God's healing touch, not God. Only God has the prerogative to withhold healing. We have the responsibility to enter in, and to press forward in prayer and ask.

> Faith is believing that Jesus is able and willing
> to heal.

Thus faith opens the way for people to receive healing. Faith clears the channel through which healing can flow. True faith does not demand of God, but humbly petitions with full hope of a response. That is childlike confidence. True faith asks of God, boldly aligns with His Spirit, and eagerly waits.

HOW MUCH DID JESUS HEAL?

The title question may sound peculiar, but it deserves explanation. Did Jesus cure mental retardation? Every time? Did He make gray hair black again? Were no babies stillborn in Judah and Israel or Galilee during His ministry? Were all hospitals/clinics in Israel and Judah empty by the time He finished His travels? Did all morticians take a three-year hiatus while Jesus was in the public eye? Were old people given youthful strength again? Did all people resemble Ken and Barbie (the American doll series) after Jesus came through? Was this His objective? Because of the final verse in John's Gospel that says, "Jesus did many other things as well," dogmatic answers to such questions become difficult to make. However, the details of Jesus' ministry are ample enough to draw the following conclusions.

1. What He Did, He Did Completely

Those that Jesus healed were completely healed. This means that no one who had faith and had been healed by Jesus left His presence in need. "The evangelists never show him counseling a sick man to rejoice or to be patient because disease is helpful or redemptive. Instead Jesus cured them all (e.g. Matthew 12:15)."[28] Granted, just because perfect healing was granted to these persons, many of them did not follow Christ. Peter Lewis takes it further to state, "There are people who have languished in hell for two thousand years. They are people that met Jesus and were healed by Him. And after they were healed, that was the last they saw of Jesus because that was all they wanted of Jesus."[29]

Jesus knew that most people He touched would not be retained as disciples. Still He healed indiscriminately. That was His unbridled love at work. He healed the ten lepers even though He knew nine of them would not even pause and thank Him let alone join Him. That is who Jesus was under His Father's command. He healed them. He did not analyze them. To merely counsel the sick on how to have faith and strength despite your circumstances would be an invalid substitute for healing. Jesus' aim was to heal them, not just to give them a positive attitude and improve their mental outlook amid suffering while leaving people in pain (that is Buddhism, not Judeo-Christianity).

The healing that Jesus administered was just what the Doctor ordered, for He was the Great Physician. He did not overlook the pain of any person. No one left Him to see a "specialist" for a second opinion. Jesus in man equals man put back together again—in other words, returned to harmony. Through the incarnation, "There is a new quality of life which is now given to men and women through the life and death of Jesus Christ....It has myriads of features, each of which sparkles with its own iridescence. The health which Christ brings is never dull or stereotyped."[30]

Jesus' authority to heal was omnipotent in terms of quantity as well as quality. In several places the Gospels say, "He healed all that were sick." In other places Scripture says, "As many as touched him were made whole."[31] And Jesus healed a multitude as easily and perfectly as He healed an individual. He was not rushing those near the end of the line so as to get finished before His "batteries" ran low.

At the same time, there are some things that "complete healing in Jesus" does *not* mean. For one, it is not a "cosmic Christian health" theory, as if once healed by Jesus one can expect to be in an enduring state of A–1 health clear to his dying day. This is the abstract and vague hope of Greek mythology, such as with the statues of the Greek culture. Complete healing does not mean permanent perfection. Those who were healed by Jesus did not feel like nineteen-year-olds when they were ninety-one. This would be promoting youth, making Jesus the fountain of youth. God's objective in healing extends far beyond physical health or promoting any worldly notions of youth. God grants wholeness. It is the wholeness that glorifies God and strengthens us with what we need to glorify God to the full.

Neither does divine healing embody nor promote the "health and wealth" trend. The healings were for a higher purpose. They are not an end in themselves, but a call to repentance, salvation, holiness, and commitment to God. Jesus healed man to glorify God, not promote man; He was not a humanist.

The health that Jesus bestowed brings tremendous joy. Healing is now but a small foretaste of the health, liberation, and joyful fellowship with God that man will have in the kingdom that is yet to come in all its fullness. Granted there are some who, upon surrendering to Christ, have their eyes opened in such a way that they see the error of their whole lifestyle: harmful eating habits, vile relationships, bad company, apathetic sloth, or financial waste. Through repentance the spiritual turnaround then results in improvements in their decisions that result in greater health and financial situation. This is a typical trend that has been dubbed the "evangelical lift." But it is not to be seen as some spiritual jackpot. It is the simple renewing of the mind in Christ that affects whole lives.

> Jesus had triumphed over sin, illness, death…death has become a transport to eternity with Jesus.

"Complete healing" in Jesus was not a Hebrew healthcare plan. Jesus' presence in Israel and Judah did not mean that leprosy was eliminated, everyone had 20/20 vision, and morticians were put out of work. Subsequently, neither did the church become the "flawless club," where everyone in every pew had two percent body fat, skin like porcelain statues, and chiseled features. Such caricatures are also the embellishments of Greek mythology and, I might add, those caught up in "Charismania," which is not the gist of Judeo-Christian theology. It is a wonder if people who seek this type of environment are really seeking Jesus, or is it a Santa Claus they are looking for (gifts, gifts, gifts, please; give me more gifts!) All those Jesus healed in Israel eventually aged and died like all others. For even though Jesus gave complete healing, death is a post-Eden passage that cannot be escaped.

In Jesus, death becomes nothing to fear. Throughout history death was man's primary fear. It is now merely the blessed passage to paradise. The apostle Paul, drawing from Hosea, clarifies this for posterity in 1 Corinthians 15:55–57: "'Where, O death, is your victory? Where, O death, is your sting?' The sting of death is sin…But thanks be to God! He gives us the victory through our Lord Jesus Christ." Jesus had triumphed over sin, illness, and death. Sin had been cancelled, illness had been healed, and death had been redefined to be a mere transport to eternity with Jesus. This was Jesus' sanction. And eternity with Jesus was to remain His followers' purpose. Ultimately then, "complete healing" releases one from the power of death.

2. Healing in the Light of His Coming Kingdom

It may seem puzzling that, with Jesus as the manifest solution to man's plight, even after His ministry in the Spirit and His granting the fullness of the Spirit, odious problems including sickness and death persist. The answer to this puzzle is having a proper understanding of the kingdom of God. Jesus announced the kingdom and predicted its future manifestation.

Jesus' ministry commenced the kingdom of God. It was like a starting gun at the beginning of a race. The race is not yet over, but Jesus' lead is insurmountable and continues to grow. Likewise, with God's hand at work there is much happening now, but there is much that is still unfulfilled in terms of kingdom blessing. Final victory will be at the finish line. God is not finished yet.

Granted, healing takes place as God moves and faith invites. But consummate healing will be at the rapture. During this present era in history the bride of Christ, the church, is engaged to be perfectly restored unto God her Creator. Then, in that day, God will permanently heal *all* who are His own in *every* way. But not before the day of His return. Until then, Christ's power and presence is manifestly here, internalized in the church. We have what we need to honor our Savior.

In time, Jesus will fully manifest Himself in the kingdom of God. It will be a dominion where there is neither sickness, sorrow, hunger, nor death. Jesus did not obliterate these problems during His earthly ministry for it was not yet time to. He offered healing and triumph *within* life's problems. This is how Jesus launched the initial assault on the kingdom of darkness. It was a precursor to what He will do completely when the time fully comes—in the Millennium and beyond (but that is a topic for another day). He asserted the kingdom of God by His ministry and message, which included healing. This was God's way of offering a foretaste of eternity in paradise.

The healing hand of Jesus is at work just the same. And believers ought to pray and not give up, for the promise of complete healing still stands. The matter of "when" all things are healed is in God's hands. God controls His children and His calendar, not vice versa. All God's own will be healed completely, when Christ returns. Yet, as the New Testament openly illustrates, many are totally healed sooner. In fact, one of Jesus' commissions to His disciples was to heal the sick. They were to keep this healing fire burning. Jesus ordered it so, "on earth as it is in heaven." And the Bible warns that disobedience comes with an awful price tag.

CHAPTER 3 ENDNOTES

1. John Wimber, *Power Healing* (San Francisco, CA: Harper & Row, 1987), 41.

2. John includes four healings of individuals and one multitude healing. But these five events are comprehensive and assert that Jesus is the authoritative Healer. John 4 and 5 have adjacent healings. In John 4 He heals the official's son at a distance. In John 5 the thirty-eight-year paralytic is healed. Note that these two healings did not take place together but John puts them together (see John 5:1) to prove that whether one is prestigious, wealthy, grieving and near death or poor, banished, chronically ill and depressed, Jesus can heal you. In John 6 the great crowd He would soon feed is impressed with His healing power. John 9 is devoted to the healing of the man born blind and interpreting that miracle as simply for the glory of God. In John 11, Jesus displays His mastery over death by resurrecting Lazarus. So even John, in his five healings, declares that the healings are pivotal for confirming that Jesus is the Savior.

3. Michael Harper, *The Healings of Jesus*, The Jesus Library, ed. Michael Green (Downers Grove, IL: InterVarsity Press, 1986), 147.

4. Keith Bailey, *Divine Healing: The Children's Bread* (Harrisburg, PA: Christian Publications, Inc., 1977), 101.

5. Francis MacNutt, *Healing* (Notre Dame, IN: Ave Maria Press, 1985), 52.

6. Ibid., 108.

7. Harper, 22-23.

8. Wimber, 38; quoted in John Wilkinson, *Health and Healing* (Edinburgh: Handsel, 1980), 33.

9. MacNutt, 93.

10. Bailey, 98.

11. F. Graber and D. Muller, "Heal," in *The New International Dictionary of New Testament Theology* Vol. 2, ed. Colin Brown (Grand Rapids, MI: Zondervan Publishing House, 1976), 165.

12. Roger Stronstad, *The Charismatic Theology of St. Luke* (Peabody, MA: Hendrickson Publishers, 1984), 44.

13. Bailey, 101.

14. Bauer, Arndt, Gingrich and Danker, *A Greek-English Lexicon of the New Testament* (Chicago: University of Chicago Press, 1979), 762–763.

15. Bailey, 98-99.

16. Wimber, 41.

17. Howard Marshall, *Luke: Historian and Theologian* (Grand Rapids, MI: Zondervan, 1970), 89.

18. Wimber, 36.

19. MacNutt, 62.

20. Wimber, 71.

21.   Fitzmyer, 585.

22.   Ibid., 586.

23.   Wimber, 106.

24.   Fitzmyer, 734.

25.   Harper, 41.

26.   Stronstad, 45.

27.   Norman Perrin, *Rediscovering the Teaching of Jesus* (New York: Harper & Row, 1976), 131.

28.   MacNutt, 79.

29.   Peter Lewis made this statement to the author personally in July 1989.

30.   Harper, 147.

31.   A.B. Simpson, *The Gospel of Healing* (Camp Hill, PA: Christian Publications, Inc., 1986), 18.

Jesus' Works of Healing: Malady, Distinction, Method, Result

1. The unclean spirit/demon is hushed and cast out of a man by Jesus' speaking (Mark 1:23–28; Luke 4:33–37).

2. Peter's mother-in-law's fever healed by Jesus' rebuke and touch (Matthew 8:14–15; Mark 1:29–31; Luke 4:38–39).

3. Jesus healed many who were brought to Him of sickness and demonization by a word and touch (Matthew 8:16–17; Mark 1:32–34; Luke 4:40–41).

4. Jesus preaches and casts out many demons (Mark 1:39).

5. A leper comes to Jesus in faith; Jesus has compassion, touches him, and pronounces him clean; he is healed (Matthew 8:1–4; Mark 1:40–45; Luke 5:12–16).

6. Bedridden paralytic is brought to Jesus; Jesus speaks forgiveness and healing to him (Matthew 9:1–8; Mark 2:1–12; Luke 5:17–26).

7. Jesus commands the man with a shriveled hand and raises it to restoration (Matthew 12:9–14; Mark 3:1–6; Luke 6:6–11).

8. Many come to touch Jesus; He heals all of disease and unclean spirits *(Scholars are not settled regarding the distinction between this multitude-healing and #23 below). (Matthew 12:15–16; Mark 3:7–12).

9. Jesus speaks to drive the demons out of the Gerasene demoniac(s) (Matthew says there were two) (Matthew 8:28–34; Mark 5:1–20; Luke 8:26–39).

10. Jesus' touch and command to rise heals Jairus' dying daughter (Matthew 9:18–19, 23–26; Mark 5:21–24, 35–43; Luke 8:40–42, 49–56).

11. Woman touches Jesus in faith and is healed of twelve years of hemorrhaging (Matthew 9:20–22; Mark 5:25–34; Luke 8:43–48).

12. Jesus heals a few in Nazareth; activity is limited by unbelief (Matthew 13:58; Mark 6:5–6).

13. All brought to Him in Gennesaret are healed by touching His garment (Matthew 14:34–36; Mark 6:53–56).

14. Canaanite woman's faith and plea have Jesus cast a demon from her daughter (Matthew 15:21–28; Mark 7:24–30).

15. Jesus heals a deaf/mute by touch, saliva, and speaking (Mark 7:31–37).

16. A blind man is brought to Jesus in Bethsaida; He heals him with saliva and by touching him (Mark 8:22–26).

17. At the father's request Jesus liberates a demonized boy by rebuking the spirit and lifting the boy (Matthew 17:14–21; Mark 9:14–29; Luke 9:37–43).

18. Through faith, blind Bartimaeus receives sight; Jesus has compassion, touches him and speaks healing (Matthew differs by referring to two men and saying this healing happened while leaving Jericho [see Mark and Luke]) (Matthew 20:29–34; Mark 10:46–52; Luke 18:35–43).

19. Jesus heals a centurion's servant by the centurion's request in faith (Luke says elders and friends implored of Jesus) (Matthew 8:5–13; Luke 7:1–10).

20. Two blind men in Galilee request in faith and receive sight via Jesus' touch (Matthew 9:27–31).

21. Jesus casts demon from a mute man and his speech returns (Matthew 9:32–34).

22. Jesus heals a demonized man, blind and mute (Luke only mentions mute) (Matthew 12:22–24; Luke 11:14–15).

23. At Galilee Jesus preaches, teaches and heals every disease in people from Galilee, Syria, and Judea (Scholars are not settled

regarding the distinction between this multitude-healing and #8 above) (Matthew 4:23–25; Luke 6:17–19).

24. Jesus is moved with compassion; He heals every sickness and disease (Matthew 9:35–36).

25. Jesus heals many of many things and says, "...report to John" (Matthew 11:2–6; Luke 7:18–23).

26. In Galilee Jesus has compassion and heals those who are in need (Matthew 14:14; Luke 9:11; John 6:2).

27. Jesus heals great multitudes in Galilee: the lame, maimed, and blind (Matthew 15:29–31).

28. Leaving Galilee Jesus heals many in Judea beyond the Jordan (Matthew 19:1–2).

29. The blind and lame came to Jesus in the temple and He healed them (Matthew 21:14).

30. Jesus has compassion and raises the widow's dead son by speaking to him (Luke 7:11–17).

31. Jesus had cast seven demons out of Mary Magdalene (Luke 8:2).

32. Jesus heals a woman with a bent back by speaking to and touching her (Luke 13:10–13).

33. Jesus touches and heals a man with dropsy/edema/water retention (Luke 14:1–4).

34. Jesus speaks and ten lepers are healed (faith is also a factor) (Luke 17:11–19).

35. Jesus touches the High Priest's servant's ear and it is restored (Luke 22:49–51).

36. Great multitudes gather near Jesus to hear and be healed (Luke 5:15).

37. Jesus casts out demons and cures people (Tell Herod!) (Luke 13:32).

38. Jesus speaks and an official from Capernaum has faith; his son lives (John 4:46–53).

39. Jesus speaks and a man lame for thirty-eight years walks again (John 5:1–9).

40. By anointing with saliva-clay and giving a command, Jesus heals a man born blind (John 9:1–11).

41. Jesus has compassion and speaks to raise Lazarus from the dead (John 11:1–44).

This panoramic chart of Jesus' healing ministry is what is referred to throughout chapter 3, "Healing in the Time of Jesus." It is adapted from the one found in the late John Wimber's *Power Healing*, entitled "Overview of the Healing Ministry of Jesus." Some of the references have been expanded to include crucial information prior to or following a healing. This way the fundamental compulsion for doing the healing and the reaction following the healing are included.

The sequence of the healings found in *Power Healing* is maintained. Students of the New Testament realize that the healings of Jesus are not presented in the same order in each of the Gospels. This is a topic of much discussion/debate within scholastic circles doing form criticism. However, since form criticism is not within the purpose of this book, it is simpler to follow the order set forth in Wimber's outline.

Mark's Gospel provides the order that the healings are in. Scholars call this the "Marcan spine." This sequence is maintained up through healing #18 involving blind Bartimaeus (Mark 10:46). From there the order alternates between Matthew and Luke. The final healings listed are from John's Gospel, for John has several healings that are unique to his account.

Peter and James healing the paralytic in Acts 3. Artwork by Gustave Doré.

four

HEALING in the APOSTOLIC ERA

THE DISCIPLES CONTINUED Jesus' ministry of divine healing with the same power and effect that Jesus had in His ministry. Healing was done. Large crowds drew near. More healings were performed and sermons were preached. People repented and lives were changed. Thousands were saved as they confessed and put their faith in Jesus' name. It is rather intriguing that this is something that did not happen when Jesus healed. It is a post-Resurrection, post-Pentecost phenomenon that first graces the apostles. In doing all this, were they acting on their own? What was their purpose? Were they building empires? Fan clubs? Some religious leaders today who do such salient things *are* building empires and fan clubs. Or were the apostles simply servants who were following orders?

THE COMMISSION TO HEAL

Jesus was intent on creating a movement that would cover the earth and last for all time. So Jesus did not keep the ministry of healing to Himself. He first passed it on to the disciples. These orders to heal began in Matthew 10:1, Mark 3:13, and Luke 9:1. He gave them the power and authority to drive out all demonic forces and cure diseases. Jesus then sent them out to preach the kingdom and to heal the sick (Luke 9:2).

> Jesus was intent on creating a movement that would cover the earth and last for all time.

In Luke 10 Jesus commissioned seventy-two others to go and do the same. They were thrilled about the results. They had demonstrated healings and deliverance from demonic power. The seventy-two were ordinary disciples who had been with Jesus and had observed His amazing authority and power. There is not one word about any of these followers having some sterling resume or qualifications. They were simply chosen. And the time had come for intense involvement in ministry. He did what they probably had not planned on. Jesus sent *them* out with authority and power, for all aspects of the gospel are meant to be experienced and shared. And these seventy-two were in for a big surprise!

But though Jesus was to leave shortly, His followers were to continue ministering wholeness to people.

The Luke 9 and 10 internships transformed these men. Up until now, they had simply witnessed Jesus casting out demons and healing. Now they realized that they could go out in Jesus' name and do these same works. They were stunned and delighted. What they did not know yet was that Jesus was preparing them to take up the whole ministry of the gospel after the Ascension.

Therefore, we can see that "it is clear that Jesus taught his disciples to take the same uncompromising stand toward sickness."[1] The disciples had now done it themselves; they had healed others and they would never be the same. The ministry of divine healing was to continue after Jesus departed. He had not come just to give temporary relief from the hand of the enemy. Satan had tormented humanity long enough. But though Jesus was to leave shortly, His followers were to continue ministering wholeness to people. The disciples may have wondered momentarily how they would continue Jesus' work. We can almost sense Jesus assuring them before He left, "I healed. I drove out demons. I will be with you. You can do this. Fear nothing."

In the Great Commission Jesus declared His total authority and instructed them to go make disciples, baptize them, and teach them to obey everything He had commanded (Matthew 28:18). A big part of what He had commanded them to do was to heal the sick. Jesus had demonstrated this. He taught His followers to model after Him. Later, as He was preparing for His final departure, He urged them to stay in Jerusalem until the Holy Spirit came over them, then go do as Jesus Himself had done. The orders were unmistakably clear.

They were told to obey all the Master's commands and preach the gospel. Healing was within that gospel. Their message was to be a complete gospel and not a partial gospel. They were not to "cherry-pick," as the saying goes and share only what was comfortable. They were to share it all. For Jesus came and liberated by preaching and healing. They were to "go and do likewise."[2] The disciples realized that Jesus was the perfect model for living life unto God in faith and practice. His healing ministry could not be ignored. They could do nothing less than continue in *all* they had learned of the power of God.

THE HEALING MINISTRY OF THE DISCIPLES

The disciples' phenomenal ministry of healing was a testimony to the transmittable, eternal, and undying power of Jesus. As in Jesus' ministry, healing served to advance the message: Christ Jesus and the kingdom of God. The brilliant attraction of healing was a means to preaching, which led to conversion and baptism in the Holy Spirit. Healing also taught a powerful lesson about God's love, which built up believers and further blessed the young church.

In Matthew 16:19 Jesus tells Peter that he will be given the keys to the kingdom of heaven. This verse foretells of Peter's ongoing ministry wherein he will be teaching, preaching the kingdom, and exercising divine healing.

In the Book of Acts, Luke records a plethora of healings that the apostles did. He begins with signs and wonders after the day of Pentecost. Chapter 3 tells of Peter and John healing the lame beggar. There were numerous apostolic signs, wonders, healings, and exorcisms in chapter 5. Chapters 6 and 8 respectively narrate Stephen's and Philip's powerful ministries. They performed wonders and miraculous signs, cast out demons, and healed paralytics and cripples, "so there was great joy in the streets" (Acts 8:8). Ananias restored sight to Saul

(Paul) after his conversion. Peter rendered back-to-back miracles in healing Aeneas of paralysis and raising Dorcas from the dead (Acts 9:32–43).

Then Paul appeared upon the scene. He and Barnabas confirmed their message of grace through miraculous signs and wonders. Paul healed a lame man in Lystra, then did what Luke called "amazing miracles" (Acts 19:11–12). In chapter 20, Paul raised Eutychus after a deadly fall. Finally on Malta, Paul survived a snakebite (Acts 28:1–10). He then healed Publius's father of fever and dysentery. Then the rest of the sick on the island came and were cured of their maladies. Paul healed the whole island, just like Jesus.

The healing ministry of the apostles bears striking resemblance to Jesus' healings.

The healing ministry of the apostles bore striking resemblance to Jesus' healings. There was continuity in the work of the Holy Spirit from the ministry of Jesus that carries into the ministry of the apostles. The Holy Spirit is the flow that links the healing activity in the Gospels straight into the apostles' work in the Book of Acts. So even though Jesus has departed, the same Spirit is now working through the disciples. While there is continuity, at the same time there is a distinction between the two healing eras.

Jesus and the apostles both preached the kingdom of God. Both heal the sick and lame. The difference is that Jesus declared Himself to be the Healer and the Way to reach the kingdom. The first name attached to the Christian movement during the Book of Acts was "the Way" (Acts 9:2). The apostles had no such agenda for themselves. For example, the apostles were never heard saying anything like, "I am the truth" or "come to me all you who are weary." They made no self-assertions. Their aim was to exalt Christ alone.

The apostles did not perform nature miracles or miraculous feedings. Remember, healing is for blessing people. A nature miracle is purely for displaying power; impressing people with God's deeds. For instance, there was more shock than joy when Jesus walked on water or calmed the sea. Granted, the healings and exorcisms were marvelous, but the apostles' motive was to bless people and exalt Christ. The apostles were merely chosen soldiers in a movement to build Jesus Christ's church.

Jesus said that His followers would *do* greater things than He had done (John 14:12–14). But He never said that they would *be* greater men. There is a monumental difference. It should be noted that "greater" does not mean "better." Neither does it mean that they will do more phenomenal things. *Mega*, the Greek word for "greater," simply means a different size or number and is not a reference to intrinsic value that is going to be amplified. The greater works were accomplished through the power of the Holy Spirit. This means that the disciples were not their own source of power.

THE MISSION OF THE EPISTLES OF PAUL AND JAMES

The Epistles do not mention healing nearly as much as the Gospels. Wherein the Gospels thrust the incidence of healing to teach the need to come to Jesus, these letters simply make a couple of references to healing to complete the biblical doctrine of healing. This is because the Epistles of Paul and James are written for an entirely different reason than the Gospels. By the time the Epistles are written, many churches had been planted; and healing was widely experienced by countless new believers. Though many Christians had not yet read a copy of the Gospels, the testimony of the gospel of Christ had been confirmed by supernatural wonders. Christians were receiving divine healing as the Spirit-directed church and its leadership ministered to them. Therefore it was unnecessary for Paul and James to write and teach extensively about divine healing. It needed no further assertion for the young church.

Paul and James wrote their Epistles to instruct people in practical matters of holy living. James reminds believers to live their faith through actions that glorify God. Paul had the delicate task of balancing and/or harmonizing the "Charismania" in certain churches (like Corinth) without quenching the work the Holy Spirit in others. Of Paul's work in Corinth, Marion Soards observes, "He refrains from displays of power, ministering in and through affliction, so that true divine power, as revealed in Jesus Christ, may work through him."[3] In short, Paul had the task of interpreting the life of Jesus for the entire church. All the people who had encountered Jesus knew how to receive from Him. Now Paul was embarking on the life-long task of teaching people how to live in Jesus.

Though little is said about healing in the Epistles, especially when compared to the Gospels, Paul and James certainly believed in it. James was an eyewitness to Jesus' spectacular healing ministry. James was Jesus' brother, lest we forget. Many of the disciples were around Jesus for "three-plus" years. James had been around Him for roughly thirty years. He was not ignorant of his brother who became his Savior, and he had not forgotten anything. Paul personally experienced healing from blindness several days after his conversion (Acts 9).

Probably the most remarkable incident for Paul is seen in Acts 28:1–10. Paul was sitting beside a fire on Malta after being shipwrecked. A poisonous snake came up out of the firewood and bit down on his hand. He survived the snakebite and later healed the father of the island chief. The natives are so impressed that all the sick on the entire island came for healing. Paul healed every one of them. Therefore we can be certain that both Paul and James knew about divine healing from personal experience. They fully believed in the doctrine and that it needed to be imparted to others.

In the Book of Acts, Luke described Paul's ministry of healing. Healing was important to Paul. His view of healing never diminished, and even though he made little mention of it in his thirteen letters, there is no reason for us to think that he changed his belief about healing. In his letter to the Romans, Paul says, "He who raised Christ from the dead will also give life to your mortal bodies through his Spirit, who lives in you" (Rom. 8:11).

Paul and James had the particular task of helping the young church grow. They believed in and practiced divine healing as did the four Evangelists: Matthew, Mark, Luke, and John. Paul and James simply present healing in the larger context of New Testament church life.

PAUL'S PERSPECTIVE AND PRESENTATION OF HEALING

Paul, in his epistles, dealt with questions that were arising among the Christians who were still young in their faith. For example, what about when someone who seemed to have faith was not healed? What about Paul's own aches and pains? Could Jesus heal them or not? And why did Paul talk about healing so little throughout his letters?

1. Healing as One of the Gifts

Healing, as taught by Paul, is one of a variety of gifts dispersed among Christians. It is not the proverbial "pearl of great price" or "holy grail," something that one is sensible or even clever to trade everything else in so to go on a life quest and obtain it. Healing is a gift that a person receives to build up the body of Christ. Romans 12:6 reads, "We have different gifts, according to the grace given us." In 1 Corinthians 4:7, Paul asks, "What do you have that you did not receive?" Later in 1 Corinthians 12:4–11, he talks about different kinds of gifts that all come from the same Spirit. These are words of wisdom, words of knowledge, faith, healing, prophecy, tongues, and others. In Ephesians 4, Paul says that it is Christ's Spirit who gave gifts to some to be apostles, prophets, evangelists, pastors and teachers.

> Healing…is one of a variety of gifts dispersed among Christians.

All of these different gifts, including healing, are diverse and are dispersed throughout the church for edification and to benefit the body of Christ. Here Paul is teaching the interdependence of the body of Christ, a place where healing is a given. By now healing is regularly experienced in the church. Paul assumes this and writes of his greater concern that Christians grow in faith and love toward one another.

Paul refers to those with the gifts of healings as practical specialists. A specific person will have a specific gift. And that person is to responsibly use his gift, healing included. Paul's teaching is similar in concept to a modern hospital. A problem with the heart or brain or bones requires a different specialist. That specialist deals with specific problems and injuries. So too are people who have been given the gift of healing in a church. They have a role that must be exercised in obedience and in the power of the Holy Spirit. They are not local folk-heroes, but simply Christians within the church who have a call to follow Christ like everyone else in the church. Their calling will then be to exercise their healing gift—no smoke, no magic—just healing and loving people; speaking peace and meeting needs.

2. Paul's View of Healing in This Age

During the earthly ministry of Jesus, He frequently healed all who were sick. But after Christ's Ascension, though sickness was tended to, no doubt it persisted in Christian circles. The church did not morph into being the divine-health-club. While healing was available, not all were healed. What were the Christians to make of this—back then and today? How did Paul deal with the dilemma? Some scholars believe that Paul's eschatology offers an answer.

Scholars have come to call this theme "apocalyptic." This Greek word *root* is where we get the term *revelation*—the last book of the Bible. "'Apocalyptic' is a special expression of Jewish eschatology [the study of the end] that was characterized by the dualistic doctrine of two ages."[4] The present age is marked by mundane, evil, drudgery, and temporality. (The Jews who were outside the church and believed that the Messiah had not yet come especially adhered to this thinking.) However, in "the 'age to come' is found the supernatural realm of the power of God."[5] The shift from this age to the age of God-rule would be distinctly marked by God's mighty intervention. The present evil age would halt and the new would begin.

The classic study of Paul's apocalyptic theory was done by Geerhardus Vos in his book, *The Pauline Eschatology*. A half century later, Oscar Cullman wrote *Christ and Time* and further developed the interpretation of "the apocalyptic." In 1987 Marion L. Soards wrote a treatment of Paul's eschatology in which he describes the Jewish "apocalyptic" concept as follows:[6]

Old Testament Era Apocalyptic Theory

GOD'S INTERVENTION

Arrival of Messiah

THE PRESENT EVIL AGE	THE AGE TO COME[6]
Messiah imminent	*Messiah reigning*
pain, disease, death	*peace, complete health, life*
periodic healings	*completed healing*

In the latter age glory, justice and peace would triumph. According to Soards, Paul's line of thinking is tied into, though not committed to, Jewish apocalyptic thought. He maintains the two distinct ages, the evil age and the glorious age to come. "But he modifies the scheme in light of the Christ-event so that there are two distinct ages that are separated and joined by an interim."[7]

It is illustrated as:[8]

New Testament Era Apocalyptic Theory

THE CROSS OF JESUS CHRIST	THE RETURN OF JESUS CHRIST
Arrival of Messiah	*Return of Messiah*
Numerous healings	*Total healing*

THE PRESENT EVIL AGE	THE ENDS OF THE AGES	A NEW CREATION[8]
Messiah coming	*Spirit equips us*	*Messiah reigning*
pain, disease, death	*partial alleviation*	*perfection completed*
periodic healings	*healing as Spirit moves*	*healing*

Paul saw himself (and us) as living between the two advents. Yes, Jesus Christ the Savior had come. Sin, Satan, and death had been defeated. The Law had been fulfilled. Creation had been won back. But there were more battles yet to be fought before all would be brought to completion. This explains the intermingling of present suffering along with the Spirit's wondrous presence and promise of Christ's return in all His fullness and glory.

So Christians live between *and* within both the old and the new eras. "Christ had become the first-fruits of the new order (1 Corinthians 15:23) but the Christian still awaits the end [of the old order] (v. 24)."[9] Therefore the final restoration of every believer's health will be in the end of time. Soards says, "Christians living at the juncture of the ages await Christ's coming at the absolute end of the present evil age."[10] In a sense the enemy of our souls has been dealt a fatal blow, but he is still affecting damage *while* he is "bleeding toward death" and awaiting final binding (Revelation 3:20). Paul wrote of this finality concept where things are perfected in Philippians 3:20–21: "But our citizenship is in heaven. And we eagerly await a Savior from there, the Lord Jesus Christ, who, by the power that enables him to bring everything under his control, will transform our lowly bodies so that they will be like his glorious body." Yes, the Spirit had come at Pentecost. At the same time God wants us to keep longing for another world.

Still some would be asking, "Why are there still sick people among us when Jesus, Who is able to heal, is dynamically present among us?" The suffering person especially would ask this. A quick answer may be offered by those who believe the "Apocalyptic Theory." It is easy to say, "Oh, we are going to be fine…soon." One truism in ministry is that the ill often do not understand the healthy. And the healthy usually do not perceive the needs and hurts of the ill. So it is important to tread lightly and not offer glib replies. For the healthy person to tell the ill to "hang on and have faith," however, this may be understandable. The painful issues do have an eschatological dimension. But we must ask, is it legitimate to conclusively tell those in pain and who are not getting better, "relax all ye sick people, you'll be fine when Jesus returns?" That is harsh. And eschatology is not the only issue in the resolution of these problems.

The adherents to the Apocalyptic Theory are right in their observation that final and perfect restoration of health will be at the end of time. They are also correct in their observation that sickness will continue and healing will not be totally completed until Christ's return. But are these solutions congruent and Spirit-sensitive within the atmosphere of what we want to call "Christian ministry?" This does not settle the question, but I will move on.

There is another slant; another question that should be asked: why should Paul employ the Jewish eschatology philosophy when he, like all the other apostles, had a new Christian eschatology given to him by revelation? The Apocalyptic Theory avoids both the teaching of a literal millennial reign of Christ on earth and the Old Testament prophecies of healings during the millennial reign (Isaiah 35:5–6). True, Paul was trained within this former style of Jewish thinking. But was it still within his mental grid? Was he just using this thinking in a tactical sense to identify with some vague aspect of the church? To those who are slightly more committed to the Jewish traditions?

> In many instances [unbelievers] became Christians after experiencing the healing power of Christ.

There are other possible explanations to the problems of continued sickness among Christians and the fact that not all are healed. A plausible answer is to distinguish two kinds of healings presented in the New Testament. The primary option is Jesus' healing of believers, and the second is the healings that occurred on the cutting edge of missionary advance mainly depicted in the Acts of the Apostles where they served as confirming signs of the gospel of Christ. By the way, such healings still occur all over the world. Amid these second types of healings are those who were healed who are unbelievers for the most part. In many instances they became Christians after experiencing the healing power of Christ.

The two-layer thinking about healing ministry is accurate. It is a strong theme of Keith Bailey's book, *The Children's Bread*. He's coming at healing ministry based on Jesus' statement to a Canaanite woman from a pagan culture in Tyre and Sidon. She asks Jesus to come heal her child of a demon. Jesus tells her, "It isn't right to take the children's bread and toss it to their dogs." (See Jesus' Works of Healing at the end of chapter 3, #14). Jesus is meaning that healing is for God's children as their normal sustenance.[11] But as is the topic, healing is also used for blessing the lost to draw them to come to Him.

Paul and James, however, in their teaching of healing, are addressing the healing of the sick *within* the context of the church. They are teaching about healing ministry among those who are already Christians. Paul's teaching recognizes the healing of the Christian to be conditional. Paul says that the body of the Christian must be for the Lord and the Lord for the body (1 Corinthians 6:13). This means that the Christian's body is the house of the Lord. Paul calls for the consecration and sanctity of the believer's body. Paul, like James, saw the necessity of seeking forgiveness and correcting behavior as a prerequisite to healing (James 5:15).

James also points out that the lack of unity and spiritual health in the assembly would hinder healing. Unlike the healings that were signs and wonders for reaching unbelievers, the healing of Christians can require the confessing and forsaking of sin. Thus healing was sometimes delayed or denied because the individual seeking healing was not right with God or reconciled with other Christians. These matters must be thoroughly examined, just as a believer's heart is to be examined prior to a breakthrough healing taking place. Of course, none of the above stipulations would apply for there to be a healing that would be a sign or an invitation to a nonbeliever.

3. Interpreting Paul's "Thorn in the Flesh"

Paul's "thorn in the flesh" is another factor in this discussion of the chronic nature or continuation of sickness. Here it is being asked again. The question does not go away: what is to be made of aches, pains, or illnesses, especially in the lives of those serving Christ where the hardship simply will not go away? In this interim period after His Ascension and before Christ returns—while the devil, though defeated, has not yet been expelled—Paul's testimony shows the menace that this situation can present to Christians. He also gives encouragement within the setting. The apostle's testimony in 2 Corinthians 12:7–9 says:

To keep me from becoming conceited because of these surpassing great revelations, there was given me a thorn in the flesh, a messenger of Satan, to torment me. Three times I pleaded with the Lord to take it away from me. But he said to me, "My grace is sufficient for you, for my power is made perfect in weakness."

This passage from Paul's personal experience is important for several reasons. First, though Satan has been defeated, he does have some limited degree of access to us. He has not yet been "locked away" and he can directly interfere to bring grief. Second, it casts a long shadow across the idea that says, "Enough faith can change anything," as if the faith found in God's children controlled God. Third, it is strong evidence against the idea that God needs people to be happy and healthy in order for God to use them and triumph through them. Fourth, it tells us that things are different in God's world. God sees and operates on a level tremendously higher than that of humanity. Because of this He will do what He must, to accomplish what He must, even if we finite and fallen creatures object to God's processes.

The definition of the phrase *thorn in the flesh* can be difficult to pinpoint. V.P. Furnish lays out the major possibilities in three general categories. First, the "thorn in the flesh" could be an inner struggle. Perhaps it was a carnal temptation or spiritual weakness; perhaps sexual temptation. "This was a favorite view in the Middle Ages."[12] Others argue it was a sense of unworthiness, guilty conscience, or agony about the Jews who would not believe. On this view, the point is that it kept him humble.

Second, the "thorn" may have been physical. It was, after all, called "a thorn *in the flesh*." Furnish says, "This is the most widely accepted view, at least in modern times."[13] Some church fathers feel it was a "headache" that Paul is talking about. Because of periodic comments made in his letters, if the "thorn" is physical, it could be a sensory problem, such as solar retinitis. He tells the Galatians that he is using "such large letters writing with his own hand" late in his script. Perhaps he could not see well anymore and needed to write big. Or maybe it is a speech impediment. In another place he talks about not having fancy words to share. It is possible that Paul suffered from a malarial fever that recurred in his travels. Paul does not say.

Lightfoot suggests epilepsy, "possibly as a result of the experience Paul had at his conversion."[14] It could be a condition that developed since being beaten violently in Jerusalem (Acts 23). Another time he is left for dead after being stoned by malcontents who hated him. There could be some lingering pain from such treatment, but theories about some sort of mentally or psychosomatically rooted illness such as hysteria or depression do come under serious question. Paul's thinking is too lucid and his influence is too prevalent to be coming from someone who is periodically delirious.

Ralph P. Martin wonders whether the problem really was physical: "With all these physical ailments suggested, one wonders…whether or not a person who was so often on the 'battlefield,' could have been so physically weak and still have withstood the rigors of Paul's life."[15] This is a valid point, for Paul was a strong character whose personal influence was felt throughout the Christian world. Could he have done all that he did and been so frail?

According to V.P. Furnish, the third possibility of Paul's "thorn" is that it is persecution from an exterior source, such as a person or group. Ancient Christian writers Chrysostom, Augustine, and Theodoret argue this. Furnish gives five reasons for such a possibility. First, note that Paul, in 2 Corinthians 11:13–15, refers to certain men who are servants of Satan. And in 2 Corinthians 12:7, Paul says that this messenger of Satan was sent "to torment me (*kolaphizein*)." Second, the only other usage of this Greek word by Paul is in 1 Corinthians 4:11. He is talking about brutal treatment from other humans. Third, in the Septuagint version of the Old Testament, Numbers 33:55 and Ezekiel 28:24 speak of Israel's enemies as "thorns." Fourth, "'in the flesh' may be understood to refer to one's whole earthly existence."[16] And fifth, because of the context, Paul is talking about hardship at the hands of others before (2 Corinthians 11:23) and after he mentions this "thorn" (2 Corinthians 12:10).

Jerry McCant takes this third point further and argues that Paul's thorn in the flesh is *rejected apostleship*. He says, "The 'thorn in the flesh' is not a physical malady but refers to certain persons."[17] This may be why ten of his thirteen letters assert his apostleship in the greetings or subscript. Apparently some opponents do not seem to acknowledge the office Paul holds. These scoffers may be Judaizing Christians (who still required circumcision), Gnostics (who claim that knowledge with certainty is unattainable), allegorizers (those who dismiss biblical stories as mere allegory, not history), or Jews from Palestine or some representative of pneumatic Christology (the belief that Christ was a spirit only and not a man with a body).

After scanning the possibilities, McCant labels Corinth as Paul's problem. He claims that by using certain literative techniques, "Paul depicts Corinth as a sick church inflicted upon him as a thorn in the flesh."[18] Paul had labored extra for them. He made two visits to their city, spent well over two years there, and was looking to visit a third time (2 Corinthians 12:14). Paul goes to great length for them. He even extends himself to the point of making a fool of himself (2 Corinthians 12:11). After all this, they are still shameful in behavior, sensual, argumentative, and aloof (1 Corinthians 12). So McCant declares that Paul's "thorn" is Corinth, or the Corinthian Church.

It seems that McCant is stretching the argument a bit. To read the text, Paul is writing to the Corinthians the second time to encourage them, not to tell them what a headache they are. If the "thorn" was *rejected apostleship* or the *Corinthian Church* in general, then Paul's statement is an irrelevant insult to the Corinthians. Why would he write to encourage and instruct, then add "by the way, you people are a real pain" as a salutation? Such a comment from their "spiritual father" would have been too much to bear. If this were the case, then 2 Corinthians is relevant to all Christians who need encouragement. It would therefore be irrelevant in regard to divine healing. If this "thorn" were an exterior problem, why does Paul refer to it as "in the flesh?" This greatly weakens the possibility of Paul's thorn being "rejected apostleship" or the church at Corinth.

By Paul leaving his "thorn in the flesh" a mystery ("thorn" actually means "stake" or "spike"), it retains its universal application to anyone in difficulty. The "thorn in the flesh" broadens our understanding of how faith can work in our lives whether our difficulties and pains are removed or not. Paul writes to encourage those in the church who are struggling with a problem or pain that God is not quickly alleviating. Paul's experience with a "thorn" tells of how God works victory in anything that is surrendered to Him.

While Satan is in the business of taking God's good things and making them bad, God is in the business of taking what Satan has wrecked and making it good again. So Satan in his usual way, full of intelligence yet bereft of insight, feverishly works ruin. In trials such as Paul's "thorn in the flesh," God can conquer by healing a situation or by working within the unfortunate circumstance to accomplish His purpose and to work for the sufferer's highest good. He can use an infirmed person to do great things, lift up Jesus, and crush evil.

A modern-day example is Joni Eareckson Tada. She was active and healthy before she broke her neck in a swimming accident and was left a quadriplegic. She now has a ministry that has blessed millions of people. Her ministry might not have been as effective had she not been confined to a wheelchair. She may not have a ministry at all. But she was "slain" and yet she held onto her hope (Job 13:15).

Fanny Crosby wrote inspiring hymns that have affected the worldwide church. Her work had such impact that she was invited to the White House and met every U.S. president between Abraham Lincoln and Woodrow Wilson. She triumphed, though she was blind.

I can remember being attacked in what seemed like a merciless manner years ago when writing a book on healing ministry. For most of three years the project occupied about thirty hours a week. I was also part-time pastor of youth and music at a new church outside New York City. There were also remodeling jobs I did to help pay bills. During these three years (remember it was while I was writing a book on *divine healing*) I received a poisonous splinter in my right hand that grew into an annoying tumor. The splinter and tumor were surgically removed. Seven months later the tumor returned as a seven-headed, Medusa-like monster. This time it required radical surgery to eliminate. The doctor got it all the second time.

Shortly after the hand incident, I sprained an ankle so badly that people thought my foot swallowed a baseball. I was six weeks in a cast. Then ditto on the other ankle. That summer a scaffold gave out on a work site and I fell, landing sideways, slamming over the top of a wall covered with razor wire. A kidney was punctured, three ribs were broken, and cuts all down my left side resembled my losing a fight to a mountain lion. An old neighbor walked over and assessed, "You'll be thirty days in the hospital." He was wrong. I was thirty-four days in the hospital! Later I had an accident that necessitated a splinter being removed from my eyeball. The next spring, with the accumulating stress of exhaustion and graduate school deadlines, I collapsed and was rushed to a heart center. My blood pressure was 40/0 (120/80 is normal)! The doctor thought it odd for this to strike someone in their twenties, but the blood pressure remained low for a dangerously long time. After twenty-four hours of monitoring and other lapses in blood pressure to dangerously low levels, I was ordered to three weeks of vacation. The book on healing was eventually finished. All the attacks on my body and soul stopped, suddenly.

One thought is, "Good thing I wasn't doing a book on salvation...who knows where I would have ended up!" Looking back, it was ironic for me to be suffering while serving our Lord in such a way. It is difficult to describe the huge temptation I traversed to quit my calling to ministry. My "thorn in the flesh" felt like twelve spears, not just thorns. It was that exasperating. But the point is that God is faithful and He carries His own through such trials. We would never know what God has planned if we admit defeat and turn away. One dear Christian, a senior citizen who heard what I had gone through and announced, "You're on the verge of encouraging countless people with what you are doing. You were attacked by Satan." I did not argue.

The simplified lesson of this thorn is that God can overrule in anyone's unfortunate situation to create a great testimony to His glory. That is, God can glorify Himself through what humans consider unfortunate. He does not need ideal conditions to accomplish His will. If Paul can conquer, and he says that we are *more* than conquerors, in spite of his thorn in the flesh, so can we. At the risk of being too colloquial, we should stare down life's enemy and the challenges that God has screened for us and declare victory ahead of time. We can have the boldness to tell the enemy, "Do your worst, I will still win. Declare a battle, you lose already. I will prevail, regardless. I will beat you because my General has already cut you off. Call a race, for I have grace and I will triumph. I will even win this race on crutches wearing a cast. Call a quiz show, I will beat you there, too—even with a migraine I will still beat you, for God guides and gives the victory." Ad infinitum.

It ought to be noted that it is not accurate to say that all health is God's direct doing and all sickness is Satan's direct doing. Surely Satan wanted to keep men like Stalin, Mao, Hitler, Pol Pot, and Idi Amin healthy. They produced more evil when they were strong. Sociologists and criminologists have found two common traits among those who are socially deviant: robust health and good vision. The question is: would a criminal have the capability to commit as many crimes if he, for example, had a congenital hip problem and very poor eyesight? Probably not.

[
Christians today need not feel they are being punished when suffering.

The quandary is that some people are more godly when they are infirmed and some are more ungodly when they are healthy. The opposite can be true, too. God wants godliness first. Yes, healing frees a person to praise and serve God more. But, for example, sometimes He may need to heal someone's gossip problem with laryngitis; perhaps hearing loss would work. Consequently however, for those who are inclined to do evil, a healing would free them up to create more havoc. Some remain thankless and self-possessed even though God heals them. We see this clearly among the ten lepers who received healing from Christ. Nine failed to return gratitude (Luke 17:11–19). I say this to caution against glib answers in this realm of ministry. Those who are suffering with such "thorns" need compassion, understanding, and love—not cold analysis and exhortation.

All of these factors must be taken into account in the ministry of healing. And by examining the "thorn in the flesh" concept, we become aware that things are not as simple as we may wish they were. As Paul's suffering served to further God's work through him, Christians today need not feel they are being punished when suffering. God can and will bring glory out of it. That is because He is God.

4. The Effect of the Asclepian Healing Temples in Paul's Day

Some scholars of the New Testament world speculate that Paul did not stress divine healing for the body because the Greek and Roman world in which he ministered was obsessed with the human body and physical health. Indeed, human body statues were everywhere. They posit that his minimal teaching on healing in his letters was his balancing via relative silence on the topic. They think that Paul reasoned (by *not* talking of it much) that the Greco-Roman world had Asclepius, the legendary god of physicians. The ubiquitous Asclepian temples were found throughout the empire. There were more than one thousand in the city of Athens. These temples were a solace for the pagan world. "Asclepius was presented as the most human-loving of the gods."[19] But unlike Christ, who healed anyone (and often everyone) who was in need of healing, Asclepius healed only virtuous people, or those who *deserved* healing (herein the concept of grace has been botched, as it is in all cults). Obviously Paul does not believe in Asclepius; Asclepius' existence is not true, but it was real in the minds of non-Christians who patronized the Asclepian facilities.

It is probably in order to mention a cultural matter at this point. Many may be thinking, "Asclepius? This can't be true. Who ever heard of this?" I personally did not hear of these temples until I had been studying theology full-time for ten years. But they do show up in extra-biblical material. And it is not wise to comfort ourselves by concluding that if something is not in the Bible then it does not affect the Bible. Most of what Jesus did is not in the Bible (see final verse of John's Gospel). Paul is writing to a Greek world with Greek culture and language and thinking. And like a wise missionary, this must be factored in to how Christ is presented to them. For example, in Athens he borrows a quote from Zeus to tell them about God: "For in him we live and move and have our being" (Acts 17:28). That is what Paul thinks about God, but it is also how Athenians perceived Zeus. So Paul uses *their* wording about Zeus to describe the God they have yet to meet. So he minimizes the healing teaching, though he believes it deeply.

American Christians will make parallel calculations even if subconsciously. For example, the Bible orders us to dance before the Lord (Psalm 149:3; 150:4). Did we obey those verses during the 1950s? And act like Elvis? Heavens no!

Did we dance before the Lord in the 1960s? No, that was what hippies did at drugged music festivals. Did we dance before the Lord in the 1970s? Our reply was, "Uh, this is a church, not a disco." Would we dance before the Lord in the 1980s? No, we did not want to be caught acting like Michael Jackson. How about the '90s? Not then, either. Dancing was for grunge-rock concerts and crazy people in moshpits. Come A.D. 2,000, and the excuses for not dancing to the Lord persist in many circles. Our resolve to disobey here has nothing to do with the Bible or anyone's love for the Lord.

Our reaction to our dance-crazed culture has more to do with our refusal to obey these verses in Psalms that order us to dance, than God does. We do not want to resemble Elvis, Michael Jackson, or anyone else on MTV. While we shun an entire aspect of the culture we are immersed in, we, by default, will not dance before the Lord either. This truth needs to be ingested.

The Asclepian Temples had their effect on their day. They had their effect on the churches. They had their effect on the early literature of Christianity, even if not mentioned. So Paul teaches healing very briefly in his letters and when he does, it is almost in passing.

We now return to understand these temples. The Asclepian sanctuaries had three essential components: a temple for sacrifice, a well or spring for washing and purification, and a place for sleeping. The directors did their best to create a healing atmosphere. Everett Ferguson writes, "The sacred precincts included trees, baths, a theatre, a gymnasium, and sometimes a library, similar to a modern health or resort spa."[20] Sometimes extensive rest or exercise would be prescribed for healing. The Asclepian temples used everything they could think of to invoke physical healing. Remember, they are pagans in the first century, so they do not know much and they are simply guessing.

> Several reports mentioned the licking of a diseased spot by a snake or a dog. Other cures can be accounted for on psychological grounds or from the medical practice of the time. In the early period the priests employed surgery, drugs, and hypnosis; later, they effected cures by courses of treatment, including beneficent prescriptions like diet, exercise, baths, and medicines. In some cases the treatment prescribed was

contrary to all ancient medical theory…Magic was also employed for healing purposes.[21]

These facilities and methods of healing had nothing to attract the Greek or Roman citizens who had recently believed on Christ. They had lived their former lives in bondage of those pagan practices. New Christians rejoiced to be free of them. Nothing in the New Testament indicates that the Asclepian temples or any other form of animistic healing (and there were others) affected Paul's ministry of healing. He did not work from a theoretical base either in his ministry or his writing. Paul was an experienced practitioner. He had had a widespread healing ministry in many cities of the Roman Empire. If the Asclepian theory is plausible, and Paul is not talking/writing about divine healing so as to offset a pagan obsession, it would be because the last thing he would want is for a brand new Christian to come to a church, note a predominant healing fixation, observe the wing or annex of the church that is dedicated to physical healing ministry and muse, "Oh, this is wonderful. Christian churches are just like the Asclepian Temples. I feel so at home here." Paul would have nothing to do with such eclectic nonsense, even by default. Had he done so, would the churches and Asclepian Temples ponder doing a merger in time? Better to leave it alone and have nothing to do with such ideas. Jesus did not need any help from the pagan world to get His work done for righteousness sake.

Granted there is a distinction between Paul's physical healing ministry as a missionary (as told in Acts) and his letters—writings that were devoted to the instruction of the church. Healing instruction is limited in Paul's letters. The Corinthian church, founded by Paul, excelled in gifts, and obviously the gifts of healings were manifested in that congregation. Did they and other churches need even more instruction on healing? Paul figures that the "choir did not need to be preached to" anymore on healing.

It has been said that if one reads only the Bible, they do not understand the Bible. The Bible was written in a Jewish culture that was encircled by a Roman world that was very influenced by Greek thought. All that said, at the same time the scriptural data does not support the theory that Paul was restrained in writing about healing due to his concern for the influence of the Asclepian temples on the Christians. That does not mean it wasn't a reality in his thinking. It simply could be that it was better left unsaid. Paul was not tapering in his priority that the Christian Church be a place of healing and restoration. Though granted, this is a popular view among dispensationalists. The Book of Acts details marvelous public healings in Paul's church-planting ministry. It was the last chapter of Acts, during Paul's final missionary journey, that he had his greatest healing "crusade." Consequently, the numerous churches he founded and instructed had been practicing healing from their beginnings. Healing was ministered in a Christian manner and in Jesus' name. There was only a limited need for further instruction on the doctrine of healing within such churches.

James's Teaching on Healing

James wrote from a pastoral perspective on the practice of divine healing. For him anointing with oil was the usual way to administer healing in the assembly and in home settings. This procedure did not counter or undo the exercise of the *spiritual gift* of healing, which was Paul's slant on the matter. However, with James' instructions, congregations would forever know that God's touch for the body was readily available. James's teaching simply concluded the biblical instruction on the doctrine of healing. The people that James wrote to were mostly Jewish and they knew the healing heritage laid forth in the Old Testament. The gospel story was filled with healings and still fresh in people's minds and was currently being committed to writing. Paul's life of mission work and teaching on healing encouraged his own ministry. Thus the teaching in James' epistle completes the doctrine of the practice of divine healing.

Establishing the Normal Exercise of Divine Healing

The apostle James has this to say on the matter:

> Is any of you sick? He should call the elders of the church to pray over him and anoint him with oil in the name of the Lord. And the prayer offered in faith will make the sick person well; the Lord will raise him

up. If he has sinned, he will be forgiven. Therefore confess your sins to each other and pray for each other so that you may be healed. The prayer of a righteous man is powerful and effective.

—JAMES 5:14–16

Under the inspiration of the Holy Spirit, James put in writing what had been practiced from the days of Jesus. Mark 6:13 says, "They drove out many demons and anointed many sick people with oil and healed them." This passage indicates that the apostles received the practice of anointing from Christ Jesus their Teacher. They were to do this for the sick.

A.B. Simpson (1843–1919) asserts that James 5:14 means, "*this is a command. It ceases to be mere privilege. It is a divine prescription for disease; and no Christian can safely dispense with it.*"[22] Being impressed with this doctrine, Simpson gathered about him a group of like-minded people committed to the ministry of healing. This group, the newly formed Christian and Missionary Alliance, boldly practiced prayer for the sick according to James chapter 5. This healing ministry burgeoned during Simpson's days while leading this bold new mission movement. (There will be more about Simpson in Ch. 5.) Simpson and his colleagues took James' passage to be for the modern day church. They preached Christ as the Great Physician.

There are three aspects of healing that are pivotal in James' orders. They are the elders, the prayer, and the oil. A confident understanding of these three elements was basic if divine healing was to be administered effectively in the church.

1. The Role of the Elders

As James states it, if anyone was sick he should call the elders. No one needed to summon a famous healer from Asia Minor or Jerusalem. Local leadership was sufficient. And these elders were to be the godly officials of the local church. They were to be men of bold faith and to be sensitive to the Spirit. "The term *elder* should not be construed simply to mean a person of senior age... Though some elders would likely be of mature age, the main qualification was spiritual competence."[23]

Since the Holy Spirit distributes the gifts according to His will and according to the ministry assigned in the body, elders would certainly have gifts of healing. Healing, from anything we learn in the New Testament scriptures, could not be ministered by mere position or office. Christ alone is the Healer and the elders are only His chosen representatives empowered by His Spirit and gifts.

2. The Role of Prayer

In the Bible, sickness is usually a call to prayer and/or ministry. It was a way God got people's attention. An illness often meant take a "time-out" to talk with God or take a rest. (In today's hurried culture, we think illness means take an aspirin—and then keep going.) And God, who desires fellowship and is constantly calling His own, sometimes needs to use an unpleasant circumstance. Therefore God wants His church to call out to Him when sickness strikes. The refusal to do so can be dangerous because it can lead to the progressive secularization of one's theological outlook. "The point James makes is that one ought not to complain or strike out, one ought not even to bear it with quiet resignation as the Stoics advised, but rather one should pray."[24] Simply put, when in pain, "come to Jesus."

When the elders anoint and pray, James says, "the prayer...will make the sick person well" (v. 15). Keep in mind that this is Jesus' blood brother talking. Mary is James's mother, too. He is a younger brother to our Savior, and he knows what he is talking about! This healing ministry is not a secret knowledge that only a few can understand. There are no secret tactics. It is the releasing of the power of God. This "prayer offered in faith" opens up the situation to divine intervention. It invites God to act. God will often not act before the prayer is offered up. Once healing has come, the patient and those ministering healing can be sure that the healing has come from God. Healing is then cause for thanksgiving and praise. The final results are enhanced relationships, vertical and horizontal.

In writing this instruction, James is aware that co-laboring with God changes a person. God could have continued the ministry of healing by the divine touch of a select few. But by involving the elders, the elders then search their own hearts (instead of searching for some healer-man), desiring personal clarity, whole-hearted devotion, and righteousness, and thus become even more fervent in pursuit of God.

James is exhorting the flock to offer prayers of faith to God from righteous hearts. And God will even use sickness to accomplish this. The result is that the Holy Spirit will move mightily and as a result His church will grow to love and know God more.

3. The Meaning of the Oil

Exactly what is the meaning of the oil? Is it a medicine? Is it a cultic ritual? Is the anointing symbolic? Is it necessary? Ralph Martin said that oil could have been included for a practical purpose such as medicine. He says, "Rituals with oil for healing were common in the ancient world."[25] This possibility pivots from the fact that Jesus tells of using oil for healing in the story of the Good Samaritan.

James, under the inspiration of the Holy Spirit, put into writing what had been practiced from the days of Jesus and before. Mark 6:13 speaks of the twelve disciples's activity after they had been sent out to preach and deliver people from evil spirits. It says, "They drove out many demons and anointed many sick people with oil and healed them." This Mark passage indicates that the apostles received the practice of anointing from Christ Jesus.

This historical introduction of anointing with oil for healing in Mark 6:13 also helps our understanding of the purpose of anointing. Grammatically speaking, the verb *anoint* is in the aorist tense, indicating an instantaneous act. This argues against the interpretation that the oil was intended as a medication. Medicine heals gradually and not instantaneously.

The anointing oil is representative of Christ the Anointed One. The application of the oil in His name brings all honor to Christ as Healer. Martin also surmises that the oil may have been applied by the elders to help in stimulating faith. The oil is not a guarantee of recovery, but a sign of submission to God so He may work. The "finished product" and God's timing in finishing His work is His option.

The anointing of oil was by no means cultic. For the word *anoint* James uses a derivative of *aleiphein*. *Chriein* is another word for "anoint" in the New Testament, but Martin says that *chriein* is always used in a metaphorical sense.[26] "*Aleiphein* thus may have been chosen...because of standard usage, yet still with the intention of conveying the thought that the anointing of oil was symbolic."[27] This would mean that there is nothing mysterious or cultic in James' orders to use oil. The oil would only mean that the Lord Jesus is now here in Spirit to heal and that it is time to exercise faith. James' use of *aleiphein* also discourages the possibility of the oil being a medicine.

James includes the section about sins being forgiven as confession is made, urging congregants to confess to each other and pray for each other so that forgiveness and healing can take place. Confession and repentance are crucial for someone seeking healing. The Holy Spirit will not bless us over willfully unconfessed sins. This is consistent with the rest of Scripture.

And what is the result of this activity? Verse 15 of the James passage assures, "And the prayer offered in faith will make the sick person well; the Lord will raise him up. If he has sinned, he will be forgiven." The section, "The Lord will raise him up" is a promise that God will act.

So what is the church to make of those who are prayed for and yet remain sick? This has been dealt with in the prior pages. Many scholars have pondered this issue. James said *He* (God) will raise them up. Is healing always immediate? At least one answer to this dilemma is the fact that James 5:15 is a conditional promise. There is a possibility that the individual anointed with oil and prayed over by the elders may not have repented of a known sin, or may have had an unresolved conflict with a brother in the assembly or was insufficiently instructed to place vital faith in God's promise. Any of these conditions would account for the failure or at least the delay in receiving healing. It is not beyond the realm of possibility that God, for a sovereign reason, delayed the healing. Healings are not always immediate. Some very spectacular healings have been gradual. James confidently states, "The Lord will raise him up." Note that *when* the Lord raises the sick is not the issue to James. The Lord will raise him up. The timing is in the Lord's hands.

> We want instant abra-cadabra healing risk-free or
> we won't proceed and obey in healing prayer.

The pastor and elders must not abandon these orders merely because they are not sure when the Lord is going to act. That may sound preposterous, but there are countless pastors in this world who will not lay on hands in healing prayer because they get embarrassed when God does not respond immediately. They want instant *abra-cadabra* healing and they want it promised to them risk-free or they will not proceed and obey in healing prayer. This is a popular resolve, albeit subconscious, for many leaders today. Just the same, God's promise of action is to trigger the response of prayer. If the Lord commands prayer, then the church must exercise praying and anointing in the name of the Lord. Neglect or omission out of fear of failure is disobedience. There is no other assessment.

James teaches that the healing ministry of Christ Jesus is to be carried on by the church of Christ Jesus, His followers. And until further notice there is to be no wavering, doubting, excusing, or ceasing from this activity. We are to pray for the sick. Our Savior told us to do this...and so did His brother.

CHAPTER 4 ENDNOTES

1.   Francis MacNutt, *Healing* (Notre Dame, IN: Ave Maria Press, 1974), 80.

2.   For the disciples, "doing likewise" did not necessarily mean to duplicate Jesus' ministry. One Jesus was sufficient. However, what this did mean was that they were to be Spirit-directed and Spirit-empowered in their ministry as Jesus was.

3.   Marion L. Soards, *The Apostle Paul: An Introduction to His Writings and Teaching* (New York: Paulist Press, 1987), 90.

4.   Ibid., 38.

5.   Ibid.

6.   Ibid., 39.

7.   Ibid.

8.   Ibid., 40.

9.   Ibid., 278.

10.   Ibid, 184–185.

11.   Keith Bailey, *Divine Healing: The Children's Bread* (Harrisburg, PA: Christian Publications, Inc., 1977).

12.   Victor Paul Furnish, *Second Corinthians*, Anchor Bible Series, vol. 32A (Garden City, NY: Doubleday, 1984), 548.

13.   Ibid., 548.

14.   Ralph P. Martin, *Second Corinthians*, Word Bible Commentary, vol. 40 (Waco, TX: Word, 1986), 414.

15.   Ibid., 415.

16.   Furnish, 549.

17.   Jerry W. McCant, "Paul's Thorn of Rejected Apostleship," *New Testament Studies* 34:551.

18.   Ibid., 572.

19.   Everett Ferguson, *Backgrounds of Early Christianity*, (Grand Rapids, MI: Eerdmans, 1987), 174.

20.   Ibid., 175–176.

21.   Ibid., 177.

22.   A.B. Simpson, *The Gospel of Healing* (New York: Christian Alliance Publishing, 1888; reprint, Camp Hill, PA: Christian Publications, Inc., 1984), 25 (page reference is to reprint edition).

23.   Ralph P. Martin, *James*, Word Biblical Commentary, vol. 48 (Waco, TX: Word, 1988), 207.

24.   Peter H. Davids, *The Epistle of James* (Grand Rapids, MI: Eerdmans, 1982), 192.

25.   Martin, 208.

26.   Ibid., 208–209.

27.   Ibid.

APOSTLES' AND DISCIPLES' WORKS OF HEALING: MALADY, DISTINCTION, METHOD, AND RESULT

The Twelve Sent Out (Matthew 10:1–11:1: Mark 3:13–19; Luke 9:1–10)

Jesus sends out the twelve to drive out evil spirits and heal every disease and sickness. "Heal the sick, raise the dead, cleanse the lepers, drive out demons." Afterward, the disciples return and give Jesus their report.

The Seventy-two Sent Out (Luke 10:1–24)

Jesus sends out the seventy-two in pairs to heal the sick. The seventy-two returned elated to realize they even have power of demons and spirits.

Disciples Attempt to Cast Out Demons (Matthew 17:14–21; Mark 9:14–29; Luke 9:37–43)

The disciples attempt to cleanse a boy with an evil spirit. He is in convulsions, gnashing teeth, foaming at the mouth, living in madness, has seizures, falls into water, and falls into fire nearly twenty-four hours a day. Jesus has to step in to finish the exorcism.

The Great Commission is Received (Matthew 28:16–20; Mark 16:15–18; Acts 1:8)

Disciples receive the Great Commission including orders to drive out demons, neutralize any deadly poison, lay on hands to heal the sick.

Signs and wonders at the Apostles' hands (Acts 2:43)

Disciples perform many signs and wonders and people are filled with awe.

Healing of Lame Beggar (Acts 3:1–4:22)

Lame beggar is healed as Peter orders him to rise and walk in Jesus' name. Result: people are astonished and Peter gives a sermon. Peter and John are arrested and five thousand more people get saved. The Sanhedrin is in an uproar.

Prayer for confidence and healing signs (Acts 4:29–31)

Prayer for boldness in preaching and to be used to heal, do miracles, signs and wonders in Jesus' name. Result: their meeting room is shaken; all are filled with the Holy Spirit and speak boldly.

Signs and wonders at Apostles' hands (Acts 5:12–16)

The apostles perform many miraculous signs and wonders. Men and women join their numbers. Numerous sick are brought on beds and mats; even Peter's shadow boosts their faith. Evil spirits are cast out and all people brought are healed.

Ministry of Stephen (Acts 6:8–10, 15)

Stephen does many great wonders and miraculous signs, so the opposition arrests him.

Ministry of Philip (Acts 8:4–13)

Evil spirits come out, paralyzed and crippled are healed. Result: there is great joy in Samaria. People are astonished at the power working through Philip.

Ananias and Saul (Acts 9:10–19)

Saul is called into ministry. Ananias is used of God to restore Saul's sight.

Peter heals Aeneas in Lydda (Acts 9:32–35)

Peter heals Aeneas after eight years of paralysis. All witnesses in Lydda and Sharon turn to the Lord.

Peter brings Tabitha/Dorcas back from the dead in Joppa (Acts 9:36–42)

Peter brings Tabitha/Dorcas back from the dead. Many people believe in the Lord.

Magician/sorcerer struck blind by Paul (Acts 13:6–12)

A sorcerer/false prophet is struck blind for opposing Paul. The proconsul witnesses this and believes in the Lord.

Paul and Barnabas in Iconium (Acts 14:1–4)

Paul and Barnabas preach and do miraculous signs and wonders in Iconium.

Lame man at Lystra (Acts 14:8–18)

A man crippled from birth is healed by Paul. People think Barnabas and Paul are gods. Paul delivers a powerful polemic sermon.

Paul raised at Lystra (Acts 14:19–20)

Paul brought back from near death after stoning at Lystra.

Slave girl at Philippi (Acts 16:16–34)

Paul casts the evil spirit out of a fortune–telling slave girl. Her owner's business is obliterated. Paul and Silas are whipped and imprisoned. In jail, their worship precedes an earthquake that looses the inmates and causes the conversion of the jailer and his whole family.

Paul at Ephesus (Acts 19:11–20)

God did extraordinary miracles through Paul, so that even cloth was used to transfer his power to heal the sick, curse their illness and drive away evil spirits. So many believed in Jesus and a number of sorcerers disband their craft.

Eutychus raised from the dead (Acts 20:7–12)

Eutychus is raised from the dead after a great fall. Many are comforted.

Paul on Malta (Acts 28:1–10)

Paul survives snakebite, then heals Publius's father of fever and dysentery. Then all the sick on the island come and Paul cures them, too.

Galatians 3:5

Paul reminds the Galatians that miracles are done among them because they believe (not because they observe the law).

Hebrews 2:4

Paul reminds the Hebrews of God's signs, wonders, miracles, and gifts of the Holy Spirit.

five

HEALING in MODERN TIMES

B<small>Y THE LATTER</small> nineteenth century, the American economy was burgeoning from the economic boom following the Civil War. An industrial machine had been assembled in America that made the world stand up and take notice. Westward expansion was full speed ahead. There was an adequate amount of slack in the schedules and budgets of enough Americans that baseball was able to grow into a full-fledged national pastime. Never before had the working class had time on their hands to the point that a "pastime" could be chosen to fill the previously nonexistent leisure time. Many futurists were musing that nearly everything that was going to be invented had already been invented. In time, humanity was going to be fine. "The Gay '90s" were the 1890s and happiness was at a premium. Perhaps America was on the verge of being permanently content. Dispensationalist Theology was becoming rooted in the minds of enough theologians that healing as a ministry was being dismissed as "for the apostles." As this perspective was gaining in popularity, many acquiesced to dismiss divine healing as a blessing that ended in the first century.

But were all people content and at peace? Indeed had all misery been dealt with in this realm, too? Was absolutely no one in need of something more? Something more that only God could deliver?

In the midst of this era with its peculiar thinking, there were people who were called upon by the Holy Spirit to relight a torch that would draw people through their dark worlds and into the light of Jesus. Crusades were held, souls were touched, and healing ministries were launched. Herein they could be saved, loved, touched by the Great Physician, comforted, and inspired in their journey. We will look at some of the key people who were instrumental in what eventually turned into a healing surge as the Holy Spirit touched lives anew. Movements of renewal were on the rise. Each played their role, but the spotlight of this chapter is going to be on Albert Benjamin Simpson, a Canadian-born minister of Scottish descent who had a greater effect on the religious landscape in America than anyone before him. Some even speculate that the affect that Simpson had upon Christendom is yet to be surpassed in the western hemisphere.

A.B. Simpson (1843–1919), by his own personal devotion, his example, his ministry and experience, and his widely read books attracted countless people to Jesus and His healing touch. Among the many things that triggered this was first, his love for his Savior. Other byproducts of this love were his passion for lost souls, his energy to see the kingdom advance, and his heart for the suffering and ill. This spurred him into a thorough study of the biblical doctrine of divine healing. What resulted was a healing ministry, which accompanied his mission endeavors wherein he and his associates, and students of his writings, ended up touching the world. As is inferred, not only did Simpson minister healing, he trained others to do so—who in turn trained still others (as is urged in 2 Timothy 2:2). His work affected Christendom in such a great way that it becomes difficult to quantify.

[Concerns of holiness usually precede healing ministry.

His zealous and rich faith spurred a ministry that led the founding of the Christian & Missionary Alliance in the latter 1800s. This brought a fresh demonstration of the biblical doctrine of healing for the body and a renewed interest to seek Christ's healing touch. Simpson's ministry affected New York City, eventually the state, then New England, and the Atlantic seaboard. His influence went national and then jumped oceans as he sent out missionaries to foreign lands. Christian & Missionary Alliance missionaries are still working in scores of countries on all six inhabited continents.

Simpson can safely be referred to as the one who head-watered much of the healing ministry that was to follow in the coming decades and across denominations. The inner circle Simpson mentored became the leaders that spurred this powerful ministry of Christ. They went on to lead a host of others; some branched off from Simpson to start healing ministries that were more healing oriented than Simpson and the C&MA he founded. The founders of the Assembly of God, which is markedly larger than the C&MA, were grateful to Simpson for the training and inspiration he provided. The Foursquare denomination, which started decades after the C&MA, was influenced by Simpson's writings. Their four doctrinal values are identical: Christ is Savior, Sanctifier (or Baptizer), Healer, and returning King. Simpson played a varying role for many other people and groups who were launched into ministry and a radical obedience to Christ's calling. His life did far more than mere addition to the church. Simpson caused there to be exponential multiplication in the kingdom.

It is in order to say that Simpson and his founding leaders were not the only factors in healing ministry in the world at the time. The Holiness Movement, which grew out of the Methodist Church in the 1800s, laid important groundwork. Concerned souls within the Methodist Church were apprehensive about their denomination drifting as they approached their second century. I mention this because concerns of holiness usually precede healing ministry. Just a note: the theology of those listed below is open to debate. Everyone's is. Please remember that God will not allow anyone's theology to be perfect. God does not need another Jesus to finish the job. So if I may offer my conjecture, He even allows people to live lives with flaws built in so as to make sure we do not worship anyone but His Son.

In the 1800s, Phoebe Palmer (1807–1874) was a key minister during the time leading up to Simpson becoming prominent. Eddie Hyatt gives a concise overview of her work in *2000 Years of Charismatic Christianity*. Though never ordained, she became the leader of the Promotion of Holiness meetings in 1840. These soon grew to include people outside the Methodist movement.

Phoebe Palmer wrote important books on the topic of holiness and during the last ten years of her life was editor/publisher of *The Guide to Holiness*. It was the most important periodical on the subject matter at the time. Thousands were saved in the meetings at which she spoke in the USA, Canada, and Great Britain. During her extensive travels and ministry, Pentecostal language that she used began replacing Wesleyan terms. That seems to be an interesting development as people began to think beyond, "Let's get back to John Wesley" who founded the Methodist Movement, and were focusing on getting the Holy Spirit in their lives. It was during Palmer's work that "the baptism of the Holy Ghost," and "endowment of power" became the expressions or slogans of an era. Hyatt calls his chapter of this time in history, "The Nineteenth-Century Forerunners of the Modern Pentecostal/Charismatic Movement."

Charles Finney (1792–1873) was a revivalist who changed the religious landscape and culture of his time. As a law student he was converted in 1821. After being in the Presbyterian Church, he joined the Congregational Church. His preaching also changed more than individual souls. Numerous communities were transformed during Finney's revival meetings. Finney himself experienced the baptism of the Holy Spirit, as he called it. And being a changed man, he went out and changed others.

His meetings were marked by powerful manifestations of God. People wept, confessed, and converted to following Christ Jesus. All over New England local businesses soon cleaned up their practices, bars closed, and the Sabbath was returned to a holy day across cities. Churches soon filled to capacity. People sang wholeheartedly, many for the first time. Charity thrived and towns had remarkably changed atmospheres. There were even people who could not get to the meetings, but would later convert to Christ back in town after simply meeting eyes with Finney along the boardwalk. The Holy Spirit was upon this man and he was mightily used.

Finney is often credited as the one who originated the *altar call*. Not being a passing fancy, the method is still used today at crusades worldwide. And God was up to something in Finney's meetings that was not humanly planned. For though healing was not a resolute practice of Finney's, people *were* being healed at his revival meetings. The convicting and powerful sermons, the

Pentecost-like movements and manifestations that took place, and the fervent prayers and conversions—automatically prompted people to pray for the ill among the crowds. Finney did not initiate this from the front, but the Holy Spirit initiated it from within the gatherings. These could be seen as precursors to Simpson's ministry wherein healing was on the program. As the Holiness Movement gave way to the Pentecostal Movement, Finney's methods of revival and crusades were retained.

A.J. Gordon (1836–1895), founder of Gordon College, pastored in Boston for twenty-five years. His ample writings on the topic of the Holy Spirit made him a major figure in the Christian scene and activities of his day. His work had great influence on tailoring the quest of the contemporary church. His writings were used and referred to by Simpson. Gordon soundly makes his case in *The Ministry of Healing* that the gifts of the Spirit were for more than just the apostles. His influence upon Simpson and other contemporary Christian leaders is noteworthy as Gordon affected the writings and ministries and many decisions of others. Simpson freely quotes Gordon in his writings.

These figures in Christendom are briefly mentioned because it should not even be implied that A.B. Simpson came along as one voice crying in the wilderness. He was not a lone voice in his desire to see the truth of Christ shining over the earth. There *were* others who had felt the marvelous wonder of walking in the Spirit of Christ. He was not the only man of his day who learned by experience the glories of serving God and His kingdom. He is, however, in my opinion, the man who single-handedly did more than anyone else to accelerate the ministry of healing in his day. A.W. Tozer would agree and more. Simpson's life ought be seen in light of all he did; not just for the healing work he did. Twenty to thirty years later there were ministers who had larger healing ministries than Simpson did. But in terms of the amassed ministries that Simpson accomplished—the writing, the leadership development, the speaking, crusade work, conversions, actual discipleship work, the healings, the healing home, the training for healing ministry, discipleship development material, training for general ministry, the mission prep, the missions sending, and funding of these missions—Simpson was without peer. Others who honestly study Simpson's life and ministry in depth come to a comparable conclusion.

In Simpson's experience, his preaching and ministry, the truth of "Christ as our Healer," was made known to him many years after he experienced Christ as his Savior. Prior to his healing experience, Simpson lived and ministered for years as a very weak and frail man with unbearable respiratory problems. This, of course, is before he learned to trust Christ's divine healing of his physical body. He had learned of the renewal of healing going on in Europe, Great Britain, and the United States at that time, but was cautious about personally accepting it. It was a pilgrimage of many difficult years that finally brought A.B. Simpson to accept Jesus Christ as his Healer.

THE PILGRIMAGE OF SIMPSON

Simpson's healing pilgrimage began amid his constant battle with sicknesses. Simpson did not have an epiphany about healing one day wherein he was then assigned as prophet to the suffering. He did not see himself as some great herald of a healing doctrine that he was going to parlay to an ill world; not from the start anyhow. He came upon healing ministry for existential reasons. Illness and discouragement shrouded him.

He had once witnessed the healing of a paralyzed man in his early days of pastoring. And this is what sparked interest in Simpson for personal healing. One leading parishioner in his congregation, however, quickly smothered his faith by encouraging him to doubt the authenticity of the healing. It was not until years later when he opened himself to personal healing that his convictions became firm.

1. Engulfed by Illness

As a young man, Simpson learned that much study wearies the body. His first physical breakdown occurred when he was a student in high school. Determined to do well, he worked himself to exhaustion. Simpson says of these days: "Beginning a life of hard intellectual labor at the age of fourteen, I broke hopelessly down with nervous exhaustion while preparing for college. For many months I was not permitted by my doctor even to look at a book. During this time I came very near death. On the verge of eternity I gave myself at last to God."[1] He was fifteen at the time. It is interesting that it was sickness and a near deathbed setting that drove him to salvation in Christ. It was a prophetic experience for him. Little did he know that nearly twenty-five years later he would begin to minister Christ's healing in New York City to assembly halls packed with the sick, handicapped, hurting, and dying. Wherein sickness drove him to Christ for salvation, sickness also drove him to Christ for healing (for himself, his family, and the world).

Simpson had just graduated from college, was twenty-one years of age, and was already pastoring a large church in Hamilton, Ontario, Canada. His ambition to study and minister effectively is what nearly killed him again. Of his first pastorate Simpson writes, "...plunging headlong into my work, I again broke down with heart trouble and had to go away for months of rest, returning at length, as it seemed to me at the time, to die."[2]

He partly recovered from this second collapse. But the now feeble Simpson became a candidate for endless medicine. "I labored on for years with the aid of constant remedies and preventives. I carried a bottle of ammonia in my pocket and would have taken a nervous spasm if I had ventured out without it."[3]

Because of his dependence on medicine, he even preached a sermon entitled, "My Medicine Chest."[4] He was always weak. A simple flight of stairs would pose such a threat that even the thought of such exertion would leave Simpson feeling anxious. After such a feat (like "simply" climbing a single flight of stairs), he says, "an awful and suffocating agony would come over me, and the thought of that bottle as a last resort quieted me."[5] Once, while in Switzerland, he climbed a flight of steps and by the top he truly thought he was going to die; it was that dire. He vowed never to do such a thing again. He was a man basically affixed to a faulty respiratory system. Gathering strength for ministry was a continual battle. In his own words: "God knows how many hundreds of times in my earlier ministry, when preaching in my pulpit or ministering by a grave, it seemed that I must fall in the midst of the service or drop into that open grave."[6] It is hard to imagine what it was like for Simpson to be preaching about a triumphant Christ who had risen from the dead, a Christ who lived in us, in our hearts—and there was Simpson, so utterly weak and always on the verge of collapse.

Simpson's constant exhaustion was further punctuated by two other total collapses in health. Like the one in his teens and at twenty-one during his first pastorate, these also were long-term breakdowns. It seemed "that the last drops of life were ebbing out."[7] Simpson had a burning heart for God. He had lofty visions. He loved people. He wanted to minister and do great things for God. But his health was taking him down a dead-end street. The future seemed grim. He was utterly frustrated with the weakness that hampered his ministry. He disdained being thought of as "frail." To him it was depressing. His congregation knew of his problem. "My good people always thought me 'delicate,' Simpson bemoaned. I grew weary of being sympathized with every time they met me. The parishioners excused many a neglected visit because I was 'not strong.'"[8]

Simpson moved from Canada to accept a pastorate in Louisville, Kentucky. Perhaps a change of climate would be of some benefit. But he continued to suffer debilitating health. He had yet to learn for himself the truth that Christ wanted to heal people, including heal him, today! He was not aware that Jesus wanted to touch him, heal him, and in turn have him touch thousands who would touch others with the healing Spirit of Christ Jesus. So on he suffered.

2. Positive and Negative Influences for Healing

As stated earlier, Simpson witnessed a divine healing while pastoring in Louisville. Thompson writes, "He had been deeply impressed by the healing of a young paralytic in his congregation."[9] At the time Simpson witnessed this healing, he himself was struggling with poor health. He said of this incident: "The impression produced by this incident never left my heart. Soon afterwards I attempted to take the Lord as my Healer, and for a while, as long as I trusted Him, He sustained me wonderfully."[10]

His health would have been preserved and the years of illness would never have been, except for two factors. Simpson confessed, "Being entirely without instruction, and advised by a devout Christian physician that it was presumption, I abandoned my position of simple dependence upon God alone, and so floundered and stumbled for years."[11] Simpson had gained a mustard-seed faith, but no sooner had he gained this faith than it was nullified by bad advice.

I wish this were an isolated incident, but sadly enough that is not so. Throughout history this has happened to many people who wanted to come to Jesus and be changed inside and out, head to toe. Jesus has all power and authority to do this, too. But too many are advised to simply bear it as if they were being punished for some reason and that this struggle was good for their soul.

3. The Inspiration to Finally Receive His Healing

In the midsummer of 1881, while the Simpson family was vacationing in Old Orchard, Maine, Dr. Charles Cullis, a Christian physician from Boston, was conducting healing services there. Cullis was instrumental in turning Simpson's doubt into faith again. In his practice, Dr. Cullis would pray for patients as well as employ his medical knowledge to assist in the healing process. "Some terminally ill patients had remarkable recoveries."[12] For this reason Dr. Cullis studied divine healing further, and became convinced that God wanted to heal the whole man.

One evening Simpson attended a service that Dr. Cullis was conducting where he "listened to at least two hundred people give accounts of their healing. [Simpson recalls] 'I had believed that there were cases of healing, but the facts did not convince me.'"[13] Simpson considered himself very committed to Scripture and not one to be swayed by people's experiences. But that same night, his doubts about divine healing began to deflate. It was those testimonies that sent him to the scriptures to examine the matter anew.

Simpson resolved that if he found healing for his body in the scriptures he would accept it as true. "I determined that I must settle this matter one way or the other."[14] He wanted an answer about divine healing and he received it that day. "At His feet, alone... I became convinced that this was part of Christ's glorious gospel for a sinful and suffering world."[15] Roughly twenty-five years after he entrusted his soul to the resurrected Christ, he trusted his body to the resurrected Christ, too.

THE HEALING OF A.B. SIMPSON

Simpson's healing was a life-changing experience for him. Divine healing played an important role in his personal life and preaching ministry. The struggle that began as a teen in school was about to end. God was on the verge of healing A.B. Simpson. The sheer fright of struggling to breathe would end very soon. And Simpson would receive this blessing and go forth to see to it that many millions received this same blessing.

1. His Covenant of Healing

For A.B. Simpson healing was not an empty theory. He accepted Christ as his Healer. For him it was as serious as when he received Christ as Savior twenty-five years prior. Right there he made a definitive covenant with God to trust Him for healing. Simpson says of that day and incident in 1881:

> And so one Friday afternoon at the hour of three o'clock, I went out into the silent pine woods—I remember the spot—and there I raised my right hand to heaven and made to God... these three great and eternal pledges:
>
> I solemnly accept this truth as part of Thy Word and of the Gospel of Christ, and... I shall never question it until I meet Thee there.
>
> I take the Lord Jesus as my physical life, for all the needs of my body until all my life-work is done...I shall never doubt that He does become my life and strength from this moment and will keep me under all circumstances until all His will for me is perfectly fulfilled.
>
> I solemnly promise to use this blessing for the glory of God and the good of others, and to so speak of it or minister in connection with it in any way in which God may call me or others may need me in the future.[16]

He arose from his covenant of prayer a renewed man of God. This from his journal: "Every fibre of my soul was tingling with a sense of God's presence... It was so glorious to believe it simply, and to know that... He had it in hand."[17] He had now accepted Christ as his Healer and was soon to learn the testing that would serve only to verify his new covenant.

2. The Testings That Came

Simpson's first test was doubting, the same test wherein he had surrendered fifteen years prior. That was back when a minister sternly counseled him *against* faith for healing. After immediately wavering as to the certainty of his commitment to Christ being his newfound healer, he was quickly reminded that this matter was settled forever. He took pause to be reassured that it was God who had led him to this point; not some selfish notion or deceptive spirit. Simpson says, "I saw that when a thing was settled with God, it was never to be unsettled...It was never to be undone or done over again."[18]

The second test came two days later. That Sunday he was asked to preach at a congregational church in New Hampshire. The Holy Spirit wanted him to testify what He had done in his life that same weekend. But Simpson was afraid to publicly take this stand. He confesses, "I tried to preach a good sermon of my own choosing."[19] He intended to deliver a normal, respectable sermon. The results were abysmal. "My jaws seemed like lumps of lead, and my lips would scarcely move."[20] He concluded the service as briskly as possible, went into a field and asked God to forgive him. He was given another chance that evening. Back in his hotel he spoke at a small service. He told them, "I had lately seen the Lord Jesus in a deeper fullness, as the Healer of the body, and had taken Him for myself."[21] He stammered, obviously disappointed with his delaying to testify, but by day's end he was obedient.

The third test came on Monday, the next day. He was invited to climb Mt. Kearsarge in New Hampshire. It was three thousand feet high! Instantly his mind flashed back to when he was left gasping for air in Switzerland. For decades a simple flight of stairs had winded him terribly. He had the enormous fear of verifying his healing and "shrank back at once."[22] Then he realized that not going would be to doubt God's healing. "I told God that in His strength I would go."[23] Remember that for decades, to simply elevate himself ten feet climbing stairs felt like a fatal assignment. How was he going to fare elevating himself a couple thousand feet on this hike? It was a daunting endeavor to say the least!

He commenced hiking and the weakness came over him as always. But against this he grew distinctly aware of the presence of God. "When I reached the mountaintop, I seemed to be at the gate of heaven, and the world of weakness and fear was lying at my feet."[24] He had embraced Christ Jesus as the new strength for his body.

Then came the fourth and most difficult test. Not long after coming home from New England, his three-year-old daughter Margaret was stricken with diphtheria. Mrs. Simpson wanted to call a doctor. The Simpsons had lost their son, Melville, to diphtheria at the same age. It was the repeat of a nightmare. Against his wife's insistence, Simpson did not call a doctor.[25] According to medical knowledge, Margaret would not last another day. Simpson was not being cavalier or foolhardy in not calling a doctor. Doctors were available when Melville died, and what good did that do? The contrast between Margaret's illness now and Melville's illness then was that Simpson had now received a gift from the Holy Spirit. He had a new level of faith. The disciples had asked, "Lord, increase my faith" and it happened. Simpson's experience was comparable. Now at his deathly-ill child's bedside, he recalls, "...with trembling hand I anointed her brow and claimed the power of Jesus' name."[26] Simpson remained at Margaret's bedside praying through the night. She was well by morning.

By now Simpson realized that God was breaking through a barrier in his mind. He had personally experienced the reality of God's healing. He was now fully equipped, blessed, and anointed to minister the message of healing to others. The tests served as verification that Simpson had moved to a whole new realm of faith in his walk with Christ. This new perspective and experience would affect the remainder of his days, his personal walk in the Spirit, and his ministry. What Simpson rose up to do in his new level of faith for healing (and missions) ended up touching Christendom in an enormous way. We will find out in heaven the amount of souls that were touched because of Simpson's devotion. Here are some of the consequences.

THE RESULTS OF HEALING

Simpson's covenant of healing entirely transformed his life. His newfound strength for ministry launched him into a whole new realm. He personally and mentally believed healing was real and a blessing for today. He embraced healing emotionally and physically. He ministered healing comprehensively and tirelessly. Healing meetings occurred weekly. A healing home was opened. Along with these positive changes came ridicule and rejection from others who were given to jealousy.

1. New Strength for Ministry

Strength for ministry was very important to Simpson. The weakness he experienced prior to being healed was his main frustration in ministry. He was vitally aware of and grateful for his new anointing to do God's work. He wrote, "I am intensely conscious, with every breath, that I am drawing my vitality from a directly supernatural source and that it keeps pace with the calls and necessities of my work."[27] He was constantly grateful and rejoicing over his renewed health.

Simpson remembered the exhaustion he experienced in early years and likened his new strength to pouring oil on the dying embers of a fire. With his usual verbal flair, Simpson describes the joy of renewed health, "As God poured his fullness on my exhausted frame, a divine strength came, full of sweet exhilaration and unwearied buoyancy and energy, and in that light and life of God I am working without exhaustion, and trust still to work in His glorious all sufficiency until my work is done."[28]

Simpson used his vigor to the full extent in the Lord's work. The thirty-eight years following God's touch upon his body were a marvel. The amount of work that Simpson accomplished in these years was staggering. A.W. Tozer, who pastored a vibrant church in Chicago and wrote profusely, felt that the volume of work Simpson amassed in life may well have only been surpassed by John Wesley and the apostle Paul.[29] To think that a bona fide, self-taught scholar such as Tozer would muse that Simpson was the third most productive servant in the history of Christendom is quite a statement.

2. The Friday Healing Meetings

After he was healed, Simpson committed himself to the ministry of divine healing. Now back in New York, he commenced upon a healing ministry that would last nearly four decades and end up playing a significant role in America's church history. The news about healing of Simpson's respiratory problem and his daughter Margaret's diphtheria spread quickly. Soon other people came to be healed. The number of those interested became so large that a regular meeting needed to be established.

Simpson was excited and challenged by this. At the same time, he was concerned that it should not dominate the Sunday services. Simpson also felt that many weekly churchgoers were not prepared for such events. Therefore he chose Friday as the day for his healing meetings. This kept them accessible, yet slightly obscure. The meeting proved to be a powerful tool for reaching people. Soon "the Friday afternoon meeting became a shrine for thousands of people connected with the churches of the city and its suburbs."[30] These meetings grew to be the largest weekday religious meetings in New York.[31]

Knowing that people were inclined to sensationalize healing and make a carnival of the supernatural, Simpson kept a tight check on these services. He was concerned that Christ remain the focus of these healing gatherings. Boredom or disappointment was no concern whatsoever. Simpson knew that God would be glorified through these healing services, so he deliberately chose Friday, a notoriously unpopular time for Christians to gather. Those who know New York City and its culture know that Friday afternoon is a time to get out on the town or out of town. Friday night is a night for dining and entertainment. So having the healing services on Fridays would immediately protect the meetings from becoming mere entertainment. Those who wanted entertainment would already be elsewhere. With the Spirit readily present and prepared for, with Simpson having thought through the factors of local culture, what else was there to happen but for the needy to gather and the Lord to bless? Simpson's biographers note, "Though Simpson was cautious as to the time and place of healing meetings, miraculous cures that electrified the audience...occurred in [these] large public gatherings."[32]

His only concern was that a proper perspective be maintained by the participants. He was aware that, in his opinion, people could easily turn into thrill seekers and make too much of divine healing; they could by mistake come to worship the healing instead of the Healer. He knew from experience what it was to think too little of divine healing—this was the story of his life for the first thirty-eight years. So Simpson did all he could to maintain a balance in his healing ministry. Second to his love for Jesus and spreading Jesus' love to the lost, Simpson was concerned for suffering people. He wanted to see people healed as well as saved. He also had a concern for the people who needed teaching and extra counseling so to receive healing for their physical conditions. This led to the realization of a plan to minister to them.

3. Berachah Healing Home

Simpson had learned of successful "healing homes" in Germany, Switzerland, London, Boston, and Buffalo, New York. His knowledge of these healing homes inspired him to begin one in New York City. Therefore, less than two years after Simpson was physically healed, the Berachah Home was opened for those needing more instruction and counsel. Many would require this before receiving healing for their condition.

The situation at Berachah, plus his experiences in ministering divine healing, were the inspiration for his first book, *The Gospel of Healing*. The book is a collection of eight articles written between 1883 and 1888. It was slightly revised in 1915. Interestingly enough, however, Simpson never changed his views on the subject. In the introduction, John Sawin tells of Simpson's grace, wisdom, and tact in the ministry of healing: "Simpson refused to impose his views of healing on others. He taught the truth as he saw it and experienced it. He only desired that his auditors or readers would understand the teaching, then examine the truth for themselves. If and when they were personally convinced and ready in heart and mind to commit themselves irrevocably to the Lord for His divine life, then and only then did Simpson consider them ready to be anointed and prayed for."[33]

Simpson had heavenly patience and a desire to wait on the Lord. He did not want even one person to enter into a covenant of healing with insufficient understanding. It was this concern that led to the writing and publishing of *The Gospel of Healing*.

Chapter one gives the scriptural foundation for healing. From Satan's work in the fall of man through the Old Testament to Christ and His commissioning, Simpson gives a brisk tour of the teaching on health that is threaded through the Word of God. Chapter 2 instructs in the principles of divine healing. In this chapter he includes his view of healing in the atonement. Chapter 3 covers the popular objections to healing, while chapter 4 gives practical direction to those seeking God's healing. Chapters 5 and 6 are selected testimonies from the scriptures. In chapter 7 Simpson gives his own personal testimony. Chapter 8 is a testimony to the work of healing that had occurred recently and was now in progress.

If any came to this healing home with little knowledge of divine healing, they were requested to read *The Gospel of Healing* before prayer was offered on their behalf.

The opening of Berachah Home ("house of blessing") in May 1883 was financed by a gift of two thousand dollars. One year later it was moved to a larger building in New York City. At this time, the home was put under the direction of two godly women: Ellen Griffin and Sarah Lindenberger. In March 1890, Berachah was moved again to a six-story building next to the New York Gospel Tabernacle on West 44th Street (currently a pizza parlor and museum that honors the fact that a denomination was founded on the premises). In 1897 Miss Griffin died. That same year the Ross Taylor Home in Nyack was purchased and enlarged to become the new Berachah Home. Miss Lindenberger ran the home and ministered healing to still hundreds and hundreds more until her death in 1921.[34]

4. Ridicule and Rejection from Others

For Simpson, the joy of ministering healing was not without rejection from peers and others who were less open to such ministry. The Friday meetings were very successful, and the Berachah Home was a lighthouse of love for the hurting. But "by many others, he was vilified and ridiculed as another quack miracle worker."[35] His zeal for the Lord no doubt left him open to criticism from the hyper-conservative and the jealous alike. Yet in obedience to the Lord, Simpson continued his healing ministry. The criticism of some toward Simpson only worsened. "Ironically, his critics were willing to let him alone as long as he struggled along sickly and weak. But when he became healthy, strong, and energetic, they bitterly criticized his ministry and motives."[36]

By his own testimony "the penalty most costly to him for his healing was a sense of loneliness."[37] It reminded him of the loneliness he felt after being filled with the Holy Spirit. Back then his friends did not understand. They were not so intensely interested in spiritual matters; including his peers in ministry. And now, in his pilgrimage with Jesus, Simpson again had to proceed alone. In short, Simpson felt deserted. As before, "the same sense of isolation overtook Simpson in the matter of healing."[38] He sums up his feeling of desertion: "My old friends seemed to leave me and for months I seemed to be alone—separated from hundreds and thousands of ministers and people I had loved and worked with all my life. I felt I did not know them now and they did not know me as before."[39] Even in all the human loneliness, his faith in Jesus never wavered. Jesus met him and ministered sustenance to him without fail. His pilgrimage was bittersweet but the love and relationship he shared with Jesus only grew more endeared to him through the years.

THE VIEW OF HEALING THAT DEVELOPED

Through the blessings and changes in his life and the ridicule that Simpson experienced, his view and theology of healing developed more clarity. In his perspective, healing was not for personal advancement but for living the life of the kingdom and continuing the work of the Lord Jesus Christ.

Simpson spells out his idea of "Christ Our Healer" in chapter 3 of *The Fourfold Gospel*, which became a compendium of Christian and Missionary Alliance distinctives. It was also Simpson's third book teaching divine healing. In chapter 3, Simpson begins by dispelling myths about healing with the following ten points.

TEN THINGS DIVINE HEALING IS NOT

1. Divine healing is not medical healing. Simpson had no trouble with people using medicine. He suggested they remain on medication unless directed otherwise by the Lord.

2. Divine healing is not metaphysical healing. It is not mind cure or Christian Science.

3. Divine healing is not magnetic healing in which a mysterious current flows from one body to another.

4. Divine healing is not spiritualism. Calling on any spirit other than Jesus Christ is *not* divine healing.

5. Divine healing is not prayer cure. This idea has the vague idea that if enough humans band together and pray, God, as if to be

swayed by democracy, will finally get the message, bend His stubborn will, and heal that person.

6. Divine healing is not faith cure. God does the healing, not the faith. (Faith is the avenue to healing that must be placed in Christ the Healer.)

7. Divine healing is not cure by will power. Divine healing is a work from the divine, not the victim.

8. Divine healing is not defiance of God's will, as if to say, "I will have this…whether He wills it or not!"

9. Divine healing is not physical immortality. It is fullness of life until the life work is done.

10. Divine healing is not mercenary healing. One could not adopt divine healing as a professional trade just like any other job; God's gifts are free.

These ten points helped clear the atmosphere of what some might read into his doctrine on healing. He continues with ten points that clarify what divine healing is.

TEN THINGS DIVINE HEALING IS

1. Divine healing is the supernatural divine power of God infused into human bodies, renewing their strength and replacing the weakness of suffering human frames by the life and power of God.

2. Divine healing is founded on the Word of God alone. Human reason, intellect, testimony, and dedication are less than worthless, if not founded on the Word of God.

3. Divine healing is always done in submission to and within the will of God. Simpson warned people against fighting that will, if indeed their life work was complete.

4. Divine healing is part of the redemptive work of Jesus Christ. It is partly the reason for the incarnation; the foundation of healing being in the Cross.

5. Divine healing comes through the life of the resurrected Christ, who bodily rose from the dead.

6. Divine healing is the healing that comes via the work of the Holy Spirit. Jesus healed by the Holy Spirit while on earth, and He is still the same today.

7. Divine healing is based on God's grace, not man's work or merit. It is a free gift that must be received.

8. Divine healing comes by faith. God does the healing, yet it is faith that enables healing to take place.

9. Divine healing is in accordance with all the facts of church history. There are endless examples of God's continuous healing hand at work from Paul to the present.

10. Divine healing is one of the signs of the age. It is the forerunner of Christ's coming and proof of God's power.

Servanthood and submission to Jesus Christ are primary in Simpson's view on divine healing. The blessings received are life changing for everyone involved; they are for His glory and for the purpose of building up the church.

1. Healing as Obedience and Not for Self-Gain

Simpson was not a crowd-pleaser. He refused to deliberately attach "the sensational" to the ministry of divine healing. God did not need any help making sensational and exhilarating blessing out of His healing touch. He was careful never to use his gift to fill auditoriums or offering plates. From what he perceived: "It is very solemn ground and can never be made a professional business or a public parade. Its mightiest victories will always be silent and out of sight, and its power will keep pace with our humility and holiness."[40]

Had Simpson put more emphasis on healing ministry, extremist groups would have been pleased. Using today's lingo, there were leaders in Simpson's original inner circle who thought he should do "extreme healing"; have healing services constantly. It was thought he could rent Central Park or ball fields for nightly meetings, and let healing be the trademark of Simpson's ministry. In truth, he could have done so. Or had he emphasized healing less, conservative groups would have been pleased. But he was concerned with godliness and obedience, not prestige or acceptance or thrill shows. Thompson wrote of Simpson, "Had he renounced divine healing he could have obtained a wider and more tolerant recognition. But that would have required a diplomacy of which he could never be guilty."[41] Simpson had committed himself to following the Lord. And he would follow in whatever the Lord directed him to do. That is exactly what he did the remainder of his days.

2. The Atonement and Resurrected Christ for the Body

"Simpson taught that the basis of faith in divine healing was the atonement of Jesus Christ."[42] He took Isaiah 53 to mean healing as covering both soul and body. Divine life came from the resurrected Christ. This life of Christ was infused into our frame, should we accept it. Jesus was more than a spiritual blessing. Simpson stated, "Not only is His spirit for my spirit, but His body for my body, touching mine into life."[43] He called Jesus "my complete Savior for body as well as for soul."[44] Simpson did not have a "superman" or "fountain of youth" perspective. Neither did Simpson teach that divine healing would grant one to have perfect or trouble free living. "The idea is too common that a person who is healed is thereafter immune from every kind of sickness. Dr. Simpson's conception of divine life for the body was exactly contrary to this supposition. He felt himself to be wholly dependent upon a vital and continuous connection with the Lord for his life."[45] If we would believe and receive, then there would be a pipeline, so to speak, that kept us on continual feed from a Triune God who never ran dry. This blessing was God's doing and for His glory. For Simpson, divine healing is not "God at our disposal." It is our believing God and, in faith, putting ourselves at *His* disposal. We would be sustained by His supply and by Himself.

Simpson's 1903 book, *The Lord for the Body*, rounded out his conviction on divine healing. It was a presentation of divine healing as found in different books of the Bible and various characters in the Bible. It is not intended to be exhaustive, only a helpful guide. Subsequent printings added material, bringing the book to fifteen chapters: chapter 12, "Natural and Supernatural Healing," chapter 14, "Paul and Divine Healing," and chapter 15, "Inquiries and Answers (concerning divine healing)."

Simpson is credited with enlightening countless people to the truth of divine healing. The notable change in the awareness and exercise of this truth during his era testifies to the effect of the one man, Simpson.

3. The Way to Receive Healing

Simpson taught that healing was available upon two conditions. First, the heart must be right with God. Second, the person must have faith. "If there is any sin…lay it at the Lord's feet, choose His will in the matter."[46] "The holy Gospel only remains in a holy life and heart."[47] After receiving the Lord's forgiveness, one must still pursue healing in faith. Simpson saw the faith necessary for healing in Jesus' day as no different from what is necessary now. As retold in *Birth of a Vision*, "The seeker must come to a definite point and cross it, put down a stake and take it forever. He will say, 'this is God's truth and I stand upon it.'"[48]

4. Continued Signs and Wonders

In Simpson's teaching and writing he regularly spoke of a "latter rain."[49] This pattern or theological theme alludes to the passage in Joel chapter two concerning when the Spirit would be poured out. The days of the apostles were the early portion of this rain. "If the "early rain" had come at Pentecost accompanied by supernatural manifestations of the Spirit such as tongues, miracles and prophecy, Simpson reasoned that one could rightly expect these "wonderful manifestations" to be part and parcel of the "latter rain."[50]

If Joel 2 spoke of the Pentecost blessing that flowed following Christ and the first advent, then 1 Corinthians 12 meant there would be a continued manifestation of gifts until the second advent of Christ Jesus. Simpson felt that from his own day until Christ returned, this "rain" would only intensify. He called the cessationist theory[51] (the view that the gifts of the Spirit had ceased) "one of the lies the devil sugarcoated…in the form of a theological maxim."[52] Whatever might be the reason God would withdraw His Spirit from the church? That thinking was nonsense. Simpson saw no reason for people to think Christ had left His church to flounder until He returned.

According to Simpson, signs and wonders were a necessity in the modern-day church. God worked healing to bless individual Christians and the church as a whole. He also saw healing as a great tool for evangelism. He taught that "...every generation of Christians needed 'a living Christ' to perform miracles that authenticated the gospel in the face of unbelievers."[53] Simpson further said, "We are in the age of miracles, the age of Christ, the age which lies between two Advents...the age of Power, the age which, above all other ages of time, should be intensely alive."[54]

Simpson felt that if we live for Christ, then our faith and works today need not be less than that of the apostles. Jesus told the apostles that they would do greater things. And writing today I would add that Jesus didn't say, "But in the last days, they won't need healing and the Holy Spirit—for they will have Power Point and amazing electronic gadgets." No, Simpson knew that the Holy Spirit would be needed for sustenance, healing, and evangelism until the end of time.

It may not have been his original intention, but a new man had emerged as a burning example and catalyst for a modern-day healing ministry in the pattern of Jesus' healing ministry. The pilgrimage and prayer life of this one man inspired untold thousands of people to seek Christ anew. The discipleship he fostered was the headwaters for millions of future conversions, countless Bible studies, churches planted in scores of countries, missionaries launched, and divine healings. At the time, Simpson had no idea that his passion for Christ and humble attitude of steadfast obedience would ignite a movement whose effects are still being felt today.

CHAPTER 5 ENDNOTES

1.   A.B. Simpson, *The Gospel of Healing* (Harrisburg, PA: Christian Publications, Inc., 1915; reprint, Camp Hill, PA: Christian Publications, Inc., 1984), 107 (page references are to the 1984 edition).

2.   Ibid.

3.   Ibid., 108.

4. Robert J. Niklaus, John S. Sawin and Samuel J. Stoesz, *All for Jesus* (Camp Hill, PA: Christian Publications, Inc., 1986), 39.
5. Simpson, 108
6. Ibid.
7. Ibid.
8. Ibid.
9. A.E. Thompson, *A.B. Simpson: His Life and Work* (Harrisburg, PA: Christian Publications, Inc., 1960), 72.
10. Ibid.
11. Ibid.
12. Niklaus, Sawin and Stoesz, 40.
13. Ibid.
14. Thompson, 75.
15. Ibid.
16. Ibid., 75–76.
17. Ibid., 76.
18. Ibid.
19. Ibid., 77.
20. Ibid.
21. Ibid.
22. Ibid., 78.
23. Ibid.
24. Ibid.
25. Simpson did not oppose medicinal assistance. He himself had used medicine. He never counseled anyone to haphazardly discard their medication. The intensity of his experience with Margaret confirmed to Simpson that only at Christ's leading should someone cease using medicine.
26. Niklaus, Sawin and Stoesz, 42.
27. Thompson, 80.
28. Niklaus, Sawin and Stoesz, 42; quoted in A.W. Tozer, *Wingspread* (Harrisburg, PA: Christian Publications, Inc., 1943), 81.
29. Ibid.
30. David F. Hartzfeld and Charles Nienkirchen, eds., *The Birth of a Vision* (Alberta, Canada: Buena Book Services, 1986), 14.
31. Niklaus, Sawin and Stoesz, 55.
32. Ibid., 42.
33. Ibid.
34. Ibid., 43.

35. Ibid., citing A.B. Simpson, "What God Is Doing in Our Age," *The Word, the Work and the World* (July/August, 1885), 209.

36. Thompson, 140.

37. Ibid., 139.

38. Hartzfeld and Nienkirchen, eds., 12.

39. Thompson, 63.

40. Ibid., 64.

41. Ibid., 79.

42. Hartzfeld and Nienkirchen, eds., 14; citing A.B. Simpson, *The Word, the Work and the World* (July/August, 1885), 205.

43. Ibid., 13; citing A.B. Simpson, *The Word, the Work and the World* (July/August, 1887), 75.

44. Ibid.; citing A.B. Simpson, *The Word, the Work and the World* (July/August, 1885), 204.

45. Ibid., 132; citing A.B. Simpson, "Editorial," *Living Truth* (December, 1906), 706; and "Spiritual Sanity," *Living Truth* (April, 1907), 191.

46. Ibid., 133; citing A.B. Simpson, *Earnests of the Coming Age* (New York: Christian Alliance Publishing Co., 1921), 118.

47. Ibid.

48. Ibid.; idem, *The Gospel of Healing*, 55, 57, (1915 edition, pages do not coincide with the 1986 edition).

49. Incidentally, his writings and preaching on the subject of the Holy Spirit and divine healing became the initial inspiration that started the Pentecostal movement. In fact, the founders of The Assembly of God denomination were a group of people directly instructed and inspired by A.B. Simpson. They were the ones who wanted even more emphasis on the gifts of the Spirit and all that it implied. And in 1906 they diverged from The Christian and Missionary Alliance to do so.

50. Hartzfeld and Nienkirchen, eds., 132; citing A.B. Simpson, "Editorial," *Living Truth* (December, 1906), 706; and "Spiritual Sanity," *Living Truth* (April, 1907), 191.

51. Cessationist theory is the belief that signs and wonders faded away after the apostles.

52. Hartzfeld and Nienkirchen, eds., 133; citing A.B. Simpson, *Earnests of the Coming Age* (New York: Christian Alliance Publishing Co., 1921), 118.

53. Ibid.

54. Ibid.; idem, *The Gospel of Healing*, 55, 57 (1915 edition pages do not coincide with the 1986 edition).

six

HEALING TODAY

D IVINE HEALING IS not a relic of the past. Against the insistence of many within Christendom, people around the world *are* being miraculously healed in our day. One author speaks about the struggle to report on *which* healings he is going to include in his next book as he sorts through thousands of astonishing healing testimonies. He became exasperated, in a delightful way, as the marvelous healing stories he was gathering began to fill several box crates.

However within Christendom the views about divine healing are still as varied as snowflakes. While some are talking of wonderful experiences they have seen that left them in awe at the hand of God at work, others speak with great reticence about failures, hurt feelings, disappointment among the ill, and those who have tried to minister healing to them.

Here is a sample of some dubious comments I have heard in recent years among American ministers: "We talk about divine healing, we pray about divine healing, but I wonder if we believe it anymore." A missionary at home on furlough commented, "There's a big gap between our theory and our practice." A young pastor in the C&MA said with concern, "I don't think the church today has the childlike faith that A.B. Simpson had." A pastor on the West Coast (USA) lamented, "God's people are running to doctors before the Lord. We are so dependent on medicine. We are forgetting to go to the Lord. He is the last resort anymore." One missionary seemed alarmed, "From what I see, there is very little healing taught or practiced in the U.S. and Canada. We dilute and deny the Scriptures when we don't minister healing. It's getting dangerous."

While these subjective comments portray personal experience and reality, there are tens of thousands of dynamic churches across the world that implement and enjoy healing ministry. And across the world there are innumerable churches with healing ministries and literally untold thousands more churches are being planted weekly. So the personal comments above represent a subjective perspective from people who are not seeing divine healing demonstrated in their own church life and personal ministries.

There is a wide spectrum of experiences and emotions among us regarding healing ministry that ranges from zealous obedience and bold faith, to quivering faith and feelings of failure, resignation, and dismissal. But wherever we find ourselves in this range, all of us acknowledge in varying degrees that God is real and active today. This truth should either confirm our present practices or spur us to walk away from past feelings of failure and inspire us to change our ways to be more like Christ in caring for the hurting. It is never wise to walk away from what we have been invited to do in God's realm.

One retired C&MA missionary sorrowfully testified to something he experienced decades earlier while serving in the Philippines:

> It was the 1960s. A man brought one of his relatives to the mission station to receive help for an illness. The sick man was anointed for healing and prayed over. The sick man was divinely healed in the presence of witnesses. The man who brought him was overjoyed at the power of God. So the next day the same man brought a friend who was blind. The relative asked the missionary to also anoint his blind friend for the healing of his sight. Unfortunately this same missionary became intimidated and declined to pray for him. The missionary told the man that he better go get help elsewhere. Perhaps some clinic nearby would help him.
>
> The missionary admitted to me that he had retreated from duty. He said that decades later his lack of faith and decision to not anoint and pray for the blind man back then was still bothering him.

As described above, most every Christian has a threshold to their faith. This is not a comfort zone that we should resign into, but an awareness that ought to arouse us to pray, "Lord, increase my faith." The scriptures still say, "With God all things are possible." And it says that to all of us. It even says that to those who claim that they do not have the gift of healing. The following are inspiring stories of people today who have personally experienced a dynamic healing touch from Christ's hand in the present day. These are included because it must be demonstrated that the view that healing ministry died with the apostles around A.D. 100 is wrong. It is defeatist and discouraging theology. So if anyone is not already convinced of this awesome truth, the following stories should help build faith. They illustrate that Christ Jesus heals our lives today. And even though He has ascended from the earth, His Spirit has not left us and He has not changed.

Each of the people below were interviewed personally by me, my assistants, or my colleagues.

Betty Gillis
Valdosta, Florida

In September of 1989 I noticed that I was gaining weight—about five pounds per week. Also I was not feeling well. After going to the doctor three times in one week, the problem could not be located. I had gained fifteen pounds by this time. My doctor referred me to a gynecologist who, upon examination, discovered I had a fast-growing tumor. I went to church and was anointed for healing by our Pastor, Charles Hartney, and the elders. That week the doctor put me in the hospital. I did not know until the anesthesiologist came to my room that I was to have surgery in the morning. I refused surgery, informing him that I had been prayed for and anointed. The next morning I was transferred to Lakeland Medical Center and put through a series of tests. The radiologist found no tumor! I feel God answered our prayers as I traveled from one hospital to the next. Years later I still have no signs of a tumor. I have gone through deep valleys with the Lord, but He has always held my hand and walked through them with me.

GARY GOODWILL
YAKIMA, WASHINGTON

First of all I want to say that this experience of mine—being brought back from the edge of death—came about only by the grace of God. I did not deserve it. In fact had I received what I probably deserved I would be beyond worm food today. But then again, God is good.

In February of 1993 I had been involved in a shooting incident where a fellow police officer had been shot and wounded by his own gun that had been nabbed by a drunk gone wild. Little did I know that experience had raised my blood pressure beyond normal. We had gone through all the steps at that time of debriefing and talking with the wounded officer and those of us who had been involved. The next step was to do a shoot/don't shoot scenario where we watched and reacted to felony stops and pretended to be the officer involved with the arrest and take down. Each scenario was set up to force the officer to choose to either shoot or not.

The date of the shooting incident was May 3rd or 4th. I had just stopped a car with what looked to be one person inside. I had talked him out of the vehicle and had him down on the ground while I was barricaded behind my patrol vehicle. I then stepped from around the vehicle and committed myself to the open. Next I noted the trunk lid of the felony vehicle moving. Just as I crouched and aimed at the trunk, a man with a pump shotgun jumped out and fired two rounds at me. I instantly engaged and fired back.

During this exchange I felt a sudden pain behind my left ear. It was a rapid onslaught migraine type of headache that seemed to eradicate my ability to think. I became nauseous, disoriented, and got tunnel vision. I felt that something terrible was happening to me. It was similar to a large electric motor shutting down and as it did, my ability to see became very restricted. I remember telling the instructor, after he asked if something was wrong, that I didn't realize the scenario was actually supposed to shoot back. It was that bad for me. I also remember repeatedly asking Jesus to "save me alive."

I really don't remember much as to what went on from then until I was vaguely aware of my wife being in my presence and that I was at the hospital. The doctor told us that they thought I had had a brain hemorrhage as the CAT-scan indicated a large dark area in the lower left side of my head. He indicated they would conduct a procedure the next morning called an arterio-gram...that was, if I lived through the night.

The radiologist explained that he had done these tests for the past thirty years and had never been unsuccessful in finding what he was looking for. They would inject a dye into the four main arteries going to the brain and take pictures to find the bleed. He further indicated and assured that they would find the bleed, bore a couple of holes in my head, tie off the bleed, cauterize it, or plug the leak. He kept repeating that he *would* find it.

The next morning, I discovered that I had lived through the night. Imagine that! My wife came to me and told me that our friends and the prayer partners at the church had been praying for me and God had told them that I had been healed. I told her I would accept that and receive it.

When the radiologist and neurologist came to get me and do the procedure, we told them that God had healed me and that they would not find anything. My wife told me later that she meant "my head was empty" and they wouldn't find *anything*. By the way, how did I survive this silly mockery?!

The procedure was to take approximately one and a half to two hours. However, after four hours the doctors returned and gave us the news that they had looked and looked, but were unable to locate a bleed; bleeding that had been clearly indicated by the CAT-scan the night before. To make sure of their diagnosis the neurologist did a spinal tap to extract fluid, which came out a darker red than a stop sign. It is supposed to be clear. Both doctors said they believed in prayer. They knew I had had a large bleed, but its absence was a puzzle to them.

During this entire period and for about seven days after I had an extreme headache that even morphine could not touch. I was in the hospital for ten days. Meanwhile I began to doubt that I had been healed. The headache was that bad. I asked my wife to call a couple I knew who had a healing ministry. I wanted them to come and pray for me. She called and they came over to the hospital that day to pray and lay hands on me. He took hold of my feet and she laid her hands on my head and said, "Dear Lord God..." She then suddenly removed her hand from my head and said that God had told her not to pray further; that He had healed me. I asked, "Why then do I have this headache?" He answered that God told him that His grace was sufficient for me. After that I stopped taking morphine and went to Extra Strength Tylenol.

Later I asked God why he had healed me; was it for some ministry he had for me? His answer? "I healed you because I love you."

That was in the spring of 1993. God still loves me.

GORDON AND JANE KELLY
ELLENSBURG, WASHINGTON

When our daughter Erica was twenty-one months old, we experienced an event which confirmed in our minds the healing power of Christ. Erica had an upper respiratory infection and was running a very high fever of 106 degrees. Her mother, Jane, was watching her closely. Without warning, Erica started to convulse. She stopped breathing, her eyes rolled back, and she turned blue. Jane scooped her up as we headed off to the hospital. As we got to the car, Jane lifted up Erica and pleaded, "Jesus, help her!" Erica immediately began to breathe. We went on to the hospital where Erica spent the night being observed. The next morning, with her fever and infection gone, she went up and down the halls visiting other patients and bringing joy to them as only a toddler can.

When Erica was three years old, we began to notice that when she really tried to focus on something, she either closed one eye or one of them would "cross." Our concern motivated us to seek medical attention. In conjunction with this effort, we sought the prayers of other believers and our elders at the church. The ophthalmologist's prognosis was not encouraging. Her eyes would not straighten with glasses. He prescribed a muscle relaxant, which appeared to work. It was a dangerous medication as it would synergize with another anesthetic, one which should be administered in an emergency. Erica had to wear a medical ID bracelet noting this fact.

After a couple of years, she began to build a tolerance to this medication. The ophthalmologist suggested taking her off the medication for two weeks in order to refract her eyes. He wasn't sure what to do because glasses still wouldn't keep her eyes straight. Again we asked believers to pray for God's intervention. She was in kindergarten at the time. Those two weeks were difficult because her eyes would cross so badly when she tried to focus. After this two-week period, the doctor examined her and declared that her eyes would remain straight with only the help of glasses. He repeated the examination three times because he could not believe the glasses were keeping them straight. Jane stated that Erica had been prayed for. The doctor retorted, "I don't know about that, but her eyes are straight." They have been since 1977!

MILLIE BENSON
MARIETTA, GEORGIA

Tabitha was a young girl in the Red Bobo tribe in Burkina Faso, West Africa. She was a Christian and was attending a Bible Camp in a small village. One evening upon returning from a meeting, she was bitten by a viper, one of the deadliest snakes of West Africa. We were called and immediately went to the hut where she was lying on a mat. There was no anti-snake venom due to the lack of refrigeration. No doctors lived in the village or in the whole area. Medical facilities were also unavailable. But God was there.

Praying for wisdom, we started suction in an attempt to remove the injected poison. Amidst the prayers by campers and the pastor, she started to bleed from her mouth and open sores on her body. This meant the venom had traveled throughout her body; death was coming closer. We spent the night alternating between praying and resting. God heard and answered. After a while the bleeding stopped, and although Tabitha felt weak for a day or two, she was soon up. She returned to her normal routine. All of us were praising God for His healing touch on her body.

We are back in Georgia at the time of this writing, but my memory of this recovery from a deadly snakebite will always be with me. God promises that we have power over these attacks.

ANONYMOUS
(WITHHELD FOR SECURITY REASONS AMID CONSTANT DEATH THREATS TO CHRISTIANS IN THIS ASIAN COUNTRY)

I live in a land that forbids the preaching of the gospel. It probably isn't wise for me to share my name or country with you but there *is* something that I must share with you. I experienced God's amazing miracle in my life when God filled my tooth around the year 2000.

I grew up in a broken family. My parents were separated when I was seven years old. It was just the two of us; my mom and me living in our home. Mom was sick often, and that made our life very difficult in many ways, financially as well as emotionally.

Hearing about Jesus Christ several times from one of my mom's friends, we made a very essential decision to accept Christ as our Savior. At first, we did not know anything about Jesus, but I personally believed and completely trusted Jesus.

I started to serve God at the very beginning of my faith in Him by getting up early on Sundays. I went to knock on the doors of some other children in my local area to invite them to come to church with me. I did this since the church I went to had Sunday school for children. I live like this because I know that God loves me. I know that God loves children, too.

As time passed, I went to university and graduated, but did not find a job. My financial situation was making life difficult. I spent much of my time praying with God. Then in the year 2000 I found that one of my teeth had two cavity holes. This was disturbing because, not only did it hurt, but I did not have money to pay the dentist for repairing the two holes in my tooth. One morning I was praying with God as I usually do. I said, "God please fill my tooth because I don't have money at all." I had heard from my pastor that God had miraculously filled the teeth of some people in a country far away called Colombia. So I asked God to please fill my tooth, too, because I didn't have money at all. I cried out loud. Then I heard a voice in my mind, "Go and look at the mirror." But I did not do that. I went on in my prayer around fifteen more minutes. Then I stood up and walked to the mirror to look at my teeth. The damaged tooth was filled in and shining very brightly! I was so surprised that at first I couldn't believe it. It may seem silly now, but I went back to prayer again to ask God if He did fill my tooth. Then I was convinced.

Since my home did not have a telephone, I ran to my neighbor and asked them to use their telephone. I wanted to call my pastor and tell him that God filled my tooth. He was happy and asked me to come to his house and show him my new tooth. Just to be sure, his wife took me to the Christian dentist that they know. He took time and examined it carefully. He told us that it was very skillfully and beautifully filled in. We told him how it happened but he seemed not to believe what we shared with him—that it was God who filled it. But we know for sure that God did it for me.

The filling is still bright and looks like new after all these years. It is still the brightest tooth I have! It really is a miracle of God. Ever since this happened, my whole life has changed.

This miracle ended up affecting much more than my tooth. I have never been the same. God is so amazing. He has done a lot of miraculous things in my life. I am grateful to God with all my heart. I love Him so much.

STEPHEN RENICKS
(SERVED THIRTY-FIVE YEARS IN BRAZIL; HE WROTE THIS FROM HIS HOME IN NORTHPORT, ALABAMA)

When I was sixteen, I was hospitalized with a duodenal ulcer. With medical treatment it was cured. However, I continued to suffer from frequent stomach discomfort especially when I was under a lot of stress. After graduating from Nyack College in Nyack, New York, I attended Jaffray School of Missions; what became Alliance Theological Seminary. While there, my wife and I began the process of becoming missionaries with The Christian and Missionary Alliance. One of the requirements was a medical examination. The physician reported that if I had a recurrence of the ulcer, an overseas assignment would not be recommended. It was 1972. Shortly after, I began to have all the symptoms of another ulcer. For three weeks the symptoms persisted and I was unable to eat without pain. I did not go to a doctor because I was afraid of the result. One evening we attended a concert at Nyack College where the vocalist sang, "He Touched Me." While he was singing, I cried out to the Lord saying, "Lord, if there was ever a time that I needed Your touch, it is now." In that moment He touched me and healed me. I went home, ate a normal meal without stomach pain, and have never had another problem.

SYLVIA THOMPSON
WILLINGBORO, DELAWARE

During a service at Summit Grove Camp in New Freedom, Pennsylvania, the Holy Spirit convicted me of my problem with anxiety. I don't think the subject was even mentioned in the message, but I was strongly convicted. I went to the altar to ask God's forgiveness and for victory over this sin of anxiety. Two people whom I did not know came to pray with me. When I explained my need, I did not mention I had colitis simply because I did not think of it. All the time the Holy Spirit was convicting me of this sin of anxiety; it did not enter my mind that my anxiety and the colitis were connected.

After I prayed and the two strangers prayed for me, we stood up. Something very amazing happened—I don't know how to explain it—but I felt nothing physically, I just *knew* I had been healed of colitis. I don't know if either of the two people noticed any change of expression on my face or not, but I stood in only a matter of seconds knowing I had been changed. They stood quietly looking at me and then I softly whispered, "I have been healed of colitis." It was so wonderfully amazing to me; I had been forgiven and healed. Praise His Holy name!

As the days and weeks passed I proved I was healed by eating corn on the cob and coleslaw, two of the delicious foods served there at the Summit Grove dining room that I had not been able to eat since the appearance of my colitis.

It may be of some interest to know that I have several other health problems. One in particular I have had most of my life and have been anointed and prayed for many times, but have not been healed from. However, this does not affect in any way the truth that I have been completely healed of colitis.

RITA HANSON
ROCHESTER, MINNESOTA

It was 1970 and God decided to heal the deteriorated discs in my spine. It started back in 1967 when I had symptoms of pain and weakness in my lower back. My health became so poor that I continuously felt as if I had just worked a twenty-four-hour shift. Everything prescribed by my orthopedic surgeon—traction, a brace, exercise, bed rest—did not change a thing. One day as I was memorizing in my Bible, Psalm 6:2 caught my attention: "Be merciful to me, LORD, for I am faint; O LORD, heal me, for my bones are in agony." Through that verse, God revealed that He intended to heal me. I had gotten to where I couldn't walk without assistance, and I had to lie on a couch at church rather than sit in a pew.

That summer, as was our family custom, we attended Big Sandy Camp. After one of my children had helped me to chapel for prayer meeting one particular morning, the camp evangelist stopped by my couch. He said to me, "Do you know what I feel like saying to you?... 'Silver and gold have I none; but such as I have give I thee: In the name of Jesus Christ of Nazareth rise up and walk'" (Acts 3:6, KJV). I looked up at him and said, "That sounds like a good idea." He assured me he was serious, so I just got up and was able to walk alone. The back pain was immediately over with. Many decades later I am still praising God for His healing power, but most of all for salvation.

KEN WALKUP
NEW RAYMER, COLORADO

The morning of February 12, 1947, dawned clear and cold giving promise of another beautiful day such as we had been having in northeastern Colorado. About the only things to remind us it was winter were the close-to-zero temperatures of the nights and the hard frozen ground that went with them. It was one of those mornings without a flaw and everything well fitted to the desires of those raised in the wide-open spaces of wheat and cow country on the prairies east of the Rockies. Norma and I were young marrieds with four strong, healthy children from twenty-one months to seven years old. We were farming near New Raymer, north of Fort Morgan. We had been having bumper crops and getting prices beyond our fondest expectations for them. Prospects for another big crop looked good. Our cattle we enjoyed raising so much were increasing and prices for beef were high. We were in a church that was thriving in every way, and it just seemed good to be alive. Perhaps it was a feeling much the same as Job had as he enjoyed the material blessings God had so abundantly bestowed on him; or Jesus' disciples had as they walked with Him here on earth and shared His victories and triumphs, little knowing how soon their bright world would be plunged into darkness and near tragedy, even as our sunshine was about to swallowed up in a few short hours by grief and sorrow.

I say *near* tragedy because it did not end that way since God is still on His throne and He is never defeated.

We had not forgotten Him or left Him out of our lives for which we soon were to be forever thankful. We were simply enjoying the good things that God has so abundantly showered upon us, at the same time putting Him first in our lives as He tells us to do in His Word. We now know after many more years of experience that it is by far the best way to live here, and the only way to prepare for eternity.

Our oldest child, Sandra, was in school and our three boys were under school age. At about 2 p.m., I backed the car up by the house as I got ready to go into town. I went in the house to see if Norma needed anything from town. I kissed her goodbye and it seemed our lives were so pleasant and wonderful that nothing could mar our happiness.

I got in the car and my father who was with us, got in on the passenger side. I started up and held my door open to watch the two older boys who were playing behind me. I felt the front wheel go over something and supposed it was a rock or block of wood. As I turned the corner, I looked in my mirror and saw Ernie, our 21-month-old son, in a red snowsuit lying where he had just been run over by our Plymouth sedan. I stopped, jumped out, and went back to find that his head had been crushed as both right wheels had run over it on ground that had been graveled with coarse gravel and rock while it was wet and soft then frozen solid like concrete during the near-zero nights.

As I picked him up in my arms, my heart felt like lead and my knees were weak, and I immediately remembered that he had come out of the house as I went in. He evidently had made his way to the front of the car and neither of us had seen him as we got in. Our wonderful bright world had crumbled in less than sixty seconds, and we found ourselves surrounded by gloom and deep sorrow.

But standing somewhere in the shadows you will find Jesus. As I carried little Ernie into the house, Norma came to meet me and instantly we both knew that our God, in whom we had learned to trust, was the only hope we had. She took him in her arms, and I arranged for my dad to go tell our faithful friends in our church that we needed prayer. There was no telephone. As dad went, I took my Bible and turned to scriptures the Holy Spirit brought to my remembrance. As we prayed, we knew that God would hear and answer us.

When some of the people in the church heard what had happened, they were not content to just pray, but came to offer any help they could. Our pastor and his wife had left about half an hour earlier to go to the Rocky Mountain District Convention in Denver, one hundred twenty-five miles away. One of the ladies in the church was the wife of the local depot agent. He at one time had served the Lord, and he knew about the miracle working power of God. When they heard of our need, they sent for their oldest girl to come home from high school and take care of the younger children while they came out to our place. He asked if I would like for him to send a telegram to the District Convention, asking for prayer. I told him I would so he wired immediately.

Our pastor arrived at the afternoon meeting just after they had special prayer for Ernie and returned with us to our home. When we got there, the miracle had already taken place and as we compared times we found that God had moved as prayer was being made in Denver. We forever praise God for this!

Here is how we witnessed the miracle take place. When Norma took him, his head was crushed flat to a mass of pulp. His nose and mouth were beneath his right ear and his right eye was out of its socket and crushed into his face. The rest of his body had escaped the wheels. *As we watched,* his head took shape again and the skull became firm. Norma took his eyeball into her hand and gently pressed it back in the socket. He was unconscious nearly three hours, but his body moved nearly that entire time. At the time they prayed in Denver, he began to cough up blood that had gotten into his lungs and stomach. After he had spit up about three-fourths of a cup of blood, he suddenly threw himself back in Norma's arms and relaxed. We thought he was gone, but instead he regained consciousness and began to breathe normally. From then on, he never appeared to be in any pain. His head was all skinned up so as it healed he itched a lot and he would rub it with his hands and dig at it, but it didn't seem to hurt in any way. Within two weeks after the accident, Ernie was up and going strong and has been ever since.

Ernie has always been strong and healthy and very athletic from then until now. By the way, Ernie turned sixty in 2005. God gets all the credit and glory, for no other person had anything to do with Ernie's healing. God's miraculous healing is just one reason why today, all these years later, God should be first in our lives. Ken and Norma attend church at Terrace Heights Assembly of God in Yakima, Washington.

LORI CALLENDAR
ONTARIO, CALIFORNIA

No one will ever be able to tell me that the day of miracles is past. The Lord has shown me several times that this is not so, but never as strong as these two following events:

On June 26, 1972, my son Jason was born in the early morning hours. After I nursed him at 6:00 a.m. he was taken out for some normal newborn procedures. At 6:00 p.m. that evening (I hadn't seen him all day), a nurse came to me and said Jason wasn't feeling well and they would feed him in the nursery. By 8:30 p.m. his pediatrician came to me looking very worried. He informed me that they wanted to run some tests and that I needed to sign consent papers. He tried to reassure me, but the look on his face was not convincing. At 10:30 p.m. the doctor returned looking even more concerned and asked me to have my husband come to the hospital. I asked why and was told they were having trouble doing a spinal tap on Jason and wanted to transfer him to another hospital that specialized in neonatal care. Later we learned they had tried more than twenty times, unsuccessfully, to get a spinal tap. They didn't want to believe it, but they were sure it was spinal meningitis. I called my husband, who came immediately. Up to this time, Jason's father had not even been able to hold him.

When we were signing papers authorizing the transfer, the nurses brought Jason to us, concerned he would not survive the ambulance ride. They were giving us a chance to hold our baby one last time. He had terrible jaundice and looked pitifully weak.

The ambulance left. My husband went home. I felt so alone and scared. Calling my prayer partner helped me to see the situation clearly as she advised me on what I had to do. God had given this child to me and I was to give him back. I prayed to God that His will be done and promised to raise Jason to know the Lord if he were given back to me. But if the Lord wanted Jason He could have him. This seems so trite, but it was the most difficult prayer I have ever prayed.

By the time Jason had arrived at the other hospital, his color had improved. When they did the spinal tap, his spinal column was completely clear. He was released three day later. A week after examining him completely all the pediatrician could do was shake his head. He told us that because of the problems he had seen the week before, he had expected Jason to be severely handicapped. Now, seeing the amazing results, there was no other explanation than a miracle!

When God heals, He doesn't go lightly—He *heals!* Not only did He heal Jason from being handicapped, He gave him extraordinary athletic abilities. He was able to dribble a basketball at two. Jason was so talented in basketball that at the age of five he had high school coaches coming to watch him play. In high school, he was all-league in volleyball, basketball, football, and baseball. In his senior year he was league Most Valuable Player (MVP) in football and team MVP in football and basketball. He was recruited by more than thirty schools for athletic scholarships.

I do not list these accomplishments to brag about my son, but to boast for my Lord. When He does something He does a great job. As we promised, we taught Jason that his abilities aren't his own, they come from the Lord. He has taken many opportunities to share his testimony with friends and teammates.

The second incident involved my daughter Amy. When Amy was eighteen months old and Jason was five, we lived in a home with a swimming pool. It was a hot summer day and the kids and I were out enjoying the pool. Jason had two friends over and they were swimming in the deep end. Amy and I had been in the shallow end and decided to get out. I took off Amy's life vest and started to run water into the pool to replenish the water splashed out by the boys. I had a timer on the table and told the boys they could swim for five more minutes. The phone rang and I ran into the house to answer it.

As I was speaking to the mother of one of the boys, I heard a horrible scream. It was Jason, and I instantly knew what had happened. The timer had gone off and he was getting out to reset it when he saw Amy lying at the bottom of the pool! He hastily grabbed her and got her to the steps by the time I reached the pool. I had never taken a CPR course, but had seen it done several times. I did know how to pray and cried out, "Jesus, help me," and started to breathe for her. She was blue and very spongy. As I breathed, Satan whispered in my mind, "She's dead. You're doing it wrong." But I kept praying. All of a sudden she started to cry and spit up water. In the meantime, Jason had run next door where the neighbor called 9-1-1.

Amy was drifting in and out of consciousness when the paramedics arrived. They took her in the squad car, not wanting to wait for an ambulance. She was stabilized at the hospital and within sixty minutes you would have never known what had happened. She wanted to get up and play. We didn't know how long she went without breathing and the doctors couldn't give me much hope as to how this would affect her in the future.

In high school, Amy took honors classes in math, English, and history and earned a grade point average of 3.7. Amy is also a talented volleyball player whose team came in fifth in the nation at the Junior Olympics.

The Lord, in both of these incidents, did not require fancy prayer—just sincerity. I am so glad and eternally grateful I serve a living God who still performs miracles!

Don Mathis
Lilburn, Georgia

At first I had headaches, which were just like any other. But they didn't stay that way long. After having a headache around the clock for two months, I went to the doctor. After much testing and examination, our doctor told me my problem was caused by hypertension or high blood pressure. I went through four different medications, with the headache persisting all the while, and still had what the doctor called "high normal pressure." Finally I reached the point of absolute agony. Further tests revealed that the walls to one of the primary arteries in my brain had weakened as a result of the high blood pressure and had expanded to the point of applying pressure to the nerves and tissue around it. Then there was concern about the possibility of a rupture, which my doctor said would most likely result in death. Medications were started, as the condition was inoperable.

A few weeks later my alarm clock went off, preparing me for another day in the office, but I couldn't get up. The lower part of my back felt like someone had pushed an ice pick right through my spine. After giving me an examination, my doctor explained how the muscles in the lower part of my back had literally pushed everything out of place as a result of the stress and tension.

Soon after this I came down with pneumonia, strep throat, and EBV II (a virus that basically disables your immune system along with various other ill effects). I was going downhill rapidly and nothing the field of medicine had to offer was having any effect. With so many things going wrong, I was missing more days than I was working and had no choice but to take a medical leave of absence starting April 1.

I had hoped that staying at home in bed would help but it didn't. After two months in bed, I was much worse. Late in the evening on Tuesday, May 31, I had been lying on our sofa in terrible discomfort. With much weakness and difficulty, I climbed the stairs to go to bed in hopes of finding some relief. But when I lay down I felt overwhelmed by it all and didn't know how much more I could take. But I soon found out.

Around 3:00 a.m. I began to have hard, sharp pains around my heart and had difficultly breathing. Within minutes I felt as if I were suffocating, and I knew, I just simply knew, I was not going to live to see the sun the next morning. My life was slipping away. I picked up my Bible, laid it on my chest, and placed my hands across it. With tears in my eyes I cried out to our heavenly Father and prayed in the name of our Savior Jesus Christ that He cleanse and heal me. I prayed, "Oh Lord, please cleanse me and heal me," over and over and over again. Although I was not well, I felt at peace and feel asleep. Around 7:30 a.m. Wednesday I woke up, still holding my Bible over my heart. When I opened my eyes, I felt a wonderful, warm, tingling sensation from the top of my head to the tip of my toes. When I sat up I felt energy flowing into my body. When I stood up, my eyes filled with tears, but they were not tears of pain, they were tears of joy. I knew that the Holy Spirit had touched me and had cleansed me and healed me. The headache was gone; the hurting in my back was gone; the virus and illness were gone; and my heart felt strong. I was not hurting at all!

As I was getting dressed, my wife came to me as she had every morning since I became ill and asked how I was doing. When I looked into her eyes, my eyes again filled with tears that flowed like a river. I couldn't talk yet. I wanted to tell her how our precious heavenly Father had touched me with His wonderful healing power, but I couldn't speak through all the tears and emotion. Without knowing how our Savior had touched me, my tears frightened her. She held me close and said, "Don't worry, honey, no matter what else happens, God will see us through; sometimes it helps to let go and cry."

It took me a few minutes to get myself together enough to tell her how He had touched me and healed me. I had seen how her worrying about me had taken its toll, but I didn't know what to do about it. But when I told her, "Sweetheart, you don't have to worry anymore because He has healed me," I could see the weight of the world leave her shoulders as we held each other and cried tears of joy.

Not only has He healed me, He has taken me to a spiritual level that is far higher than I have ever been before. He has filled my life with a beautiful, sweet peace and joy that goes far beyond anything I could have imagined or know how to put into words. I can feel the Holy Spirit working in me every day and can feel Him pulling me closer to His side. I feel a love that I have never felt before and have truly learned how He will make me first in His life as I make Him first in mine. Now I understand what it is like to have a love relationship with Him, one that is real and personal. It is hard to describe this beautiful closeness. All that matters anymore is my love for Him, my wife, and my children.

It was fun to see the look on the doctor's face when he examined me and said, "All I can say is that you are healed. You are well! When do you want to go back to work?"

BILL HUNT
ELLENSBURG, WASHINGTON

I became a Christian in May 1959 while serving in the United States Air Force. We attended a small Nazarene Church in Big Springs, Texas. We had just had our first child in January. Tim was our delight and we were thrilled to be parents. I was discharged from the Air Force on November 3 of that year, and Tim contracted polio on November 23.

He was in the hospital for three weeks. When he was discharged he was paralyzed from the waist down. This was devastating to us, and all we could do was hold on to the Lord.

On January 23, 1960, our first daughter, Mona, was born. The doctor told my wife and me that something was wrong, but he could not make a diagnosis. In the summer of 1960 we heard of a therapist in Boise, Idaho, who worked with polio victims so we decided to move to Boise so that Tim could get the best therapy possible. While we were preparing to move, Mona died in her sleep. We were devastated. The coroner accused us of smothering her with a pillow. Our doctor was out of town and did not return for a week. When he returned, he was able to clear our names with the coroner because an autopsy showed a spinal block had been the cause of her medical problems since birth and her death.

Things went well in Idaho and on March 21, 1961, our second son, Bill Jr., was born. On June 8, 1962, our third son, Daniel, was born. Bill Jr. developed ear problems at three months and had earaches most of the time. After his first birthday, we had to take him to the doctor every day to have his eardrums lanced. At about 1:30 one morning, I was walking the floor holding him. He had a fever and was crying. I knelt down and said, "Lord, I just can't take it anymore." Billy instantly stopped crying. I was fearful that he had died. I checked him. He was sleeping peacefully and his fever was gone. The Lord had completely healed him and he never had another ear problem. Praise the Lord!

When Daniel was about two years old he was in the back yard playing and put a glass under a leak in our furnace fuel barrel. He drank four ounces of diesel fuel. In checking on the boys, my wife discovered something was wrong and immediately rushed him to the hospital. The doctors pumped his stomach but said it was too late; he probably would not live over two hours. Once again God stepped in. Not only did he live, but he grew to six-feet-four and was given divine talent as an artist!

On December 23, 1965, our daughter Joanna was born. After a minor complication with strep throat, she was able to go home, healthy; there were no problems!

On February 2, 1966, my wife had taken Joanna to the doctor for a checkup, and she was doing great. Driving to school to pick up Tim, my wife hit a hole in the road and ran into a parked car. As a result, Jean, Bill Jr., Daniel, and Joanna were put in the hospital. Jean and Bill Jr. had brain concussions, and Daniel was bruised. Joanna had suffered a fractured skull all the way around her head. The soft spot was swollen to the size of a hen's egg. She was in very serious danger, and the doctors had to insert large needles into the soft spot five times in a twenty-four-hour period to relieve the pressure on the brain.

On the evening of February 3 my boys and I got down on our knees in the living room and asked God to heal her. A short time later I went to the hospital. The neurosurgeon that had been called to evaluate Joanna said that she had to be operated on immediately. They took Joanna down the hall to the surgical room, but did not return for some time. We became very concerned. Finally the pediatrician, who was a Christian, came back and told us that when they put the needle in to drain the pressure, the soft spot went down on its own and there was no pressure! Joanna had been healed. We took her to the neurosurgeon four months later. After examining her, he said, "Don't ever bring her back. We can't even find scars." Today Joanna is the mother of four children and is happily serving the Lord.

(THE LATE) MRS. BESS WILLIAMS ALVIN, TEXAS

I was born in 1924 and raised in the Alliance Church in East St. Louis, Illinois. When I was two I became very ill. My mom wrapped me in a blanket, got on the trolley car, and took me to the parsonage. The pastor, knowing immediately that it was diphtheria, prayed with my mom. I was healed instantly.

When I was four and my brother George was two, mother was expecting another baby. Complications mounted to such a degree that the doctor said an abortion was absolutely necessary or the baby would be physically or mentally disabled. "God has given me this baby, and He will take care of it and me," mother proclaimed. The doctor did not argue with such a woman of great faith. All went smoothly and we had another brother, Bob.

Some time later Bob developed rheumatic fever. At that time the advances of modern medicine were not available. A man came to town and held healing meetings in a tent. I do not recall names or denominations. Mom decided to take Bob to the tent. Since Dad was not a believer, she went alone, carrying the boy in her arms.

Later, as I was in the yard with my father, we heard Bob yell, "Hey, guys, look at me!" He was running home as fast as he could. All the pain and swelling in his joints was gone. When Dad saw him running he put his hands on his hips and quietly said, "Now I *know* there is a God!" I'll never forget that scene as long as I live.

(Bess's widower telephoned late in the 1990s to share that Bess had passed away. Her story is left in because it is inspiring and for the fact that she relayed it to me when she was alive.)

LISTO BELL
JAMAICA, WEST INDIES

I came to the United States in 1985 in order to create a little better way of life for my family. My dream was to have my husband join me here in the States. Unfortunately, he died suddenly on April 24, 1987.

I worked in Brookhaven, Pennsylvania. It was my practice to pray for protection before I drove off each day and thank God whenever I reached my destination. The morning before my accident was no exception.

That afternoon I had to return to work as I had forgotten some things. Driving down a busy main street in Chester, Pennsylvania, I suddenly blacked out for a few seconds. I didn't know what was happening, but I realized the car was pulling hard to the right. I became frightened and, missing the brake pedal, I stepped on the gas pedal. My car went across an embankment going fifty miles per hour and slammed into a tree.

Before I hit the tree I knew I was in danger and said, "I will now see my husband just eight days before the second anniversary of his death." After I hit the tree I felt my feet become as cold as ice. I knew

I could not live. I raised my right hand to heaven and prayed, "Lord, have mercy on my soul."

My eyes closed, my head fell backward and I knew nothing more except that breath suddenly left my body. I saw my spirit going upward. It went up...up...up and then it began to descend, re-entering my body. I became conscious and immediately opened my eyes. My face was hurting so I spat in my hand and found my partial denture was broken in two and all my front teeth had been knocked out. I unhooked my seat belt and opened the door. Experiencing pain all over my body, I just sat there. I began feeling numb and just then a tall white man about sixty years of age, came up to me and said, "Lady, I was out jogging and I saw everything. Don't move!" Then he touched me and I heard him gasp, "My God, she is bleeding all over."

God was good to me, for although I was traveling on a very busy street, no vehicle was coming nor going when the accident happened. Just as the man (a retired policeman) came to help, other cars came and people began to stop. I heard him say, "This lady is badly hurt. Call the ambulance. Don't crowd her."

Within seconds the ambulance arrived. The attendants took me out of the car and placed a neck brace on me. Then they placed me in the ambulance, and I heard fear in their voices. My blood pressure was falling.

They rushed me to the hospital trauma unit. The nurses and doctors ran to my side, cut off my clothes, and inserted a tube in my mouth to take out some of the blood. They were all doing everything in their power to keep me alive, but all through this I kept saying, "Let me give my children's phone numbers before I lose consciousness." No one understood what I was saying because of my accent and so many broken teeth. Finally an Iranian doctor understood and asked me for the numbers. I gave him two of them. He asked me all the necessary questions. I gave all the answers. He turned to another doctor and exclaimed, "Have you ever seen anyone reel off answers like this is such a condition?!" After twenty-one X-rays I was placed in intensive care. I vaguely remembered seeing three of my children and friends from the church who had arrived.

My pastor, Joe Broze, told me he came to pray for me. The doctors directed him back to the waiting room and told him to go and prepare my family because I would not live. Pastor Broze then looked intently into the doctor's eyes, "I didn't come here to bury anybody." His intensity made the doctor freeze in his tracks. Pushing past him, he opened his bottle of anointing oil and arrived at my bedside. I opened my eyes, saw him and said, "Pastor Joe, pray for me." (Pastor told me this later. I remember nothing of it.) He said he anointed me and prayed for me. He then turned back around and told the doctor the Lord had told him I *would* live otherwise. He went out and prayed with my children in the lobby without telling them what the doctor had said. I am not sure if it was the same day, but I know I felt someone touch me.

My right kneecap was broken. My feet were cut badly. There was a problem with my throat. So while the orthopedic doctor was repairing my knee and seeing to the cuts on my feet, another doctor was working on my throat. I am told I spent four hours in the operating room. I remember while I was in ICU a dentist came to extract the teeth that were broken and put some stitches in my mouth without using anesthetic! It hurt badly.

The third day I was taken out of ICU and placed in a room. That same evening an attendant came to take me to the therapy department. As he placed me on the stretcher, I saw the attendant, the nurse, and two televisions start spinning. I was crying and begging them not to push me over. Then gradually the whole world began to spin, slower and slower, until it stopped. I guess I was reliving the accident.

I later learned that the Emergency Room doctors were so hopeless at my condition that they had declared that I had less than a minute to live. My pastor arrived just then. He asked to see me. The doctors spoke in low tones telling him that he best wait outside and be ready to comfort the family because I was not going to make it. He pushed past the doctors, approached me, anointed me with oil, and essentially brought me back from the brink. Pastor told me later that it was slightly humorous that as my slide toward death halted, the doctors wondered, even demanded, to know what the "magic oil" was that he had put on my forehead when he prayed for me! Praise God the prayer came just in time and the healing began that moment.

The third day after I got out of ICU my stomach began to hurt. When my doctor, Dr. Afshari, came to see me he found a very hard lump and sent me for an ultrasound. He discovered I had pancreatitis and placed me on an IV. After several days, my condition was not improving, but I was kept alive by prayers and God's amazing grace. Pastor Joe had all the C&MA churches all over the United States praying for me. Other pastors who also knew me had their congregations praying, too. My son, who is a pastor in Jamaica, had every Christian back there praying. The other six of my nine children called daily from Jamaica and prayed without ceasing.

There were other operations, for I had broken ribs and my liver had been damaged and was decaying; the fluid from it was now penetrating all over my insides. The doctor removed the affected portion and treated the infection, then removed my gall bladder and appendix (right before it would have ruptured!). He also had to make some repairs to my intestines. After this operation I was taken to the recovery room, then to the ICU.

In recovery I listened daily to the scriptures on audio tape. Although I could hardly catch my breath, I was now able to sing my own favorite songs: "Hiding in Thee," "Because He Lives," and "Near the Cross."

The accident occurred on April 16, 1989, and I left the hospital May 10, 1989. I never went back for a single therapy session, but rehabilitated myself at home in the bathtub. What power there is in prayer! First we were told I would not live, but I did. Then I was told I would have terrible complications, I don't. I was told that I would not walk. Then that diagnosis was withdrawn and they thought I might learn some mobility but with a walker—someday. Today I walk without a limp.

I look back to when I was in the emergency room and, medically speaking, without hope of surviving, with only a minute to live. I know God did all this for me, not because I am anyone good or special: He healed me for a purpose and for His glory.

God has been so good to me. He is using me to care for needy men and women and has blessed me with a wonderful ministry through my job that allows me to read the Scripture and pray with those who want me to. My horrendous medical and dental bills have all been either forgiven or paid by friends!

There is neither pen nor paper nor words enough to describe the pain and suffering I went through. I cannot fully explain the experience I had when my life was snatched away from me and then given back. I thank my God for giving me a second chance. Psalm 31:15 says, "My times are in your hands."

(Mrs. Bell telephoned me after her story was publicized in another writing I had done in 1996–1998. She was thrilled to share that her testimony was shared nearly verbatim from the above story. The excitement was that much of the church was elated and renewed in their faith by her story. Also, there were five who gave their lives to Christ after hearing her story of miraculous healing. I reiterate, as Luke makes it a point to illustrate, healing and salvation are linked truths and blessings in Christ.)

NANCY PERSONS
REPORT GIVEN WHILE SERVING AS A MISSIONARY IN BANGKOK, THAILAND

Larry and I were living in Fairfax, Virginia, working at Arlington Memorial Church. We had a wonderful two and a half year old son, Evan, who was such a joy that we had decided to have another child. My pregnancy was going along normally, but a sonogram done in my fifth month showed a very irregular heartbeat. A follow-up done in my seventh month reassured us that the baby's heart was fine. The doctor did, however, question whether I was sure of my dates. Apparently, our baby was extremely large. In fact, the doctor estimated the baby would be full term by the end of July, although my due date wasn't until August 23rd. When our son was born on August 22nd he was ten pounds! There were difficulties during labor (meconium in the amniotic fluid), so a couple of neonatal specialists were called in just in case there was a problem with the baby's lungs. This was good because ultimately, we needed those two doctors and a nurse to lie across my abdomen in order to push the baby out. It was a very difficult delivery requiring high forceps. Finally his head crowned, but his shoulders were so wide that his collarbone broke during the birth. Those of you with any medical knowledge are surely asking, "Why wasn't a C-section done?" Indeed, it should have been done, but God's purposes are beyond our understanding, and this event was clearly in His hands.

Once Drew was born however, he didn't cry or breathe. A full resuscitation was done and we finally heard a high-pitched little squeak. His Apgar scores, we later found out, were low—5 and then 7. Drew was immediately rushed to the Neonatal Intensive Care Unit. The next day we were told that several X-rays had been done on his neck. I was very worried. Why would they need an X-ray of his neck? We were also told that his cry was very unusual, called stridor. The X-ray showed his esophagus was very, very narrow. The doctors also noted that when he cried he would turn blue, and he had extreme difficulty feeding. In the beginning it would take him two hours to drink four ounces of milk. Every moment was a struggle.

The doctors insisted that we learn infant CPR right away. We, who had three years earlier come home from the hospital with a perfect little boy and knew all we thought there was to know about caring for a new baby, would now be coming home with a baby attached to an apnea monitor, a machine that would ring a loud alarm if Drew didn't take a breath every twenty seconds. A book full of new rules on childcare was part of the package. Now, for example, I could never take a shower if I was alone in the house. If I did and the alarm went off, no one would ever hear it. Also, there had to be at least two adults in the car any time we went anywhere with Drew in case there were ever a need to resuscitate him before the driver could pull over. We were to do everything possible to prevent him from crying as he could choke on his saliva. Add to this that Drew was very colicky. To be honest, I was already a rather anxious person even under normal circumstances. All of these rules and the possibility that Drew could die in our arms made us, and me especially, very anxious!

On the second day we had to take him from the hospital in Fairfax, Virginia, to Children's Hospital in Washington, DC, to be examined by heart and lung specialists there. After performing a laryngoscopy, they discovered that his vocal cords were paralyzed. We were told that since this was such a rare occurrence, they had very little information on how he was going to fare as he grew up. There was hope that as his body and organs grew, his airway and esophagus would also grow, but there were no guarantees.

All of this was very upsetting as Drew was only four days old. About this time the elders from our church came to pray for Drew. They gathered around his bed in the NICU and lifted him up to God in prayer. At that same time I was filled with the most wonderful peace. God truly gave me His peace that passes understanding, a peace that had seemed so elusive. I would look at the green light blinking on the machine and I would think, "He's going to be okay. I don't have to worry about this, he's going to be all right."

I did notice right from the very beginning, though, that whenever I held him, Drew never looked into my eyes as other babies do. He did have a startle reflex that was normal, but if you shook a rattle by the side of his head, he wouldn't turn to look at it. I had mentioned this to my pediatrician a few times, but she just brushed it aside saying he was fine. But I knew something was wrong. He wasn't smiling or responding as Evan had.

Finally when he was two months old, we couldn't ignore it any longer; he wasn't following anything with his eyes. Larry and I took him to a specialist, and he examined Drew for two full hours. Finally, we were settled into his office to hear the news. We were told that Drew showed no signs of vision at all. The doctor felt this was very unusual because his eyes were structurally normal. This indicated that the problem had nothing to do with his eyes. The problem had to do with his brain. His brain simply was not perceiving objects in front of him. When I asked if this meant Drew was mentally retarded, I was told, "You'll just have to watch and wait and see."

We went home and I totally fell apart. That wonderful peace of God that had been guarding my heart and mind for the past two months evaporated, like a mist. Gradually, the truth about our son was sinking in deeper and deeper. Larry and I were having a hard time facing the facts. The panic attacks I'd occasionally had in the past returned with a vengeance as I tried to envision what would be entailed in raising a blind, possibly retarded child. I would get short of breath and my heart would pound like a hammer whenever I dwelled too long on Drew and what kind of life he would have.

After Drew was born I stopped attending the mid–week ladies' prayer group because I was so busy caring for Evan and Drew. However, we received a great deal of support from our church. One woman in particular was a nurse who was qualified in teaching infant CPR. She gathered and instructed eleven people in this life-saving technique, just so I could begin attending church again on a regular basis.

One night I was unusually anxious and at prayer group asked the ladies to pray for me. I wanted either God's help in accepting that this was the way things would be or to have God heal Drew. I expressed to them how completely overwhelmed and drained of strength I was. They sat quietly, as if listening to the Spirit. Finally the leader looked at me and said, "No, I don't think we'll pray for you, Nancy. We need to pray for Drew." I sat in a chair, in "proxy" for Drew. They gathered around me and laid their hands on me and prayed, some praying in tongues (other languages), some praying in English. When they were finally done praying, two women simultaneously said, "My child, it is done." Remarkably, I felt a total sense of relief and peace in my heart. I was no longer anxious! I felt and believed everything was completely taken care of.

That night it was my turn to sleep next to Drew. He woke up at 3:00 a.m. hungry, so I rushed to prepare his bottle. As I fed him in the darkened room and looked into his eyes it almost looked as though he was staring into mine. But since I was so sleepy, I forgot about the prayer prayed for Drew only six hours earlier. I put him back down when he finished and went to sleep.

At 6:00 a.m. he woke up, and as I held him in my arms to feed him, he looked right into my eyes! I couldn't believe it! Soon he was asleep. Had I imagined it? Yet a little later, around 9:00 a.m., he got up again and this time he was definitely looking into my eyes. I laid him on the floor, took a rattle and passed it in front of his eyes. Left-right, right-left. His eyes tracked it! I held it at the side of his head and shook it on either side. Drew turned his head both ways. He just lay there smiling and cooing. I ran to the phone and called Larry and told him everything that had happened. I kept screaming, "Drew's okay! He's healed! He can see!" I was totally excited and thrilled beyond words! I laid Drew back on the floor and during the rest of the day he rolled over five times. This, too, was something he had never done before.

After Larry came home and we talked about what happened that day, I expressed to him that I was sure Drew's vocal cords were healed as well. We decided to take him back the next day to Children's Hospital to have him examined. The doctors were surprised because they had seen him two weeks prior and the laryngoscopy they had done had showed no changes. We asked them to do another scope. They did and found that his vocal cords were working perfectly! Both sides were vibrating normally. I tried explaining everything to the doctors about God's healing Drew and the power of prayer, but they were very skeptical. The doctors had no belief that any miracles had taken place.

Three days after Thanksgiving we dedicated him to the Lord. It was a wonderful time for everyone because we had so much for which to be thankful!

Drew seemed to be "socially" delayed about three months, compared to other healthy babies. This, however, seemed completely natural since everything was a brand-new experience of sight and sound for him. But by age one he was developmentally on track. Now, no matter where we go or what country we are in, people are always commenting on how beautiful his big, blue eyes are or how far his voice carries and how beautifully he sings.

These words are the Lord's gentle reminder to me, "Remember, I did this for Drew. I gave him his sight. I gave him his voice." The miracle has become a wonderful witness to friends, Christian and non-Christian alike. To this day I still wonder, "How can anyone live without God? How do people face crises without Him?" God is so faithful! Look at what He did for Drew! And how He built my faith through His love and compassion!

Some people once asked Jesus why a certain man had been born blind. He responded that it was so that God would be glorified in the man's healing. Why didn't I have a C-section? So that God could be glorified. All praise to Jehovah Rapha, our Healer!

ELAINE ENOS
SUNNYVALE, CALIFORNIA

This answered prayer happened in 1994, but it was such a miracle, it is always fresh in my mind. I had been operated on for a brain tumor three months earlier. The surgery left one of my eyes "out of kilter," permanently pointing off to one side rather than aligned with the other one, making normal vision impossible. I had to wear a patch over it.

My prayer to God to heal and restore the wayward eye took place on a freeway in Washington when I was driving my four-month-old granddaughter to a place I had never been to. I was struggling to find the way through detours, heavy commute traffic, bad weather conditions, and my lack of depth perception. I was constantly praying for God's guidance and protection. As I prayed, I reflected on the fact that when Jesus walked the earth, He healed people continually, from all kinds of ailments, even when not with them or near them. Hebrews 13:8 came to mind: "Jesus Christ is the same yesterday, today and forever." So...since He healed then, He could heal now. My prayer changed to asking Him to heal my eye, even to heal it immediately because I needed it right then. He didn't, but He did guide me to the destination safely. The next morning when I awoke, my eye was straight, perfectly aligned with the other one! It blew the socks off my son and his wife (baby's parents), my neurosurgeon, my ophthalmologist, and all the family. God has given me countless opportunities to tell this story.

DIEP MILLER
SELAH, WASHINGTON

When Bill came to the adult home, he made it very clear to me that he didn't want to learn anything about Jesus. He was an atheist and he wanted to stay that way. He was suffering from terminal cancer and we had placed him in the hospice program at our care facility. During his first few months with us, he isolated himself in his room. He was bitter and angry, complaining about why he was suffering with cancer.

I knew that I was supposed to introduce him to Jesus, but he slipped into a coma before I had a clear opportunity to witness to him. He would be gone soon. As I sat next to his bed, I sadly watched as Bill was breathing very slowly. I was so sorry that I had missed my chance to tell him the good news; the love of Jesus Christ. As I sat by his bed, something clicked in my mind and I started praying to God, "Please, God, I really messed up because I didn't get the chance to introduce Bill to You. Now help me wake up Bill so I can tell him about You." I kept praying to God, this time as if I actually was Bill. "God, I represent Bill. I repent for him. I told Bill, 'I know you can hear me, and you need to accept the Lord Jesus Christ.' Then I asked Bill to forgive me because I had been judging him as the world had been judging him. People had been cruel to him and life was cruel to him.

Before too long, Bill started to blink his eyes. I tapped his shoulder and asked Bill if he wanted to accept Jesus Christ. He nodded his head and listened without reservation as I explained the gospel story to him. He prayed and accepted Jesus Christ as his Lord and Savior. Bill lived another six months and was pain-free before he left this Earth for his home in heaven with Jesus. He was a completely different man and his family was so happy with the change. He interacted with the other residents. He visited in the courtyard with the other residents. It was the total opposite of the isolation he craved the first two months he was with us. Before he died, Bill said I was the best nurse he ever had.

BILL MYERS
GLENBURN, CALIFORNIA
(GLENBURN COMMUNITY CHURCH)

I had gone to a nearby ranch to deliver bad news to one of our elders. There were complications with his daughter's pregnancy and she was being rushed in for an emergency caesarean section. Our church's prayer chain was activated and we waited for further news. The initial news was great. The surgery, rushed though it had been, was entirely successful and mother and child were doing well. It was early the next morning when I first heard the concerns the doctor had about a lump that had appeared under the child's jaw, but also a combination of perilous blood abnormalities. During the next two days, waiting for test results, the rapid decline of the infant's health had everyone alarmed.

As the elders and I answered the parent's call and drove to the hospital, my concern was how to comfort these young parents, recently renewed in their faith, who would soon face the loss of their first child. Even as the elders and I prayed in a small waiting room down the hall from obstetrics, I was searching for the right words to say to explain what would appear as God's actions in robbing them of this joy.

When I walked into that hospital room and saw the faces of this family I loved, God spoke very clearly to my heart. His words were, "Tell me, Bill, why do you think this child should die?" Trembling at my Lord's rebuke, I prayed with a faith for that touch, that healing, that I had never known before. (Even now, writing these words, trying vainly to describe the sense of God's undeniable promise to those people at that time, in that place, for that healing, my eyes are filled with tears.) I prayed words that were not mine nor do I recollect them; words that a compassionate Father wanted delivered to a pair of His children that afternoon. It was a powerful moment.

Before we arrived that afternoon, the doctors had made the decision to transport the infant to a larger medical center before his condition could further deteriorate. Their concern was deepened by the fact that after our prayer with him and his parents, he slept for the first time since his birth. He received no other treatment before being whisked away. The expert examined, tested, and X-rayed. Early the next morning the young father's voice was on the other end of the phone: "They said they can't imagine what the people down there were thinking about. They want to know why our hospital sent them this healthy baby."

The blood abnormalities had been corrected. The lump beneath his little jaw, thought to be a thyroid tumor, was nearly invisible by ultrasound the next day. He was held for observation and released to his parents. He is one of the biggest, healthiest, happiest little boys I've ever known. Jesus reigns. He saves and He heals.

CHUCK DAVIS
REPORT GIVEN WHILE SERVING IN BAMAKO, MALI, AFRICA

We witnessed a tremendous healing while serving in New Jersey prior to being sent to France for language study. A young family had experienced new life in Christ. Part of His redemptive work in their lives was to miraculously save their marriage. Several times the wife had packed her suitcase to leave, but each time the Lord intervened.

In the spring of 1988, their new experiences of God's victory caused them to have unlimited faith in the Lord. During this time, their three-year-old son broke his leg. They had the break confirmed through emergency room X-rays and the leg was set in a cast. The father was not satisfied with this intervention because of hearing a series of messages on divine healing at his church. He called the pastor and asked him to pray for the complete healing of his son. In faith, he returned to the doctor to have the leg re-examined. The second set of X-rays showed no sign of the break. Another X-ray was taken, confirming the results. The doctor was amazed and could not explain it. He was baffled in the face of the new X-ray as the father asked for the cast to be cut off.

Later, we were in the midst of language study in France; a daily ten-hour regimen of intense study. During this time, we experienced many attacks from the enemy. One such attack occurred when Ingrid, my wife, developed a severe neck problem. The pain became so intense that she could not remain in class nor give herself to her studies. We discerned this was a physical attack from the enemy to discourage us and to hamper our missionary training.

Before leaving America, Ingrid had experienced many back and neck adjustments by chiropractors. We were concerned about going to France, as most French chiropractors used New Age principles of healing, which we interpreted as dangerous and demonic. We were also concerned because our destination was Mali, West Africa, where chiropractors could not be found. With this problem, we sensed that Ingrid would not be able to continue.

During a Sunday evening worship service, organized to encourage us missionaries studying French, we set aside a time for people to come to the front for prayer. That night we gathered around Ingrid, laid hands on her, binding the spirits who desired to torment her and invited the Lord to divinely intervene. During the prayer time she experienced a warm sensation in her neck. We accepted it as the Lord's intervention. She has not been restricted from working because of neck pain since.

LISA CONNORS
BOZEMAN, MONTANA

After a week's hospital stay in 1973, I was diagnosed with multiple sclerosis. I was not informed I had MS; I was told I only had a virus. I always knew that something was wrong but could never pinpoint the trouble. I did not know Jesus Christ as my Lord and Savior at this time.

In 1991 I went blind in my right eye. After several months of numerous medical tests, including an MRI (brain scan), I was diagnosed with optical neuritis, caused by the MS. The shock was terrific, but by this time my husband and I had come to the Lord. We knew where to go for strength and guidance. Soon I began to feel an incredible peace and saw God's protective hand on me, even back when I didn't know Him. I would not have been able to handle the truth about my MS condition had I known about it back in 1973. God, in His mercy, waited until I knew Him and was able to handle such news.

My vision slowly returned, but by the following winter I had another attack of optic neuritis and went blind for the second time. It was a very painful condition, yet God was right by my side once again, enabling me to sleep without pain. During this time my medical records were sent up from California and the MS diagnosis was revealed. Despite the slow return of my vision, there was permanent damage to my right eye. Nothing could be done to improve the dark film over it. God drew me closer to Him, to a sweet dependence on His unfailing love. I began to have trouble with my arms and hands, mainly weakness, numbness, and pain. I also had nerve damage in my leg from the first attack. My greatest battle was with fatigue and total exhaustion.

Despite being anointed and prayed over several times, nothing changed, including my peace about the situation. When I heard about the healing service at Riverside Alliance I had no intention of attending. I saw Mike Phillips a few days before the service and he insisted that I attend. At the conclusion of the service, I came forward for healing, resting in whatever decision God would make. When I was being prayed for, I felt overwhelmed, and I could only repeat Jesus' name over and over. When the spirit of infirmity was bound and commanded to leave my body, I felt the weight of the fatigue lift. When I opened my eyes, Reverend Bill Putnam stared straight at me saying, "This is a complete healing, and in the morning you will know it." It was true God had chosen that service to heal me. The next morning the dark film had been removed and my eyes were normal and completely clear. *Praise God!* And since then not once have I experienced any MS symptoms. My hands and arms are strong with no numbness, and my left leg is strong after being damaged for twenty-one years. My energy level is amazing. This is such a blessing. My husband says the same.

VARIOUS HEALING MINISTRIES

We see the work God is doing in people today as a testimony to His loving kindness. While it is true that some churches and denominations have abandoned the practice of healing, others are experiencing a renewal in this work of Christ. God is not just doing His work in isolated individual cases. He is using churches, crusaders, and evangelists, giving them thriving healing ministries as they pray and plan to minister the whole Word of God to the lost (and to the saved!) who need God's therapeutic, saving touch.

Below are some churches and ministries who see scores of people healed in the name of our Lord Jesus Christ each year. Note that leadership and pastoral involvement is a key to a vital healing ministry in the local church. When the pastor is convinced that Christ still heals today, that conviction will be reflected in his preaching. He will also take time to train the lay-elders in the theology of divine healing and in the actual practice of healing. Like A.B. Simpson these pastors do not view healing as a fringe issue. They understand it to be a gospel blessing accompanied by vital evangelism and personal growth in holiness. The exaltation of Christ who heals his children today is a necessary component in the worship and practice of a healthy Christian assembly.

The following accounts of local church healing ministries show divine healing to be alive and well in the twenty-first century.

OPEN BIBLE CHRISTIAN CENTER
YAKIMA, WASHINGTON

The Holy Spirit is up to something in this congregation that has parishioners on the edge of their seat. Pastor Mike Lyons says that something is going on that clearly indicates that the Lord has come over this body of believers in a new and powerful way. One great plus is that they have a medical doctor, Dr. Sunny, who attends and ministers at Open Bible regularly. He can define, quantify, and verify that healing is indeed happening at Open Bible. Dr. Sunny practices medicine in the Yakima area. He unabashedly employs prayer with his patients in his medical practice. Pastor Mike and Dr. Sunny will testify that their church began to seek the Lord for more of His blessing. And that in the search for a greater pilgrimage into His will, they were noticing that there was a growing number of people who had debilitating problems. As these issues have been brought forward, God has moved in mighty ways. Here are a few of the stories.

First from Dr. Sunny, who is a believer, member, and teacher at Open Bible Church in Yakima.

DR. SUNNY

We as a body of believers have pursued God's purposes and we found out that one of His purposes for the current world is that He wants everyone well. I personally have walked with the Lord, trusting Him since the eighties. I am from India and I was a part of the Anglican Church in India. We came to know and experience the charismatic renewal movement that flooded through

India during the seventies and eighties when I was filled the Holy Spirit and started to believe the Word of God for what it says. I have seen God use me in various parts of the villages bringing people to the Lord. Seeing the glory of God at work, I have seen demons flee and tremble at the name of Jesus. During those years, even though I have seen people being set free from demons, I have not seen many concrete healings. A few miracles happened here and there but it's like the saying goes, even a blind squirrel finds a nut once in a while.

In 2006 at Open Bible I received a unique revelation about the grace of God. I found out that I need not beg God to do something to heal people. I need not beg God to heal the people who were coming to me on a regular basis. I found out that God in His grace has already carried all the sickness on the Cross of Christ. As in 2 Peter 2:24, "By His stripes, we were healed." I understood that it was a finished fact when Christ said, "It is finished," the job to handle our sins was done. The job to handle our past was done and the job to carry our sickness was done. And I started seeing that I am not twisting God's hand in prayer but I am agreeing with what God has already done but just bringing healing into manifestation. I recognized my role in the divine plan of God. Matthew 10:1 says when He had called the twelve disciples, He gave them power to cast out demons, to heal all kinds of sickness and all kinds of diseases. What attracted me as a physician is that He had given the disciples power over all kinds of sickness and all kinds of diseases. The word *power* actually means authority and there is another scripture in Luke 10:19 where Jesus says, "Behold I give you the authority." Here Jesus is not only talking to twelve, but to the seventy that He sent out. Jesus declares that they have been given authority to trample snakes and scorpions and to overcome all the power of the enemy. He assures, "Nothing will harm you."

(As Dr. Sunny continued sharing the revelations that spurred him into his healing ministry, the "electricity" in the room surged in our hearts as we simply listened to him.)

All the power—and we have it! The enemy has no power that God has not matched and exceeded in you; in us. And nothing shall overcome you. This was amazing to me. This authority that God gave to me was not only over demons attacking people, but over all the power of the enemy: powers of possession, depression, anxiety, sickness, anything that is destructive to human beings is included in that the power of the enemy. Jesus goes on to say that nothing shall by any means hurt you.

Another scripture, Matthew 28:16, was not only for the disciples present, but verse 18 applies to everybody. This is the church that believes people that are receiving the Great Commission have all authority as has been giving to Jesus. We must not miss the part that the spiritual authority, "...*has been given*...," that means this transaction *already* took place on the Cross, in heaven, and on Earth. So we are to make disciples of all nations. Our Open Bible Church recognizes that God has given us, the believers in this current day and age, the authority to not only bring people to the Lord by sharing the gospel but also to heal the sick, raise the dead, and cleanse lepers. We have freely received so we give it out freely. And once I started to receive this revelation and meditate upon it, it started to change my thinking. It revolutionized my whole life. It has even given new light to my medical practice.

With this fresh inspiration we started a Friday night home group with about six people. It increased in number and was moved to the church. We started to see great transformation in people's lives.

In June 2006, I was in my clinic having a very busy day. I was seeing my last patient around 4:00 p.m. It was a friend of mine so we were chatting about various things. Suddenly there was a frantic knock to the door of the room. The nurse popped in her head, "Dr. Sunny, we need help!" There was a person in the post-procedure room who had collapsed and they needed somebody to come take care of him—quickly! Not knowing what I was getting into, I hurried with the nurse to the post-procedure room in the basement. As I entered the recovery unit, I found a man lying on a stretcher, completely limp. His hands and arms were lifeless on the side of the stretcher, his eyes were rolled up, and to my best assessment he was completely dead. I checked the carotid pulse and could find none. No breathing. His oxygen level was around seventy and falling. (It must be more than ninety to maintain proper oxygen level in the body.)

The nurses told me that this person had just come out of a procedure and was doing fine, then just minutes before I saw him he had gone into cardiac arrest. I initiated the protocol to try and resuscitate him. The nurse was panicking. I was giving orders (in a controlled panic!) trying to set up the defibrillator, oxygen, and other necessary items to connect the gentlemen and resuscitate him. It was close to four minutes by now that I had been with him. I was scrambling trying to get some access to his airway. Precious time was melting away and the patient was not responding. Suddenly I decided that I should do something unorthodox and drastic, outright extreme. I paused and stood facing him, with his head to my right and his body, legs, and feet to my left. I made a fist and I firmly declared, "In the name of Jesus, you come back to life!" and I hit his sternum/chest bone with full force. His eyes opened. He looked at me, said nothing, then slowly drifted off and closed his eyes again.

Meanwhile, his heart returned to normal rhythm. After hooking him up, he was completely restored to a regular cardiac rhythm. He went by ambulance to the nearest hospital and ultimately survived a heart attack.

I, the doctor, was left in shock. I didn't know what had transpired. I knew that he was either dead or close to death and I had resuscitated him; brought him back to life. It was not done by medical technology but by Christ's power. I call it CPR: Christ Powered Resuscitation. The news spread in the clinic as the nurses talked about what had happened. The management called and asked what really happened. They shook their heads and said thank you for helping us out. The nurses who saw what happened started coming to our church's Friday meeting to learn more about Christ's power and what it means in the lives of those who seek Him.

It is in order to tell you of our mission trip to India that happened two months after this CPR event. I was so excited because I knew I would be ministering in Tamil, the local dialect, to large groups of people that varied between five hundred and two thousand. In this church they had advertised two full days of healing services.

At the first service on day one there were around six hundred people filling up the church. As I was sitting before the time to preach, I saw a lady who was probably in her fifties make her way in to the healing service. She was clearly a practicing Hindu. She had a *bindi* marking (the red dot) on her forehead.

She came in carrying her handicapped son. I estimate he was close to thirty years old. I watched her take this "kid" to the corner of the church and sit him down. He flopped in a heap like a folded pretzel. His scrawny legs had no strength. His arms and legs crumbled up under him. His fingers were gnarled and bent in all directions. The mother did not mean to be gruff. She was simply exhausted and it was clear that she was in need of some changes in her family's life.

The message ended with an altar call. We were blessed as twenty-seven Hindus, who had never come to a church prior to this night, came forward to receive Christ. I had preached that Christ loves every single person: Hindus, Muslims, Indians, Americans, and all kinds of people in the world. As the people were coming forward, that specific woman hoisted up her son and lugged him to the front. The ministry team was already busy leading people to the Lord and this mother received the Lord right along with the rest of them. Her heart overflowed with joy. Her eyes sparkled like gems in the sunlight. Her face was happy as her eyes gleamed with expectation. She believed for her son to become well also. But in our excitement about the salvations we missed this subtlety of her second desire; her son to be healed.

This unrelenting mother came back the next day. And the next night we were all there again. As the worship was going on, the same lady came again with her child and again sat him in the same corner. From the front I could see the hope and anticipation in her eyes as the evening proceeded. During the course of the service, she began working her way through the people to bring her son back up to the altar.

The astonishing moment came that night during the ministry time. I was systematically praying through the 150 or so people who had come to the front and were standing, waiting to be specifically ministered to through prayer. Suddenly the whole group of one thousand people started to shout. Looking around puzzled, I didn't know why people were shouting. I turned around again and there was the obvious reason. The kid had gotten up and was standing on his own. I say "the kid" because his mother had been caring for him as if he were a one or two year old. Then the mother started to scream.

I ran to the son, held his hand, and asked him if he was ready to walk. He said he was ready. We walked up and down the church rows again and again.

The congregation was frantic with excitement. I told the woman, "Your faith has made your child well." Above the excited rejoicing and shouting, I heard a man shouting over all the noise, "I am the dad! I am the dad! I need Jesus." Then the father of the crippled boy accepted Christ. Demons were sent out. People were set free. I started to pray for another girl with mental retardation. The demonic spirit came out, she fell down, the spirit left, and she got up and she could talk well. She had been labeled the maniac of this neighborhood. But she was fine now. When I saw her parents, the father told me, "This is my daughter. She was mentally ill for the past thirty years, now she is okay. I need this Jesus, too."

There was such a commotion that the pastor that came out saying to me, "You have no idea what you have done for our neighborhood. The cripple who was the beggar of the neighborhood is now walking around and telling everyone that Jesus has healed him. The maniac who was given food by people in the neighborhood is well. Jesus is her healer. Hallelujah!"

Then I came back to Yakima after the mission trip. We had recorded these miracles on amateur video, which I showed to friends and Pastor Mike Lyons. Our expectation for a greater move of God increased and we wanted to see these things happen in Yakima. We felt that if these things can happen over there, then they can happen over here.

Three or four weeks later, I had the opportunity to assist Sharon Lyon, Pastor's wife, in the worship service, which was my first time to help in this capacity. We talked about it and we prayed about it. During the service, we were singing songs and praising God. Our theme in the celebration was about being led of the Lord.

Suddenly, one gentleman stood up and started to shout frantically, "Pastor, Pastor, look, look, look!" We looked into the congregation. A lady in a wheelchair stood up. I ran to this lady and asked if she was ready to walk. She said, "Yes," and she started walking with me to the front and back of the church. Mike Lyons took over escorting her back and forth. People were calling their families by cell phone and cheering and crying. This lady had a stroke more than seven years before and had not been able to walk since. She was using a motorized wheel chair. This was her first time to walk in seven years! What had happened in India was now happening in Yakima, Washington!

Miracles have been happening beyond medical explanation. People have been getting excited about the Word of God and His truth. We are not twisting the hand of God or the arm of God, as the saying goes. It is not our prayers that manipulate anything. We as a body of believers recognized that Christ has borne our sickness, carried our pain, and triumphantly said "It is finished." All we do is stand and speak to the problem and the problem has to change. Healing has to come because Christ has done it all.

In January 2008 Open Bible started an outreach in Toppenish among the Yakama Nation tribal people, and we were having a service in one of the local churches there. We were presenting what the Lord had put in our hearts. A lady came who was short and stubby. Two friends brought her up to the front. She had multiple medical problems. She had suffered amputation of both legs below her knees and multiple fingers were amputated. I asked her, "Ma'am, what can I pray for?"

She said, "Sir, I have had diabetes since the age of seven. I'm losing my body parts and vision in my eye. More than a year ago, I completely lost my vision in that eye. Now doctors say they have to take the eye out because it is starting to disintegrate. Can you pray for my vision?"

I looked at her. I wanted to know how much she could see. She could not see me out of her bad eye, just some light. She was legally blind in that eye. I told her, "Christ has already carried our sickness and our pain. Do you believe that?"

She agreed, so we agreed to pray for her healing. I clasped my hand around her bad eye and I started to speak to the eye. I started to yell at the top of my lungs, "Eye, you will open up in the name of Jesus Christ." I spoke to the retina, the optic nerve, and various other parts of the eye. I stopped praying. No lightning bolts had gone off, no significant signal that anything had worked, but I felt I should check her again. I held up two of my fingers in front of her eye. She said she could see the two fingers. People around started to scream. I told her, "Close your good eye and cover it with your hand." I held up my fingers using a different number and walked farther away from her. She was seeing correctly and clearly up to twelve feet away. She could see what the number of fingers was and what the color was and she was able to see me clearly as well. The place was in an uproar and we were praising the Lord. The next day she came back and said the bad eye was now better than the good eye. She asked, "Can you pray for my good eye?" We did. Friends, God has done it all.

A couple months after the miracle of the blind lady in Toppenish seeing again, the news had spread. People from all parts of Yakima were coming out on Friday night to the healing service. So here we were, two months after when another blind woman appears at the healing service. She was legally blind. She had been blind for more than twenty years from macular degeneration. At the end of the Friday night service, Jeff, one of my ministry teammates, went to her. It was spring 2008 by now and we told her about the miracle of the blind woman seeing back in January. He asked if he could pray for her eyes. She was a little reluctant at first. But after pondering she figured, "why not?"

By the time he was ready to pray, Brian and I had joined Jeff. We agreed with each other. She had a problem in the left eye. Jeff examined her vision situation and confirmed that she was not able to see anything except vague light. And Jeff did the same thing that he saw me do two months before. He placed his hands on her eye and started to speak to the eye and commanded it to open. After praying for maybe a minute, he stopped and checked her eyesight again. When he showed two fingers to her she said, "I can see two fingers." Jeff was ecstatic! People observing nearby started to shriek with delight. Amid all the excitement we kept our heads about us and continued testing her vision. She was able to see clearly for more than ten feet. By this time everybody in the area was screaming and rejoicing over what God had done. This woman had been so amazingly blessed. And so were the rest of us who witnessed this miracle.

We again connected with her in early summer of 2008. It was about three months after her healing. She said that she was still doing wonderfully with her vision. Praise the Lord!

A friend named Valerie, who attends Open Bible, has a few ladies get together and pray at her work. She said that in June 2008 a lady who was six months pregnant came into their prayer group. The newcomer was anxious, weeping, and distraught. When they inquired as to what was distressing her, she said that her doctor had checked her pregnancy a few days before and had told her that her baby was dead. There was no heartbeat and there was no movement. The doctor had recommended medical termination of the pregnancy because the baby could become toxic to the mother. She didn't know what to do. So she came to the group of ladies for some help.

The first thing Valerie said to her in the prayer group was, "Your child will live. He will not die and you will declare the works of the Lord." She prayed with the mother and gave her a small testimony booklet of Dr. Sunny's young child, Elizabeth. Then they said their goodbyes.

A few hours after the prayer time, Valerie got a call from the mother. The mother was rather frantic. Through her breathing she was able to say, "I read the book. As I was reading it, the Lord clearly spoke to me through this book that I should not heed my doctor's latest advice; that I should *not* terminate the pregnancy." Valerie agreed that she should follow the Lord in this.

A short time later the clinic called to schedule the abortion. She didn't set it up because she wanted to get a second opinion. A few days later she went to another clinic in Yakima requesting this second opinion. The doctor at this other clinic did an ultrasound. While he was doing the ultrasound, he turned to the mother and asked, "Who told you the baby is dead? The heartbeat is strong and the baby is moving. This baby is *not* dead." The mother was on cloud nine!

She called Valerie and said what the Lord had done. Three or four weeks later her regular doctor called her back because he wanted to see how she was doing. He was concerned because she had not come in for her prescribed abortion. So she told him the story of what had happened. Despite her testimony her doctor asked her to come in. Her doctor did the ultrasound and turned to the mom and said. "Ma'am, I am confused. I can see the heartbeat. I can see the baby growing appropriately. I don't know what to say but your baby is alive."

Hallelujah our God has done it again!

The following are a few stories of people (in their own words) who have experienced divine healing at Open Bible:

WENDELL

Wendell, who attends Open Bible, had a constant and sharp pain in his shoulder blade area for about ten weeks. Then one morning during the worship service someone gave a message; it was like a short word that was in another language. Then there was the interpretation. The woman said, "Someone is here with a shoulder pain and God wants to heal you." I took that to mean me. Whatever that all meant I wasn't sure yet. The pain continued through the church service. Then after lunch it was getting worse. I refused to doubt and kept claiming the Word of God to be true and the word that was spoken about my shoulder area that would be healed. At about 3:00 p.m. that afternoon, I noticed that the pain was gone completely. Praise God! The pain has never returned.

JERRY

Jerry suffered with a degenerative arthritic spine for thirty years. His condition had become so severe that it left him disabled and unable to work at his profession. Before a Sunday service Pastor Mike felt led to pray for him. Jerry reports, "So Pastor Mike approached me, told me about his being prompted to pray, and pray for me he did!" I sensed nothing notable at the time, but a little later my friend Gordon came and told me to "receive my inheritance." I realized it was a prophetic word when in his hugging me he pulled at me sideways. For the first time in a very long time I could feel no pain in my back! It was an amazing change in my spine. For years any gesture or movement like this would have caused immediate pain in my back. I realized by the end of the service that my pain was truly and completely gone. I am still pain free today. Praise the Lord!

RORY

Rory's sciatic nerve was pinched. He had trouble walking, bending over, even laying down gave him problems. What is a man to do when there is virtually nothing to do and no place to go to escape the pain? It had been this way for over four years. I shared with Pastor Mike about it and he laid hands on me and started praying for my healing. I told God, "I believe, and I receive." All at once I felt awash in warmth. It was God coming over me. I had never known His touch to be like this before. I was being wrapped in a heavy blanket so to speak and I could feel it! The sensation started at my head and went to my feet. Instantly the pain in my leg was gone, and my back pain faded away. I am truly thankful to the Lord for my healing. Hallelujah!

ROSEMARY

The doctors told Rosemary in the winter of 2008 that she had a bad viral infection that was attacking all of her internal organs. Her liver was getting the worst of it. How long could she hang on with this problem? It was anyone's guess. The last report was that her liver was completely out of control. Rosemary thought that this problem warranted a double assault so she called Pastor Mike *and* Doctor Sunny. She remembers two distinct things as each of them prayed for her. Pastor prayed first. As he prayed, peace came over her. It was like when a doctor talks to you right before he begins a treatment. He tells you what he is going to do and assures you that you will be fine. And his words help bring relaxation. That was the peace I felt when Pastor Mike prayed. Next, Doctor Sunny prayed. There is no other way to describe what happened except that a weird feeling went all through my body. There was nothing to compare it to. I had never felt anything like this before. I couldn't say, "Oh great, it's working. This is just like the last time when my infection was prayed for." It was a *new* feeling and I could tell that something extreme was sweeping through me anew as Doctor Sunny prayed. The words in his prayer took command over the infection and began to reverse it. Looking back, I knew that that is what happened. The next day the liver doctor said that my liver was back to normal. Can you believe it? One day later! Within a week I was holding food down. The doctor stated that I would be out of work for at least two months but I was better in much less time. Thank God for His servants who are here and remind us to come to Jesus and receive His healing touch through prayer.

KAREN

Karen fell at work and it turned out to be quite an eventful "splat" which did a good deal of damage. Her left knee twisted out. Her back and head hit a counter and cupboard on the way down. She landed on her tailbone. There was immediate searing pain that burned all through her lower back and went down her left leg. We all know that phrase, "What a difference a day makes." Well for Karen it was "what a difference a split second makes!" If it were over within another second that would have been one thing. But the pain lingered and served to entwine her body and her life for three weeks. When Mike and Sunny prayed for her at church, Karen says the healing began right then. A soothing sensation of warmth came over her. It felt like healing oil was pouring all down her back and legs. The relief was instant though the healing sensation (that could almost be called "a tranquil burning") continued. "The warm burning sensation continues still as God rejuvenates me," Karen says. It is a marvel how God touches us when we ask Him to. I can bend freely. My knee is healed. I can stand on both feet and sit. None of this was possible during weeks of the suffering! God has healed me and I give Him all the glory! Alleluia!

GEORGIA

Georgia testifies, "I praise God for the wonderful gifts that He gives us. Through the years I have called on Jesus to help me and guide me. He has always been there for me during major surgeries. He has helped me through the grief I have suffered from the loss of my mother and both of my children. Then just two years ago I lost my husband. Jesus was there helping me through these painful times.

After the loss of my husband, however, I became a very depressed person. Doctor Sunny noticed this in me and spoke with me about attending his Friday night Bible Study and ministry time. So I attended. Then shortly after that I began attending Open Bible Church. This opened my eyes to a whole new life. I thank Jesus for guiding me in the right direction. After attending church there for several months, I gave myself to God and was baptized. It was December 9, 2007. It amazes me that I had been with Jesus and he had helped me during the suffering over the years but that I had not totally surrendered my life to Him before then. Now I was His child.

Being newly and truly committed to Jesus, I became alert to so much more. Prior to this, I had grown accustomed to the pain that was so prevalent but there was a new motivation to take this pain to Jesus for healing. You see for many years, up to this point, I had suffered pain throughout my body: namely in my back, my legs, and my knee. I have taken many different medications for these problems. The excessive dosages and chronic usage was making me feel drugged to where my mind was not functioning right. I was very distressed and had not known where to turn for years. But now with my faith at a whole new level, I prayed for specific guidance and healing; I asked God to help me with my pain problem.

I will always remember that miraculous morning late winter 2008 when I awoke to a pain-free body. I have had no pain since! Praise God! He is always there for us. All we have to do is ask. I am witness to the Lord's work for the healing He has done for me. My prayers were answered. He has always been there. I just had to learn how to ask. I thank You, Jesus, for all Your great blessings.

For what it's worth, the numerous healings that have occurred at Open Bible *during* the publishing of this book, that missed the publishing deadline, far outnumber the healings that have been reported above.

Allegheny Center Alliance Church
Pittsburgh, Pennsylvania

This congregation founded by E.D. "Daddy" Whiteside in the late 1800's has in recent decades enjoyed a revival of healing comparable to the early days of this great work. Pastor Rockwell Dillaman affirms evident manifestation of God's power to heal the sick in the congregational life of Allegheny Center Church. He attributes this blessing to the consistent preaching on healing and the participation of the elders in this ministry. Elders are at the altar prepared to pray for the sick at every service.

The pastor observes three aspects of the healing ministry of their church. Anointing with oil, the laying on of hands, and prayer are regularly practiced in the church's ministry to the sick. Often persons are healed before they can be anointed with oil. Such healing takes place during times of intense worship and praise to the Lord. The exaltation of Christ in these times of praise quickens the faith of some resulting in instantaneous healing. Times of prayers for those bound by evil spirits have resulted in some remarkable healings. During one such session of spiritual warfare praying, a lady who had suffered seven years with phlebitis was completely healed. She had also been afflicted with hemorrhages. Both problems were healed at once.

This historic church does not see divine healing as a mere artifact of days gone by, but as a reality for now. Instead of dying as many such urban churches are, Allegheny Center Alliance Church is a growing, active congregation in the central city of one of America's great metropolitan areas. Their vital healing ministry is an integral part of their outreach to needy people of all races and social classes in the greater Pittsburgh area.

First Alliance Church
Lexington, Kentucky

The First Alliance Church in Lexington, Kentucky is a growing church with a dynamic outreach to its community. The congregation is composed of professionals, college and university students and professors, physicians, middle-management people, plus people from all walks of life. Pastor Ron

Gifford is excited about the renewal of the ministry of divine healing going on in their midst.

It began with the elders of the church. At a weekend retreat the elders became convinced that they needed to take seriously their responsibility to biblically carry out the ministry of divine healing. During the months that followed, these elders studied, prayed, and sometimes fasted in preparation for an effective ministry of healing to their church. As time went by the intercession of the elders and pastoral staff was heard and took effect. Marvelous incidents of healing began to occur.

Over time there developed the concept of healing as a vital part of pastoral care. While opportunities are given for anointing with oil and prayer in the public services and at the monthly communion services, much of the healing ministry is initiated as members relate to their elders. The elders have so developed their gifts and sensitivity as to be able to inspire faith for healing and to relate healing to the spiritual needs of the members who approach them. The results of this method have been phenomenal.

The success of this approach to healing has created a whole new level of trust in the congregation. Members feel free to go to the elders for prayer and counseling when they have physical needs. The compassion and active faith of these dedicated elders is conducive to presenting Christ as Healer who works in our bodies today. Their biblical understanding of this gospel truth equips them with insight and discernment that really helps the seeker meet Christ who heals. The spiritual aspects of the seeker's condition are not overlooked but wisely dealt with by the elders.

The testimonies of extraordinary healings are making an impact on the whole church. Pastor Gifford says that a side effect of the revitalizing of divine healing has been the spiritual renewal among the elders engaged in this work. So many outstanding healings have taken place that an effort is now in progress to compile a book of these up-to-date testimonies of physical healings.

EAGLE CHURCH
ZIONSVILLE/INDIANAPOLIS, INDIANA

Healing is happening in well-established churches as well as in newer churches. Eagle Alliance Church (Eagle Church) on the northwest side of Indianapolis began in the early nineties and has a Sunday attendance of between six and seven hundred. Kerry Bowman, the pastor of this mission-minded and growing church, is convinced that physical healing is an answer to prayer and is active today. Eagle Church's praise and ministry service is designed to equip and inspire believers to carry on the work of Christ in word and in deed during the week. Doing the work of Christ is far more than a Sunday activity. A focus on ministry to the needs of people includes encouragement to pray for physical and emotional brokenness. Kerry himself has been involved in deliverance ministry prayer efforts throughout his ministry.

The church strives to sustain a successful neighborhood life and small group ministry. One group is composed of people with a great burden for intercession (intense prayer ministry). Here people are encouraged, trained, and equipped to pray for those bound in complex problems as well as for others with physical needs. From this group, there are individuals who assist the pastors and small group leaders. They visit the homes of those in need of personal intercession and prayer for healing. The church has also recently established a twenty-four-hour prayer room for reflection and prayer. This room provides a gathering place for people to intercede for one another and to pray for any needs, including healing.

The scriptural teaching of "Christ as Healer" is a truth concept that many people in society have never taken the time to investigate or consider as a reality that is to be experienced in our world today. For instance, there was a medical doctor who came to Eagle Church in the earlier years. She was quite skeptical about divine healing until she saw a miracle of healing. A young boy in the church (this doctor's patient) was diagnosed with a brain tumor and had no real hope of recovery. After anointing and prayer he was healed and lived well and at home with his family for a significant number of years. The doctor then went on to incorporate prayer and intercession as a very practical means in her life and ministry.

It is exciting to see how the blessed truth of Christ as Healer is an important factor in the growth and spiritual health of this mission-active church of young families. The work of the Eternal Christ in healing the sick and loosing those who have been trapped or bound is a reality in the life of Eagle Church and a demonstration of God's ongoing work of grace among his people.

HILLSIDE CHAPEL ALLIANCE CHURCH DAYTON, OHIO

In the late 1970s a small Alliance Church in Dayton was led of the Lord to relocate in Beavercreek, a growing suburb of Dayton, Ohio. From the beginning this congregation began to grow and experience the blessing that comes from preaching the fullness of Christ. Pastor Nelson says that divine healing has been a part of the ministry throughout the years. During the early years of this ministry, a member of the church was diagnosed by medical doctors as having terminal cancer. After anointing and prayer, the man was clearly healed. As the church increased in size, Pastor Nelson found it necessary to devote some of his messages to healing in order to instruct the newcomers and the new converts on the doctrine of healing. Consistent instruction has been a part of the methodology used in the Hillside Chapel healing ministry.

The elders are taught and trained to carry on a healing ministry. The church, in addition to its public healing ministry, often goes to hospitals or homes to pray for the sick. At every communion service there is anointing and prayer for those suffering physical needs. At the Sunday evening services, testimonies of healing are often heard as people tell of God's healing touch on their lives. During the interview for this article, the pastor shared his personal testimony. Recently after anointing and prayer he was definitely healed of a serious back problem. Needs are being met and Hillside Chapel continues to grow. The preaching and practice of the whole gospel is at the heart of this church's ministry. Divine healing is a normal activity in the life of Hillside Chapel.

Thirty years after relocating, Hillside continues to support a ministry of healing by regularly praying for individuals. At times, the results are noteworthy, including a young couple who struggled to begin a family. Due to medical complications, physicians raised serious questions about the feasibility of a pregnancy. Within a few months of praying with the elders, the couple discovered that they were expecting twins! At other times, God has worked in much less sensational ways, not necessarily giving the healing that was sought, but instead giving His gifts of perseverance, patience, and courage versus continuing on a path into despair.

In recent years, Hillside has broadened the ministry for healing to include prayers for individuals who face needs such as dealing with emotional trauma, relational disruptions, behavior addictions, and more. Believing that God is concerned about the whole person, Hillside Chapel regularly invites individuals to request prayer for *any* situation wherein healing is desired.

As an example, during the fall of 2007, current senior pastor, Chuck Moore, was sharing a series of messages on the topic, "Extreme Makeover: Spirit Edition." Prior to the celebration of communion in one worship service, Pastor Moore invited the congregation to request prayers for healing for any areas of their life that could interfere with the outgrowth of the fruits of God's spirits. Three altar benches were then strategically placed at the front of the church where individuals could come, be anointed with oil, and receive prayer. The response was tremendous. Many individuals came to the front to request prayer for God's help in overcoming addictions, reconciling relationships, family struggles, healing emotions, and more.

In order to achieve the goal of developing a community where such responses occur, Hillside works regularly to talk about the importance of honesty, transparency, and vulnerability in a context of grace and forgiveness. Central to Hillside's practice is the belief that the Body of Christ must carry on the ministry of Jesus in a way that affirms the gift of healing to the whole person. The pastor concludes, "Christ Jesus truly meets us as we come to Him. That's what we are seeing happen."

GENESIS CHURCH
FOLEY, ALABAMA

Pastor Donald Young and a layman from his church had no idea what was coming as they prepared for a trip to visit and minister in the Alliance churches of Chile, South America. In the midst of their excitement at visiting a mission field, God poured out His Spirit in an unusual measure upon these visitors and the Chilean church. Not only were people saved and filled with the Spirit in large numbers, but the Lord was also pleased to heal the sick and set free those who were bound and oppressed. Glorious days of revival followed the initial outpouring. It was a life-changing experience for these men. They laid hands on the blind who were healed; their sight was completely restored. Miracles became the order of the day. In awe this pastor and his elders stood back and watched the hand of God work on a level seen in the book of Acts. The leadership of the Chilean church wept for joy. It was a memorable, life-changing experience for all who were there.

For the next chapter of this story one must go to Elberta, Alabama, the location of Donald Young's church at the time. The Lord had been blessing the Elberta congregation with new life and growth but now a new era was about to begin. As the men came back home from Chile, they were pondering the revival they had just experienced and wondered if God could do a work like that in Elberta, Alabama. The answer to that question came very soon. The first Sunday back, as the congregation gathered to hear the report from Pastor Young and the elder who went with him to Chile, a mighty wind of revival began to blow. The same glorious work they witnessed in Chile occurred in the Elberta church. Souls were saved, believers were filled with the Spirit, the sick were healed, and demons were cast out in Christ Jesus' name.

The moving of the Holy Spirit on this church brought them deep spiritual change and a revitalization of the ministry of healing unlike anything the church had previously known. How marvelous are the works of God! He still confirms His gospel by the supernatural healing of the sick and the exorcism of evil spirits in Christ's name. Revival is obviously the key to the renewal of healing in this church.

The above happened in the late 1990s. What about today? Since those glorious days of renewal and revival between Chile and Alabama, Pastor Young and George Woerner have been back to Chile a number of times. Pastor Young has traveled throughout Chile and has seen continued revival. Many hundreds of people have been converted and hundreds more healed and delivered from satanic bondage. The Chilean church is strong, and revitalized

Marriage Encounter seminars have given God a platform to heal literally thousands of marriages around the world. By the way, this version of the Encounter movement started in Chile.

Marriage Encounter came back with Pastor Young to Elberta. And since the inception of the program, more than one thousand couples in the area have lived "the forty-eight hours of love" experience. Dramatic healings and deliverances of marriage have taken place and God continues to move by His Spirit in awesome ways.

The Alliance church in Elberta has since moved to Foley, Alabama. They are eight miles west of the previous building. They have changed their name to "Genesis: A Church of New Beginnings." This church continues to impact large crowds of people on a weekly basis. There are Spanish ministries, Relief Ministries in Waveland, Misssissippi, and a new satellite campus site in Lillian, Alabama, that provides venues for renewal and healing to hundreds of people.

The anointing of God is still on the two main churches in Temuco, Chile, and Genesis Church (the former Elberta Alliance) as the miracles continue. Recently at Genesis, halfway through the sermon, the speaker stopped and said, "God is impressing on me to pray for someone here with diabetes and imbalance." So he stopped and prayed for this situation. After the service, a woman came forward and testified, "This was my first Sunday here in this church and in this area. I have never met your pastor and there is no way that the speaker could have known that I suffer from diabetes. In fact, I can hardly walk because of vertigo. During the prayer, I felt a warmness all over my body and I know I was healed."

This dear lady and more than a dozen others in the morning and evening Spanish services were healed. There has been a month of healing and deliverances throughout the church. It appears there is a continued line of anointing that extends from Chile to Alabama. These are great days and we bask in this awesome work and power of God.

seven

THE DAY "THE FLOOD"
POURED OVER MY LIFE

A s I RECALLED the events of this chapter, it became apparent that I needed to blend my testimony with that of my associate, Nigel Thomas. Therefore this chapter is told in the third-person for the sake of clarity.

ON-SITE MINISTRY CRISIS

"Now...now is the time, start!" Those words bellowed in Drake's soul: loud and clear as a bell. It felt like God was commanding him to step off a cliff onto an invisible balance beam and walk across the Grand Canyon (no safety net!) and to start immediately. His heart skipped a beat. For a moment he couldn't breathe.

> God, please...God, what if I pray and nothing happens?

His English friend, Nigel Thomas, and he were in a rural church outside Kiev in the Ukraine countryside. The church had a couple dozen seriously handicapped people among them. They expected Drake and Nigel to deliver the cure. Drake froze. "God, don't do this to me. Can't we start out slow?" he stammered. He was apprehensive yet challenged, eager yet ashamed. He had waited for this moment all his life. Here it was and he was quivering like a hamster dipped in ice water! "God, please...God, what if I pray and nothing happens?" He was panicking, to put it mildly.

There before him were a few dozen people who couldn't speak a word of English. They were distressed, in pain, and they wanted relief. And they wanted it right away. When they asked Drake to pray for their healing, he hesitated at first, then breathed out, "God, go with me. God, guide me *please*." So he took that first step, and crouched down to pray with the first one in line; a lame woman!

FRESHFIRE IN EUROPE

Over two weeks prior a dozen people had flown across the Atlantic Ocean to minister with the FreshFire Evangelism Team from Canada. The first week was spent at a prophetic conference in Dudley, England. The second week was spent at a crusade in Kiev, Ukraine; formerly part of the Soviet Union.

PREPARATION IN ENGLAND

The worship that first week, the prophetic teaching, ministry time, the healings, blessings, and fellowship were awe-inspiring. Speakers in Dudley, England, were Paul Keith Davis, Shawn Bolz, and Roland Baker. Roland was the local pastor who coordinated the conference. The ministry team the people had joined was touched by God as they touched others in ministry. Lives were truly changed. It felt like a mini-Galilee experience.

Nigel and Drake would later look back on the week in Central England as vital training time. They were trained to simply be ready to move into the unknown and be ready to be used by the Holy Spirit. Nigel later realized how God molded his heart and his thinking the week before they went to Ukraine.

During the training, Nigel felt the inadequacies that the rest of the team had felt. There was always the first time that a sick person would wave over a team "expert" to pray for them. After all it was "the team" who had come to assist with the healing evangelism. Everyone had experiences where they prayed and...nothing happened. Then what? Tell them God is not here yet?

Wait? Try again? Move on? Nigel mused that what came home for him in the evening meetings was the reality that sometimes healing is a mystery of God. Should they separately categorize successes and failures as they prayed down the rows of people? Some were getting healed and some weren't. They would discuss these matters later back in their quarters. They all had high hopes but all of them were puzzled at how stories developed night after night.

Did I truly have a heart to see people healed?

Nigel shared, "As I thought and prayed through what happened each night, instead of God giving me answers, God began to question me: What *was* my reason for signing up for this trip? Did I truly have a heart to see people healed? Was I just after some great stories that I could 'wow' everyone with when I got back to my home church?"

Nigel confessed that these were just the sort of God-questions he needed to hear to bring him and others back down to earth. He said, "I resolved from that night on to seek God for a heart of compassion for those in need and to make sure He got all the glory—not me." It was a decision that would bear great fruit over the rest of the trip.

HEALING IN ENGLAND

Nigel had an experience in England that helped prep both him and Drake for the flood of healing that would come later that next week. On the final day in England, Nigel was praying for a lady who was deaf in her left ear because of an operation three years prior. This procedure made it utterly impossible for her to hear again as it removed a diseased part of the inner ear. Her three tiny ear bones had been surgically removed and, medically speaking, hearing was not a possibility; it was "history." But then again, nothing is impossible with God. There was something about this lady that touched Nigel's heart. He just couldn't stop praying for her. He thought he was more desperate for God to heal her than she was!

After praying with her for more than thirty minutes and trying every method of healing he could remember from his training, she suddenly began to get a strange sensation in her left ear—and her hearing returned. God had performed a miracle. How did God do it? What was the secret? What method had God used? Which or what method of mine was it? Was Nigel's question legitimate? He had no idea. God did what He does best, He surprised them. Sometimes healing truly is a mystery of God. But what is not a mystery is God's goodness. Just when Nigel was ready to give up and go home, God's "surprise" had raised his faith and that was enough for him.

What had happened for Nigel was just as astonishing as trying to key-start a car that had no engine under the hood. You could turn the key and hear clicking or no sound at all. The car is not going to start. One of the passengers could ask you to pop the hood. You do so. He raises the hood and looks at an empty cavity where an engine once *was*. After that he walks around to the driver's window and asks if you are Einstein, Sherlock Holmes, or Bozo the clown. "There's no engine under the hood, buddy! Where's your mind anyway?" Just then another soul appears. You both look at each other and wonder, "Who is this?" This surprise guest closes the hood with both fists. The stranger orders you to get in the front seat, and for both to buckle the seatbelts. He gets in the backseat and orders, "Start it, let's go."

Though feeling foolish, the key gets turned, the engine roars and the car soon accelerates to full speed. That would make anyone on earth wonder if they were asleep and dreaming all this, or question, "Are we in the 'twilight zone' yet?" Or one might muse as to what galaxy they were in.

If automobiles could be compared to ears, this is exactly what had happened to Nigel! He was ready for the Ukraine. Little did Nigel and Drake know that they were about to get knocked off their feet, but hey, these things are up to God not people.

ONWARD TO UKRAINE

Rain came down as the team departed Birmingham, England, for Holland and then Kiev, Ukraine. While bussing through the Ukrainian countryside, Drake noticed that the scenery resembled much of the World War II films and videos he had watched during school days. The crusade in Kiev was held at the Ukrainian Olympic training facility. Ukraine's professional soccer team trained in the field adjacent to the center.

> The local perspective was that their healing would come from God or not at all.

For four days and nights it was the most rousing worship, teaching, preaching, and ministry Drake had experienced in nearly forty years of being a Christian. The musicians were local. All the songs were sung in Russian. There was no overhead or words to follow. "Jesus never spoke English either," he mused. This worship was so wholly anointed and enjoyable. The delighted faces at the crusade were a bright contrast to the dour faces of the people who ambled through the streets and markets of Kiev; the latter being faces that were dreading the imminent bite of winter during this last week of October 2005. Maybe they had premonitions for the temperature did drop to minus forty degrees in Kiev, winter 2006!

The speaking each night was about an hour. No notes or script, just a blaze of good news in the Spirit and the Lord was powerfully present. It was fascinating. The ministry times were straight out of the Bible. People were called up by revelation given to the speaker. There was no prior prompting. Many were told what their ailment was *before* they described it. Then came the flood: The deaf could hear again—one after another. Limbs were healed. Internal problems ceased. People who were carried to the crusade later walked home under their own power. People in paralyzing pain were set free! Night after night it was the love of God administered in large doses.

Nigel noted the push to get to the front and be touched by God's servants. It was a feverish atmosphere that Drake and Nigel rarely observed in church functions. The local perspective was that their healing would come from God (here in Kiev) or not at all. Most of the people in that auditorium had no access to health care like people do in the West. This was their only chance to be healed. It didn't matter which one of us prayed for them. All that mattered was that God wanted to heal them, and if they came down to the front, then healing would become a reality.

Each night the team couldn't move because the crowd wanted them to stretch out their hands and pray for them. Most of them spoke no English at all and with only a handful of translators around, the people made gestures trying to indicate what they wanted healing for.

Nigel shared his way of ministering when there is no way to communicate English to Russian and vice versa. Step one: smile, nod your head, and look like you know what you are doing. Step two: pray loudly and with confidence, something like, "God, You know what is wrong with this person's health, so heal them now in the name of Jesus." Step three: rejoice as God comes and heals them. It was simple and effective.

This ministering/praying/healing cross culturally in a foreign language was a powerful and humbling lesson for the team. For example, they were praying for a kidney and somewhere during the prayer a translator would wander by them. The person they were praying for would look relieved and grateful and begin speaking very excited and briskly. The roving translator would overhear and stop to tell them, "He says thank you! He is very happy and wants you to know that his spine isn't hurting anymore. He has been in pain and waiting eight years for this!"

Those praying would think, "Spine? We were praying for his kidney—hey, Praise God. He's better now." They would shake their heads, look at the floor, chuckle, and go to the next person. The lesson: God does not need great minds and prophet-level insight to use a person. He just needs an obedient person emptied of any selfish agenda.

God showed His merciful power. He was there night after night. The surprises were nonstop. Mysteries unfolded before their eyes. They realized that God often doesn't do things by the book. They realized that they, the healing team, were virtually incidental in this whole ministry. They were not the reason why people were being healed. Their methods were trivial, though subconsciously or not they kept groping for the perfect method. It wasn't even their faith that was the pivotal matter in all these healings that were taking place. And there were hundreds and hundreds of healings going on! It came down to the fact that the people pressing to the front were 100 percent certain that if they were touched and prayed for, they would be healed. And so they were healed. The team felt like one of the "four friends in the Gospels" who was bringing people to the feet of Jesus and letting Him do what He does best; heal and save people.

The people on the healing team seemed to be getting touched, blessed, and changed as much as the people who were experiencing healing in their bodies. For many on the team, it was the most amazing moments of their lives. God answered their prayers. And He translated them too—especially when they were praying for the wrong part of bodies to be healed. They rarely knew what people were asking or needing to be healed. God knew and the Holy Spirit prayed through them and for them. About the most wonderful change for many of them was that they came away from each meeting more like Jesus and having His heart of compassion.

The nightly bus ride back to the hotel was pure joy. Team members sang, shared stories, and marveled at what God had done in the latest gathering. As the nights went by, more and more people filled the auditorium. They came to anticipate what was coming. Long before the invitation to come forward was announced, people began to stand, move out, and were waiting in the aisles. The level of faith and expectation in that place was so high, they could feel the presence of God. Drake experienced first hand what Luke had written about in his gospel, *"And the power of the Lord was present for him to heal the sick"* (5:17).

One cannot help but be amazed at spiritual gifts that are employed in such a powerful way. The speaker one night wore leather, a do-rag, and had a ponytail; he was a "biker." Drake didn't understand the regalia. And he didn't need to. One service, some "surfer" spoke. A lanky Englishman spoke at another.

Each one preached as powerfully as John the Baptist, who prepared the way for Jesus. One of the nights during preaching we heard of a young boy who was healed of Down's Syndrome a couple months prior at a crusade in Central America. The preacher continued, "Prior to this I had prayed for a thousand people with Down's and nothing had visibly changed. Then, surprise, this one is healed!" The child was spontaneously healed by Christ while sitting up in the stadium. No one even knew about it until the mother ran to the front shrieking with her healed boy to show what had just happened to her son.

It struck Drake again—who can explain the ways and timing of God? This is good to keep in mind as one is wondering if and when such blessing in ministry is going to grace *them* in their service. "Do not become weary in doing good, for at the proper time we will reap a harvest if we do not give up" (Gal. 6:9).

THE NIGHT BEFORE "THE FLOOD"

On Saturday, October 30, 2005, members of the team had been invited to speak in Kiev churches and around the region and were preparing to go. Drake volunteered to preach. The evening before, the FreshFire Team laid hands on Drake as had been done to thousands of others that month. He admitted he didn't remember what was said. He didn't remember where this happened. He didn't remember any details of the laying on of hands except regaining consciousness later. How much later, he did not know. Drake was on his back and looking up at the ceiling wondering where everyone was and how he got there. Was he slain in the Spirit? He honestly didn't know and wasn't concerned. It seemed a strange new step of faith. He didn't try to interpret anything or cover for himself. He just pondered it all.

What Drake took from this experience was that he was heading into very unknown territory and that his perceptions, thoughts and mind, and prior experiences were insufficient to deal with what was coming. Drake was to "let go." He was to forget about his skills, decades of theology training, his need to be directive in ministry; forget everything. He was to discard his agenda, persona, personal insecurities, notes, and surrender to God who would take over—just as soon as he yielded. Drake was sobered to perceive that this would be an adventure through new terrain in ministry. With holy fear Drake felt ready (for the first time) to surrender the steering wheel and get out of the Holy Spirit's way. Frankly he didn't know exactly what he was sensing but within twenty-four hours it all made much more sense. It was just as well that he did not know what lay ahead. The Holy Spirit was preparing to surprise and utterly astonish all of them.

THE FLOOD IS UNLEASHED

Then came Sunday morning, October 30, 2005, the final Sunday of the crusade. A Russian translator came by taxi to pick up Drake and the good chap Nigel Thomas from England. They drove out from Kiev and northeast through the Ukrainian countryside. In every sense of the word, Drake did not know where they were going. Something felt ominous as Nigel and Drake learned that they were almost close enough to see the ruined power plant Chernobyl. Were it not for one chapel between them and this place of the famed nuclear disaster, they *would* be in the closest church in the world to Chernobyl. It turns out they were at the second closest. They were not close enough to be in danger of radiation. But a different type of radiation *was* gathering force.

> The Holy Spirit was preparing to surprise and utterly astonish all of them.

They arrived and walked into their assigned church. It was a scene out of the early 1900s. If you have ever seen video footage of Russian life in a rural setting during the early 1900s you will know the scene. The clothing in this congregation was tattered and patched up. No smart suits or posh clothes. They looked like they were just in from the fields. Most wore thick, puffy coats. Many had the rabbit-fur hats. Women had the babushka headscarves. Many men were unshaven, and children had mussed hair. Most had dirty fingernails, all had beautiful eyes, and honestly when we walked in, love filled Drake's heart. The piano was out of tune and everyone literally sang their hearts out.

Drake's next sentiment was that he felt embarrassment about the state of many American churches. He was ashamed at how distracted many Christians, including himself, had become in the USA. Many churches and their leadership staff in America are obsessed with the bulletin, outfits/robes/clothing, lighting, parking, finances, appearances, breath-mints, legalism and/or liberalism, the facility, numbers, colors, seating patterns, timing, acoustics, ad nauseam. Drake inwardly confessed that he was not immune to these Americana-church concerns—petty concerns that have little or nothing to do with Jesus, His kingdom, missions, evangelism, the Holy Spirit, and/or the knowledge of the holy One.

So here they were at this church outside Kiev. They didn't recognize one song or one word as about fifty people sang like there was no tomorrow. Not only was the piano out of tune, it looked like it was used as a barricade during the war. Some of the people were tone deaf. God didn't care and neither did any of the Ukrainians. They were so crazy-in-love with Jesus. That was all that mattered to them. Drake and Nigel were humbled and on the verge of tears. Drake sat among these people wearing one of the finest suits money could buy (it was a gift) from one of the finest stores in the world. He thought, "God help me. They think I'm some great Christian evangelist/healer when it is they; these people here, who love You more than I do." Drake honestly felt about two inches tall.

First there was the music, next it sounded like announcements and church news of a sort, then Nigel's testimony. That occupied the first hour. Somewhere in there Nigel admitted that the reality hit him. They were on their own. There was no experienced evangelist in the background to cover for them if they faltered. They could not pass off the difficult cases. There was no one to come forward and share the prayer weight. They learned later that a whisper was sent around the local church that there would be two great healing evangelists coming that Sunday; one from London, one from America. That boosted their faith. Honestly, they were glad they didn't know of any expectations.

There were just the two of them, three if you count the interpreter, although she didn't look like she had much experience in praying for healing. No, it was just Drake and Nigel and if God didn't show up and cover this ordeal, it was going to be a long day! If they had known that the locals had dreams as big as a cathedral, they would have felt like church mice (only smaller!).

Nigel was up first and gave a short and simple talk for the children. It was all about trusting God even if we couldn't see Him. We can know that He really is there for us. Nigel said that if ever in his life there was an occasion when he needed to listen to his own talk, this was it! He was telling himself, "God is here even if we could not see Him."

A BUMPY SERMON

Drake was invited up during the second hour. The topic was "Get to Jesus" (do what needs to be done to get to Jesus). Push through the crowd, trek the road, burst in where there is no welcome, do the hunt, send a messenger on ahead, punch a hole in a roof, get your friends to lower you on ropes if you must, get to Jesus! It was all taken from stories in Luke where people had a part in their healing. Their faith needed to be displayed in order for Jesus to act on their behalf.

The message was translated line by line into Russian. Drake admitted he felt a bit off kilter; correction, he felt *very* off kilter. An interesting thing happened during the sermon that further eroded his self-confidence. He looked out and most of the congregation was shaking their heads. To an American it seemed like gestures of intense disapproval. He perceived them to be thinking, "Where'd this clown come from?" Drake ruminated in his discouragement, "Great, now they think I'm a loser." The next few minutes forced him to surrender the remainder of the service to the Holy Spirit as his eyes blurred. He literally could not read his notes or Bible. One-inch tall letters would have been too small!

They were coming to a spiritual vortex or something. Nigel confessed later that he didn't hear much of the talk. His attention had been drawn to a lady who was obviously blind—and he started to panic. Wonderful, huh? Two "great healing evangelists" had come from the Western world. One was having a panic attack and the other (who was the speaker that morning) was losing his mind. And he couldn't see either! Drake tried to remain calm and keep preaching. Nigel's mind was racing, "What if she came up for prayer? What would we pray? Oh dear." Both men didn't know that their faith was about to be transferred from the proverbial "little red wagon" and put into space shuttle mode.

Drake had not caught on to what God was up to yet. Trying to continue impromptu through the frustration, he got scrambled and began to pathetically mush stories together. It must have sounded something like, "After Noah's ark of the covenant rested in Bethlehem the animals came off. Then David parted the Red Sea so the whale couldn't take Jonah across the Jordan before Shadrach, Meshach, and Joshua returned from the Tabernacle to release the lions who were trying to eat Daniel's lunch of five loaves and two fish..." Yes, it was that bad—it was getting scary. Was his mind melting? Drake was becoming anxious in preaching. It had never felt that before. First they didn't like the message. Then he couldn't see. Now he couldn't think straight either. And Nigel was panicking too! What a skit.

Simply put, God did a wonderful job of unplugging both of them that day. Flabbergasted, Drake finished as quickly as possible and wrapped up what he thought was the most erratic and nonsensical sermon of his life.

Against protocol, Drake turned to the translator and asked how to the end the service. "Do we sing a song? Close with prayer? Do more announcements?" He felt like a total failure. It seemed the congregation thought Drake was a flunky and then when his eyes blurred (they are normally 20/15), it seemed God Himself was also telling Drake to give it up and sit down. He was experiencing "three strikes and you're out." Such utter discouragement! Drake wanted to crawl out a gopher's tunnel, if he could just find one. Really, he badly wanted to disappear. It was the first time he had ever felt that way in forty years of public speaking.

> Little did the men know that though the service had gone past two hours, it was not nearly half completed.

In the middle of his trying to figure out how to leave the premises before people started throwing potatoes, the translator gently requested, "I think people would like you to pray for them specifically; for healing of their illnesses."

"Uh, me? Uh, wha—I beg your pardon!" Drake confessed that his sentiment was pure defeat. Then Drake fatalistically thought, "Why not? I've crashed everything else." In truth, God was decreasing him. And He had done a thorough job of it. Just the same, Drake agreed to pray for a few. So the translator explained that it was going to be a healing service now.

Nigel recalled that it was now time for action. No more talk. The people lined up politely and waited for the men to start praying for them. It was all very reserved; unlike the second night of both crusades and every night thereafter wherein people knew what was coming next. At that moment there seemed to be not great level of faith—yet. They seemed to be holding back and waiting to see what kind of ministry they would now be delivered before committing themselves to being prayed for. Nigel "shot up a prayer" like an arrow asking God to give them something easy to start with.

Little did the men know that though the service had gone past two hours, it was not *nearly* half completed. The first two hours were what one might call "doing church." The next three hours was going to be New Testament turbo. But not knowing this left Drake quite dejected and Nigel a tad spooked.

Drake did not know that according to local culture, the shaking of their heads (during the message) implied amazement. The people later told them that the general feeling during the sermon was appreciation. They were fascinated with a strong feeling of motivation to "get to Jesus." They knew they needed to get to Jesus, but weren't sure how to.

Drake had completely misread them shaking their heads. When Americans agree with anyone who is talking, they nod up and down. When Americans disagree, they shake their heads left and right. So Drake thought they disagreed with him, and wanted him to know they disagreed by shaking their heads. He was wrong. But think about it, Americans do the same gesture although Drake had forgotten this cultural subtlety. When Americans share something truly amazing with a friend, show off a shiny waxed car, share a new tech-gadget, sample a fantastic meal, we whistle slowly "whooo-whoo," take a step back, and shake our heads in agreement and approval. Yes, do we not?

These Ukrainians were *more* than agreeing. They were touched in the heart and motivated to emulate the Scriptures and do so today. They wanted to get to Jesus!

It is interesting that the Holy Spirit was intent on keeping both men very dependent and drained of any self-confidence. There Drake was *thinking* these dear Ukrainians were wishing the men would hurry up and leave the building. Drake couldn't blame them either. The message was bumpy as an old dirt road. Then again the translator probably cleaned it up. Who knows?

TREMBLING BEFORE THE FLOOD

However they came to this point, the healing ministry time began. And Drake felt out of it and weak at best. The quandary immediately deepened as the first person carried forward for healing was a woman over seventy years old. She was placed in a chair because she was lame. The pain in her legs and feet was so intense she hadn't walked in ten years or so. Drake's stomach dropped and Nigel felt about the same. They wanted to disappear through the floor. Drake moaned to himself, "God, can't we start with a migraine or sore elbow or something minor? I've already blown the message, now I'm going to be remembered as the Kiev cuckoo; Russia's false prophet, the new Rasputin of the third millennium." Audible words can hardly describe how alarmed he felt.

> The Holy Spirit was intent on keeping both men very dependent and drained of any self-confidence.

"God, get me out of here!" Nigel's feelings were equally hoping for an easier start, but as he said, "no such luck."

Nonetheless, they proceeded cringing as if ministry were bad medicine. Drake felt like an empty suit. He stalled with one last pathetic question, "God, do you want me to pray for her?"

"Yes, start, now!" God bellowed in his soul. It felt like they were being ordered to walk an invisible balance beam across the Grand Canyon, and to start immediately. "God, don't do this to me. Surely, we can start out small?" Drake paused again. Though challenged, he felt anguish, even ashamed. He had waited for this moment all his life, here it was, and he seemed to be turning into a quivering hamster that had been dipped in ice water. What a pathetic scenario!

Despite all the fears, they could remember what they had been taught the prior week to not pray as if begging favors of a God who was a million miles away. And not even to pray as if He were *next* to them waiting and wishing they would get it right, or hoping they would say or guess the right words. No. God is *in* us; speaking through us. God "unit-verse" or "single-speaks" things to be. Thus we call the universe, the "uni-verse!" That is what it is because that is what God did. A single phrase was spoken and there it was. He spoke it about. So Drake and Nigel were pressed in training to do the same. Since God speaks in, speaks to, and speaks through us, speak for God. Say His words. Don't speak *about* things—speak things about. Don't drone on wishing and pleading like a dejected salesman peddling worthless trinkets. Never. They were to speak creatively and with authority.

Authority has been imparted to us to create new life in people because the Spirit of Jesus works within us. Jesus told His disciples that all authority in heaven and on earth was given to Him (Matt. 28:18). And then He gave His disciples orders to go, do and teach all He had commanded. Among all this "going" there would be healing. He didn't say, "Go, and ask Me to heal." He ordered us to do it. We are to cut any false piety and to minister to people with all our hearts wholly dedicated to Jesus and surrendered to doing things His way.

"Hmm, great," Drake thought sarcastically. But there was this lame woman before them plus several dozen other people who couldn't speak a word of English. All were in pain, they wanted answers and relief. And they wanted it right away. Drake hesitated momentarily and the Holy Spirit again hammered His bell, "Now is the time—start! Are you going to work with Me and for Me or not?" It sounded like God's final offer, and it was loud and clear. Then Drake breathed out what he knew he needed. "God, go with me. God, guide me please. If I am going to look like a fool today, cover me and be a fool with me!" That was it. And he crouched down to heal this old woman's feet.

THE LAME WOMAN

The instant Drake said, "God, guide me please," a ray of confidence in the Holy Spirit came over his soul like a light beam of ten million watts. He took off her shoes and wrested his hands on her ankles and moved them for her. They felt and sounded like gravel and nails grinding in a Christmas stocking. She immediately cried out in pain for Drake to stop. Undaunted, the men heard the reminder, "Nothing is impossible with God." Drake felt as assured of his calling and placement there that day as a referee presiding over a sporting event. The prior hours served as proof that it wasn't Nigel and Drake acting in self-confidence so all was well. The men were cleared to proceed. Nigel prayed with all the fervor he could sum up in the Spirit.

Knowing God was with them, Drake spoke new life into her ankles, shins, and knees. They declared words of new creation, regeneration while working her shins as if to be warming and softening up clay. They were glad no one in the room spoke English as Drake prayed, "God, if mechanics know how to install new brakes and shocks, then you know how to install new ankles." So Drake called down for new ankles to be "installed" for this woman. Drake paused momentarily, stunned at what he had just said. "Does this really happen?" he mused. Drake looked away at the floor in embarrassment. He had been talking to her feet as if they had been her ears! He said it without thinking. Was he going nuts here? It seemed Drake would be run out of town and labeled a vodka-headed fruitcake. Remember, no one had been healed yet! Maybe they did bring in a charlatan that day? What was going on? What were they saying? Just then they chuckled to remember that no one in the room spoke English except the translator. So forward they went into uncharted territory, praying fervently.

> Jesus didn't say, "Go, and ask Me to heal."
> He ordered us to heal.

A couple of minutes later, Drake rose and placed his hands on her knees. Crouched like a baseball infielder, he looked her in the eye and flatly declared, "Jesus says it is time to rise and walk." That was his version of Acts 3:6–7. People crowded in to see what would happen. By then all doubt from the prior hours had evaporated. There was no question as to what would happen next. She looked into their eyes, then at the ceiling, then at her feet. Her face gestured, "Okay, God, here goes." She leaned forward in her chair, pushed down on the armrests, and rose to her feet. The bustling room fell silent. People gasped as she began to take baby steps toward the podium. She climbed the stairs up onto the podium and walked across the front of the church. She was stunned, as a deer in the headlights. She was walking for the first time in ten years and in no pain! She slowly began to grin and praised God. The young school children especially had *never* seen this woman walk before. Holy smoke! God was in the room and had gone to work!

She wasn't the only one praising God! God in His mysterious way knew exactly what He was doing. The sight of that old lady, lame for years, up and walking around took the level of faith in that room up several notches (Drake and Nigel included). God was in the building, there was no doubt. The people were getting excited about being prayed for, and Drake and Nigel were excited at the opportunity to pray with them for healing power to fall on all.

For a split second Drake and Nigel wanted to pause, marvel, and share in the delight about this first lady in line who was brought to church lame and now walking. But many others had pressed in to be healed. There were dozens of others wanting the same touch of the Almighty. Drake nearly swooned and looked at his palms. "God? You? Me? Why are you using me?!" Just then a delighted and yet urgent sentiment akin to, "Can I be next?" flooded through the room. The entire congregation pressed toward the center, toward the empty chair from which this woman had just arisen.

LAMENESS AND PARALYSIS

Nigel and Drake looked at each other with anticipation. The next lady in line was upper 70s in age. She too was lame but also paralyzed on her right side from a stroke. Their minds raced a moment but then the same words shot through them again, "Nothing is impossible with God." Their hearts thumped so hard Drake could feel it in his throat as they went straight to her. They were wholehearted and eager to see God bless another. Their eyes blazed with full confidence that God was not going to let up now. Though they could not verbally communicate with this dear grandmother, their eyes told her point blank, "And you are going to be the next one on your feet."

Before Nigel and Drake began with her, she explained about being captured by Nazis at the beginning of "the war." Most of her village was executed at point blank range along with six of her relatives. She was forced to watch her father dig a grave *for her*! Just when something seized the attention of the guards she escaped into the woods with her parents. They hid in the forest for six months. She recalls no food or water and no way to bathe during this half year of hiding. She confessed that she had spent the next sixty-five years hating the Nazis. The hatred did not subside with the years like she thought it might. As decades passed, pain, arthritis, and paralysis crept over her body. She hadn't walked in more than fifteen years. She still hated the Nazis. She wasn't a Christian. She didn't know Jesus. She admitted that her hatred about murdered family and terror during World War II had consumed her for sixty-five long years. She couldn't break this obsession. Then several years ago the stroke hit and paralyzed her right side. As her misfortune deepened and her mobility had ceased, she was sinking into despair.

When they asked how she got to church that day, she said that she had been carried in that morning. Imagine this woman, near eighty, not a Christian and being brought to church by others who carried her there. It was just like in Luke chapter five. But there had been no advertising of a healing service (so they thought). God had orchestrated all this! They didn't know she had prayed and received Christ in her life that morning *during* the service. Drake wondered, "How did she get blessed through such a choppy sermon?" Drake would have gotten a C-, maybe a D+ in preaching class for that "dud-bomb" message! She snapped them back to reality when she said that getting to Jesus was what she wanted. She told of feeling warm all over after forgiving the Nazis who had tormented her sixty-five years prior. She spoke of a tingling sensation that had come over her body. Even the right side of her body that was deadened by the stroke felt the new sensation. Then she looked us straight in the eye and insisted, "If God can touch me and make me feel this way, then He can make me walk again." She pointed to the seventy-year-old woman pacing the front and finished, "I want to walk like her."

"No problem," Drake muttered with soft confidence. What was he saying? Was it even him talking?

The first woman healed was still walking in an oval pattern up on the platform as they lowered to knee height and touched this brave woman's right shoulder and elbow, her right side, knees and feet. Drake spoke for the reversal of her stroke, paralysis and pain; they declared those things to be over with—and they were. Drake felt like a herald in praying, "God, you preserved this woman during the war, brought her through the darkness, sustained her, redeemed her life from the pit, you've touched her body, it's time she was fully restored and came to her feet to walk anew with you." They rose, took her hands and summoned her to rise. She stood to her feet, handed her cane to a grandson, and calmly told him, "Here, I'm done with this."

People were wide-eyed as they watched this paralyzed woman, who did not know God when she was carried into church that morning walking out without aid. She walked all the way home with her new Savior, strengthened, healed, and joyfully venturing into a whole new life and a whole new eternity!

A HEART IS HEALED

As they made their way down the line of people, Nigel was drawn to one lady in particular. It did become evident that some of them were there for healing; others just wanted them to lay hands on them and pray for them. That one particular woman was especially uncomfortable with her appearance; clothing and all. Nigel could tell that this woman did not have access to functional bathing facilities. As Nigel approached, he heard God say that she just needed to know that she was loved. Standing in front of her he knew what he had to do. It wasn't prayer that she needed. She needed to be hugged. So he hugged her and held her.

He looked her in the eye and flatly declared, "Jesus says it is time to rise and walk."

There was no immediate response, so Nigel kept on hugging her. Seconds turned into minutes but he would not let go until he knew she had felt God's love for her. Finally she put her arms around Nigel in return. As she was hugging Nigel back, she broke down in tears. At that moment he knew that God had touched her heart. It wasn't a physical healing she received, but a healing of the heart. What can be more wonderful than someone knowing—truly knowing—that they are loved and accepted by God in every way! Nigel shared that of all the healings that day, none was more precious than that one.

DEAFNESS

Then a ninety-one-year-old woman came forward. The translator told the men she was 95 percent deaf. By then the men were feeling like kids at a carnival who had a pile of tickets to cash in on the rides. God in all His power was definitely present like is described in Luke 5:17. God had begun moving through His people, doing what only He can do. It was a rich atmosphere. Nigel and Drake marveled at what was happening right in front of them. They were in Christ Jesus, walking in intense obedience with His Spirit. God was getting all the glory. Again, Drake clearly remembered how pathetic he was during the sermon earlier so he knew it wasn't his own "power" at work.

People in line were filled with faith and hope—and time was not an issue. The Spirit was very much present and virtually everyone was staying to witness Jesus' healing Spirit touch His children. And He was using these two young chaps in odd clothes who couldn't speak Russian. Figure that one out!

When they learned that the next person had trouble hearing, Drake tagged Nigel as if to say, "You're it." They had both remembered that Nigel had that marvelous experience the week before in Dudley, England, with the utterly deaf person. Nigel had prayed for this woman who had no medical chance of hearing and then she could hear. This boost of faith from the week before emboldened Nigel, especially in view of who they were to minister to next.

And they both clearly remembered it. With this in mind, Drake grinned and with relieved assurance smacked Nigel on the back and said, "Nigel, you're the 'ear-man,' take the lead on this one."

They both laid hands on her while Nigel prayed. She was a dear old gem with work-worn hands. She was still laboring at an orphanage nearly thirty years beyond what a Westerner would call retirement age. She just wanted to hear again and their hearts went out to her. They prayed on. Drake prayed a bit then Nigel prayed some more. She still couldn't hear. At first it seemed like "two out of three isn't bad." They hadn't failed; they just didn't know why she couldn't hear yet. They weren't troubled—they just didn't know what to make of it. Many were pressing to the front. So Drake thought maybe they could "put this lady on the back burner and let her cook on low" so to speak. They were just guessing what to do next. It became one of the most memorable healings of Nigel's life but there was more perseverance to be employed before breakthrough hit.

After ten to fifteen minutes, it felt about time for Drake to move on to another who was suffering. He mentioned, "Nigel, you keep after this ear patient while I go start on the next person."

Nigel agreed to persist with the ear. Talk about praying with all his heart. Nigel put his heart into this one in a huge way. He prayed every prayer he knew. He spoke to the deafness. He commanded the ears to open. He cast out every spirit he could think of. All seemed to no avail. Nigel grew desperate to see her healed. Meanwhile Drake approached the next woman in line.

MORE LAMENESS IS HEALED

Imagine it. Up next was another lame person; a senior citizen who hadn't walked in so long that no one could remember or say the number of years since she had been on her feet. Drake proceeded to pray solo for her while Nigel kept ministering to the woman who couldn't hear. Without much ado or time-lapse this elderly soul that Drake was praying for was on her feet and people were marveling. God was raising many that day. There seemed to be no let up in sight.

Meanwhile the first woman healed was still pacing the stage. This was her first exercise in more than ten years and she was becoming fatigued. She cut in loudly, "May I sit down now and rest? I am getting tired." Most of the room chuckled, taking pleasure in her new problem of needing rest. Friends gave her a hand as she stepped off the stage and sat with her family. What a day this was turning out to be! It was so easy to rejoice and be glad in it.

HEARTACHE AND HEART TROUBLE

To the front came a sheepish fifteen-year-old girl. Something was wrong, but Drake couldn't tell at first what it was. She told what her pain and distress was but he inquired for more. Drake perceived in his spirit that there was something deeper going on. Her problems seemed spiritually rooted, not genetic or physical or even biotic. She hunched terribly, especially for a young girl. Drake forgot how the following news came to him, probably just because it came by revelation. He was told none of the following by the translator.

This teenage girl was abandoned as a two year old. The alcoholic father had cut out and disappeared thirteen years prior. Her mother did what she could and persevered admirably, but still the girl was besieged by heartache and feeling abandoned. The heartache was so bad that it was becoming diagnosable heart trouble. In addition, her spine was very bent over. Her posture gave her the stature of someone very old, with acute back trouble and with one year to live. Though the lumbar of her spine was vertical, the top third of her spine was nearly horizontal. The girl spoke Russian and no translator relayed this to Drake.

Again, they were in a room of people who did not know a word of English. There was no cardiologist and no orthopedic specialist to say exactly what was going on. The truth was that there were multiple things that were very wrong. So it was time to take this young woman to the throne where Christ knows what to do. Christ loves and understands, and He is very able to heal her. That was Drake's diagnosis.

With confidence that would stun a medical student and have him labeled as reckless, Drake walked behind her and did a couple manipulations of her spine. After ten seconds and *"click, click, click, thump, wham,"* she stood up straight and exclaimed something in Russian. The translator squealed in delight and quoted her that she was feeling much better. The young girl asked Drake via the translator what he had done to make her back straight and take the pain away. He had no human answer and it was probably better that way—God could do His work all day with no distraction. But Drake did shrug for her and raise his palms to say with eyes wide open, "You got me...what happened?!" She did get the message that it was God at work. Drake was simply an English-speaking American who was trying to cooperate and not get in the way of the Spirit.

The young girl's heartache was still with her though her back had straightened up. So Drake placed a hand between her shoulder blades and put a second one at the base of her neck where the collarbones meet. Praying words of a loving father (Drake has many children of his own and wants all of them well), he called for God her Father to receive her heart and touch her heartache, then declared that it would be done, and that her heart was in fact being restored. Psalms 27:9–11 came out of his mouth without even thinking. It seemed the Holy Spirit was flying him like a remote-control airplane.

For most of those hours praying with Nigel for those folks, Drake was *hearing* words come from his own mouth. His mind was being bypassed. Many of the prayers said that day, Drake had never heard himself pray like that before. His prayers were not prior thoughts. They were news to him as well as everyone else in the room. The interpreter translated as she saw fit.

About then Drake could see a hazy vision of a shrink-wrapped heart being squeezed and having trouble beating. Then what looked like unyielding "cellophane" was gently cut away and discarded by a mystical hand of surgery with gloves and scalpel; Drake could see it. Opening his eyes again, he looked and the girl was taking deeper breaths. Relaxation, relief, and color came over her face. She broke into a grin and said that the pain was gone. She wanted to know something from him but the translator told her that there were others who needed healing and that he needed to move on. She asked again, "What did you do?" as she slowly moved her arms. She was flapping like a bird in slow motion. She hadn't moved like that in a long time and was doing a careful test. Again, she asked Drake, "What did you do?" All he could say was, "God bless you, dear. I don't know what I did. God did it and you're better."

HEARING RESTORED

Back in the middle of the room, Nigel was still with the deaf woman and had refused to give up on her. The compassion of God was so strong it gripped his heart. He just had to keep going. When his best prayers had dried up, he cried out to God with everything he had, begging God to come and heal. Then her miracle arrived without warning. Her hearing returned and a shout of victory arose. The woman, who was ninety-one and deaf, could hear again! God opened her ears and she could hear perfectly! Her healing took twenty minutes instead of three minutes. It was a good thing that Nigel had felt bold and experienced enough to see this woman through to have her hearing restored.

This miracle was a wrestling match and the answered prayer lifted spirits like no other event that day. The room was filled with shouting and Nigel was dancing and praising God (this is an Englishman here!). Nigel could have prayed for anyone and anything, he was so confident after this. If there were a handful of Lazarus situations brought through, Nigel might have raised them all. The spirit was that jubilant in the room. Jesus' compassion had touched down in the room. It was affecting the men and people were getting healed.

VARICOSE VEINS

Drake was directed to the next person amid the cheering. He was a man about sixty. He pointed to his legs, said something in Russian, and pulled the left leg up on his pants. On his left calf was the most horrible case of varicose veins. Not really knowing what varicose veins were, nor what was wrong, how they got that way, nor what to do about it, Drake was again beyond his mind pondering the remedy.

Without a single thought Drake pointed to the floor and told him to get on his back and put his leg in the air. What was his hunch? What was his cue or clue? What was Drake's plan? He didn't have one! So he dropped to one knee like a home-base umpire and held the man's leg in a similar fashion that a string musician holds the neck of a cello with his left hand, forearm and wrist.

Drake erupted into fervent prayer. "God, You made this man to walk with You," he began. "You made him to walk in Your will and in newness of life, to walk the straight and narrow according to Your Word. Now this will all seem more real to Him as his leg is healed and the circulation is normalized."

Drake spoke that the veins shall be pulled straight again. Somewhere in there he did it again; he started talking to the leg (oh dear!). Drake spoke to the veins and told them to stop straying and cooperate again. Good grief! Thank God that none of them spoke English! Frankly, he felt that with his words and gestures, he was a student in an art class pulling on strips of material and laying them in a straight line. The day was turning into the craziest adventure they had ever been on.

The man looked up at Drake with a confidence in his eye that whispered, "Thank you, brother, I am glad you know what to do." Drake tried not to laugh because it felt like he was zooming down the road with an iced-over windshield, begging God to keep steering for him. All day long he and Nigel never knew what the next minute was going to hold. Often the next five seconds wasn't even clear to them. The phenomenon continued. Many of the words spoken, Drake heard himself say *before* he was conscious of what was being said. It was definitely a different level of ministry than Drake had ever surfed through before.

The prayer ended as Drake clapped his leg with two hands and snapped an "amen." Now it was time to see what God had done. Drake pulled the pant leg back from the man's calf a mere three minutes after he pointed and told him to get on the floor. The huge purple veins were gone! His calf looked as normal and healthy as a college age track runner. The man gasped. He was as stunned as the onlookers. He sprung off the floor as if it had turned into a hot griddle. He looked at his leg, then at Drake, at his leg, at Drake again. The man couldn't stop the tears. He was beyond joyful. He hugged Drake again and again. He hollered and motioned for his family to come over.

In Russian-speaking culture it is customary to greet others with three kisses; right cheek/left cheek/right cheek to signify and bless them in the name of the Father, the Son, and the Holy Spirit. Even during the seventy-year Soviet era, people kept greeting in this manner, though they had forgotten its origin.

Well, three kisses weren't enough gratitude for this man and his family. Drake received the Russian triple-shot. He smacked Drake on both sides three times and kept going. He kept crying and kept hugging him. His wife wept. His children and relatives jumped up and down while the younger ones tugged on his coat and shirt saying, "Thank you, thank you, thank you (*spaSEEba*)!" They were so grateful. "Hey, it was no problem!" Drake thought.

SHOULDER PAIN

Another couple who had a need was in the front. The husband motioned them over while pointing at his wife's upper arm. Her shoulder was so damaged that it was all she could do to raise her arm to level. The grimace on her face radiated excruciating pain. Completely unintimidated, Drake and Nigel figured it was time to end her agony. Not once did they halt and ponder, "Gee. I hope God can handle this one. Maybe this one's too difficult. What if it doesn't work this time?" No way!

By now they had long realized that words and the communication Drake especially was so accustomed to employing in life was a moot issue. They didn't need to decipher any medical history or symptoms, just call on God.

Prayer came to them again like electricity comes to a bulb when the switch is thrown on. Drake admitted that all his life prayer had been an effort-filled scramble to find the right words. But there he was feeling like a volcano of intercession. Prayer flowed out like lava from the center of the earth; without any thought or mental effort. All day they heard themselves say words and prayers of "arms," "the arm of the Lord," "bones," "renewed joints and tendons," "new heart," "spine," "to hear again"—the prayers simply came over them and were spoken. For flash moments, Drake felt beside himself watching it all happen. It seemed surreal. Periodically Drake checked his hands to see if it was indeed *his* hands that were touching these people. Somewhere Nigel exclaimed in his thick English accent, "The Holy Spirit's reeally doooing things here today!" It was a good moment to pause and laugh.

The "amen" at the end of praying with this couple led Drake and Nigel to demonstrate and move their own arms in a circular motion; doing "windmills" if you will. Their eyes invited her to try the same with her arm. As she waved her arm like a pendulum on a grandfather clock her eyes popped wide open in astonishment. Her shoulder pain was gone. Then she got bold and began spinning big circles with her arm. She looked like a referee at a football game signifying "start the clock."

Everyone all marveled again. But why wouldn't God be able to repair, renew and restore what He has made? It's not just His ability. It's the tidal wave of love that flows from His heart. That's what they were seeing all afternoon.

BARRENNESS

They spent over three hours ministering to those wonderful people *after* the scheduled church service had ended. But it felt like thirty minutes because there was so much of the presence of God in the room. However there was still more blessing to come. Drake was with their interpreter ministering to another man, when Nigel arrived at the final person in line. She signaled that she just wanted to be prayed with, so Nigel began. As he was praying for her,

God gave Nigel a picture of two young boys playing in the garden. Nigel then shifted to praying for her boys.

The woman had been quietly standing there receiving prayer. But the moment he began to pray for these boys, she suddenly started crying out. God was clearly up to something. Nigel kept praying while she kept shouting and after a few moments the pastor and the interpreter came over to find out what was going on. The interpreter spoke to the woman who told her that the Holy Spirit was moving in her causing her to spontaneously cry out.

The interpreter turned to Nigel and asked what he had been praying for. He told her that everything had been fine and calm until he started praying for her two boys. (Remember he is praying in English with a woman who speaks Russian and cannot understand prayers in English. Nigel and this woman were not able to communicate in typical manner.) At this point the pastor, who understood minimal English, looked amazed and told Nigel that the lady didn't have any children. She and her husband had been trying for many years but she was barren. Now Nigel was amazed and then "the penny dropped" (it all made sense). She didn't speak any English and had no idea what Nigel was praying and yet as soon as he prayed for "the boys," God started moving. Nigel was able to encourage her that God had heard her prayers and that she wouldn't be barren for much longer. Two healthy boys were on their way!

ARTHRITIS

There were many who were healed of many things that day. What they remember as the last miracle was an elderly couple who simply wanted alleviation of the arthritis in the woman's fingers. Drake took her hands and made the same motion a cook does when making hamburger patties; press, squeeze, rotate slightly, press, squeeze, rotate, and so forth. Drake spoke for God to send His rest and peace to her joints, to break up the calcium/mineral deposits, or whatever arthritis is.

Her hands didn't *look* different when they had finished. Still she exhaled long and slow and offered that she had greatly relaxed while they prayed. Her hands did move more freely. The stiffness and pain had softened markedly.

There was one person however who was not healed that day. He was a blind boy. He seemed to be ten-years-old at the most. At some point early in the healing time they noticed him near the exit door. Drake saw him for just a few seconds. It impressed them that he was being coddled, almost shielded in a sense, by his mother. They were clearly outside the group that was pressing forward to have their lives changed by the Holy Spirit.

During the first hour of the healing session, it crossed their minds to wave them over; to come get in line. The boy would obviously need to be led forward by his mother. But the gripping electricity during the healing time was so powerful, the urgency for each person to be the next in line overrode any thoughts they had of this blind boy whom by now no one could find.

A couple of hours later Drake remembered these two; the blind boy and his mother. They inquired as to where they had gone. Did they leave? Did they not know that Jesus was moving among the people today? How could they have left in the middle of what was happening? The translator explained that they had slipped out during the first hour of ministry time. They were told that the mother usually grabs her son and leaves as quickly as possible most Sundays. Nigel and Drake were chagrined. They knew the verses wherein time and again "Jesus healed them all." They knew Jesus had not singled out this boy for quarantine against being healed. Jesus had not agreed to touch everyone *except* him. How could this have happened? Where did he go? If they were running a spiritual hospital today and God was there in power, who told these folks that God was healing everything except eyes? They were really bothered by what still seemed like an oversight on their part.

They were frustrated when they realized that the mother had taken this boy away from the event before they could pray for him. As Drake and Nigel were discussing this, the translator explained that this woman *did not want* her son to be healed. They were incredulous. They were told that if there were any parallels between the Gospels and this setting today here outside Kiev, that this woman saw her situation as the man by the Pool of Bethesda saw his (John 5:1–9). Remember the man who sat by a healing pool for 38 years. Jesus asked him if wanted to get well. Jesus asked him that because the man didn't want to get well and didn't want to reckon with his subconscious desire to keep sitting there forever.

The locals assured Drake and Nigel that this woman's refusal to have her son healed was her choosing. It was not their error or oversight. She was careful to slip out of the church when Nigel and Drake were not looking. She did not want her son healed, and she did not want to be asked to have her son healed. That would have "pulled back the veil" on her agenda and forced her to submit to healing in her family. Or it would have forced her to openly reject the offer of healing in front of her friends in the church and community. Each was an unacceptable option to her and so she disappeared quietly. Last, the people explained that if her son was healed, he would have had to amp up, so to speak, and become functional in the community and she would lose her leverage for sympathy among friends. The current unfortunate scenario was apparently more important to her than dynamically encountering the Lord and consequently doing her part in the neighborhood and in her church.

With that explanation clearly laid forth, Nigel and Drake realized it was too late to do anything different. They'd missed their "window" with this young blind boy and it was no fault of theirs or God's. The mother didn't want him to see, so she spirited him away before the Holy Spirit could change the lives of both of them. They could but sigh and groan at this regrettable revelation.

There came a moment of stillness and calm. What at first seemed like a tremendous fatigue coming over them when they sat down for a moment, clearly became the Spirit telling Nigel and Drake to rest now. It had been five hours since they first walked into that church. The clear orders to get started hours ago came to a crisp halt. "That's all for now," fell on Drake's ears like a whisper.

The remaining elders and members in the church honored them beyond what they had envisioned. They had an envelope; a gift to present to them. They asked them to sit in the front row. Kneeling directly in front of them, the leader placed their gift on the floor and announced, "We lay this at the apostles' feet."

Drake and Nigel both were overwhelmed and greatly humbled. What the people gave them would have cost a local worker over two month's wages. They discussed as quickly and as quietly as possible how to handle this gift. "Good heavens, we can't take this," Nigel insisted quietly. "We have to give this back," Drake agreed, also speaking softly. They pleaded with the translator for some guidance. It was embarrassing. They didn't come here to "take the money and run."

Their interpreter came close to their faces and said, "Let them thank you. There are numerous people here today who have been given their lives back. Their pain is gone. Many can move, hear, feel, and are free to live again from what you have shared. You *must* receive their gratitude."

So they graciously accepted and thanked those who were still there. Later that day they gave this offering to an evangelist who was heading into Uganda to work at a crusade; preaching to the masses and ministering to orphans.

Nigel reflected, "What can I say in summary? Those ten days of healing and crusades took me beyond my understanding of healing and into God's heart of compassion. It wasn't about practicing ways of healing but discovering how to connect with the One who heals. Drake came home with some great stories of healing, but so much more than that. God changed his life. He learned that the opportunity of healing comes for God to heal us, not just the people He heals through us."

The next day was Monday, October 31, 2005. On the flight from Kiev, Ukraine, to Holland to Chicago to New York, the team was reminiscing about all that God had done those last two weeks. One gentleman shared from an email on his computer about a crusade in India that prior week where millions had been in attendance. They talked about the new churches that were springing up in China, Nepal, Iraq, and all over the Andes Mountains. They remembered about how the missionaries in Brazil were pulling out because the locals were getting the job done themselves. Symbolically speaking, there is no longer any need to hold a match under a log that is burning on its own, is there? God is cracking open countries that have been closed to the gospel for centuries. Countless people throughout Muslim lands are having dreams about crosses, Jesus, and salvation—a salvation that does not exist in Islam.

CLOSING THOUGHTS

Some are having visions about a massive thrust of revival, healing, and evangelism in the last days; healing that will flow from a prominent city located at a great crossroad in Eurasia, where East and West meet and a river running through that city is the demarcation line between East and West, in a city named "Kiev." I [Drake] am not one to despise prophetic utterances. What I do know is that what I saw that week will stick with me and inspire me for life.

Yes, we truly are involved in a vast and gigantic enterprise. And it is mere obedience to launch in the Holy Spirit, traverse the world, spread the name of Christ Jesus, and do all that He has commanded us to do. And we are to teach others to do the same. As we headed home each member on our team marveled to ponder where God would take us next.

We hope these testimonies strike you the same way they did us while we were experiencing them live. For all of us are to be involved in God's work: the advancing of the kingdom of God, spreading the name of Jesus, and doing so through the power of the Holy Spirit. Remember Jesus told us that in order to receive the Holy Spirit, just ask Him. He is altogether eager to give.

eight

WHERE to NOW? WHERE to NEXT?

THERE ARE AMPLE Bible stories and teachings about healing from the Bible authors, plus a tremendous number of modern-day testimonies of healing. There is enough verification to convince any honest man that divine healing is a current reality. One author who was finishing a book on healing a couple years ago was challenged to decide and choose *which* healings to include in his new book. He had received so many healing stories that he was inundated with testimonies; all notarized by witnesses and verified to be authentic. The testimonies from people who offered their stories were so plentiful that it became a stack of paper two feet high, and it was still growing after he chose which healings to publish! This is just one writer. Books for sale today on healing are too numerous to count. Healings are happening worldwide to millions each week. People are being blessed and saved and God is doing it. And He invites us to join in His labors.

MOVE PAST DISCOURAGEMENT

Still there are many who are discouraged. Some have abandoned praying for the sick. Others claim they have been going to prayer meetings for years, decades, a lifetime. Every week they are praying for a "laundry list" of ill people. They keep praying for the sick in this manner because they know that...well, they know that they *should*. Pastors tell me it feels more like an exercise in willpower to pray for these ill people on their list than it is the flexing of their faith. And over the years these weekly prayer meetings have turned monotonous—they all sound and feel the same with no surprises. They are kind of like school cafeteria food in the 1950s. Millions of people personally believe in healing, but claim they have never seen it. This is usually confessed with weary disenchantment.

Be not dismayed. There is more that God wants to show us as soon as each of us is ready. Who but God knows, we may be just one last item or issue away from overcoming, one more prayer of faith, one more bold step away from the breakthrough that will vault us into a whole new ministry of healing and restoration.

PRESS FORWARD IN BOLDNESS

To move to higher ground in healing ministry, we must lay out some final principles on how and why we are to do like Jesus and heal the sick. My objective is to encourage each one to keep believing, to press forward in faith until we are thinking about divine healing the way God sees this ministry. To proceed in divine healing, it is also in order to list our own apprehensions about fearlessly praying for the sick. Basically it is time to name these fears, lay them at Calvary in prayer, call them over and done with, and walk away from them. There is a whole Bible full of reasons to be healing, plus a world full of reasons to start healing. There is a world full of struggling souls. That alone, with Christ's command, is enough motivation to respond to God's calling to heal and save. One missionary friend tells me from Africa, "Drake, there are miracles just waiting to happen, waiting to be prayed to life all over this land. They are here for the taking. Just come and minister in the middle of it all. God is going to give these lands and tribes to whomever shows up and asks of Him." Americans like to walk down aisles in shops and stores and pick out things. My friend says we could be walking through villages and handing out miracles. That's a switch, isn't it?

HEALING MINISTRIES TODAY

It is obvious, even to those who doubt, that healings happen as God moves. Healings happen today and they are happening in a big way. Anyone who denies that miraculous healings happen today lives in the bleak and grim stupor of willful ignorance. There is no other explanation for such unbelief. The people I encounter who have healing ministries simply share that they

asked and God gave. I do not see a hint of arrogance in their spirits or personalities. Their attitude is so humble, and it is inspiring. They asked and God
gave and that is about it. Bill Johnson in Redding, California, is very transparent to testify that God just answered his desperate request as he prayed for
more of Himself. He asserts that God hides His blessings, gifts, and healings
for us not *from* us. He and his leaders and congregation see hundreds and
hundreds of healings each week.

Randy Clark was simply preaching in Canada and God arrived dynamically. The few meetings he was scheduled to minister at ended up going on
for several weeks as the Lord came down in power. The training in healing
he offers is a marvel. The truth is that God can do whatever He wants with
whomever He wants, when He wants. The late Smith Wigglesworth was
twenty one years old when his wife taught him to read. After reading his Bible
for twenty-six years, the Holy Spirit filled him dynamically. Then for decades
he shook hearts, the church, and souls the world over.

See more about these people and many others in *Recommended Reading*
in the back of this book. I highlight the above because I have met some of
them, witnessed their work, and trained under and collaborated with them
in crusade work. Before going further, I will say that encountering any of
the above, in person or print, will thrust whoever desires God into greater
involvement—right into the thick of it all. If we are serious about it, God
will take us!

HOW TO HANDLE UNCERTAINTY

Many more Christians wish they too were involved in healing ministry, but do
not know what else to do to get involved. Many people feel like they need to
do something mysterious or religious before they can have the gift of healing
given to them; pray this, kneel this way, visit some place. Many wishing for a
healing ministry feel intimidated, like a child trying to jump onto a merry-go-
round that is already spinning too fast. Starting a healing ministry can seem
equally daunting. They think that if they do not do things just right, God is
going to cast them out, the same way a merry-go-round will cast off young-
sters when it spins too fast.

Sadly, such pointless thinking, though not true, is very real to many people. They then become weary and seem to stall versus moving further up and further in with God. And stalling, even if subconsciously, may seem the only option as they pray on year after year. This may seem a viable resolution were it not for the hundreds of scripture passages that testify consistently to God healing His people throughout biblical history. And there are the many reasons God did what He did in healing.

It is God's character to heal. Perhaps we ought to change ours to better match His. What else are we to make of the suffering and need all around us? Even in this era of superb medical advancement, millions upon millions, even billions of people are afflicted. And there is the never-ending healthcare debate. This simply proves that a solution will come from a divine Source— not a political, nor a medical, nor a financial, nor a legal source.

Obey Christ's Command

So there is plenty of reason that we are to heal people as our Savior did: the main one being—He *told us to* heal. People come up with a myriad of reasons to *not* reach out and heal people. But all of them are irresponsible excuses that do not excuse us from our duty to minister to the ill and care for the suffering. We are to see them well again. This is no time to give up versus proceed into healing ministry for God's glory. We will either obey our Lord, knowing He is with us, or we will not obey Him. It is one of the strongest ways we can make an assault on evil in the world, shine light, show love, and bless people.

Still many persist in not praying seriously for the sick. They will not go to the sick and lay hands on them as the New Testament orders us to. Strangely enough, some comfort themselves with, "Oh, I would pray for the sick and dying, but I'm not comfortable with that." The question is, how long will the suffering around us be forced to remain in anguish and despair while we who know where the power is shy away from them in their distress? How long will we withdraw from the dynamic commissioning that comes with encountering the Holy Spirit in this way, the way that is required to administer healing? How long shall we resign ourselves from dynamic ministry and into a life of the relentless pursuit of personal comfort and "security?" We must face that this is the obsession of most in the free world: the pursuit of comfort—not the pursuit of God, nor saving the lost.

SETTING ASIDE SELF

Remember the horrid scene from the 1997 movie *Titanic*, when the last of the ship disappears into the subfreezing waters? (Remember, salt water gets well below thirty-two degrees.) As portrayed in the movie, each of the lifeboats held more than sixty people, but some lifeboats only had twelve in them because certain of the well-dressed passengers who escaped the floundering ocean liner insisted on the special comfort of extra legroom. They did not realize how evil their demand for comfort was until they saw the whole of the one thousand, five hundred people flailing in the water and briskly freezing to death.

There is an intolerable similarity between that scene and church life today. Many Christians would do more to comfort others with the love, salvation, and healing of Christ were they not preoccupied with the tenacious quest for personal space, amenities, "security," and privacy. This calls for a colossal change in priority. We have this life today to alter it or eternity to regret not doing so.

We as Christians have the Spirit power. As a body of believers we have access to all His gifts. The U.S. Center for World Mission has recently stated that there is presently ten times the manpower and ten times the financing available to finish the job of evangelizing the world. For doing healing ministry we have an even greater supply in Christ. Being backed the way we are, we have what we need to launch out in ministry and lay hands upon the ill and pray for recovery. This is to be an ongoing omnipresent worldwide ministry until Christ returns.

HANDS-ON HEALING

Yes, the long distance prayers are a part of our duty, but when we are able, the laying on of hands is vital. It demonstrates that we mean business as New Testament Christians!

I remember in 1991 when I crushed a kidney in the falling accident I described earlier. I never knew a human could be in so much pain and still be alive. The procedure that would remedy the situation was too risky. Doctors opted to watch and wait to see if the kidney was going to heal on its own. The prospect of removing the kidney was avoided because of my young age. A Christian nurse spent the first night at my bedside praying, "Oh God, please, he is too young." Thus the kidney did not need to be removed. But things were very perilous for thirty days. If I lay extremely still, it might heal. Every week or so any slight movement would burst the fragile healing process and the internal bleeding resumed. This happened a few times. Specialists, interns, medical students, nurses, and face after face after face would show up to analyze another aspect of the debacle. There were easily two hundred professionals that came, made a judgment call, stuck another needle, changed an IV, or did another X-ray, and then left. Each doctor seemed to end his visit with a tenor of doubt. I kept hearing tones of "Well, maybe, that will work. We will watch, wait, and see." It became evident over the weeks that the kidney could not repair on its own.

After thirty days it became evident that the risky procedure had to be done to patch the kidney from the inside or I would bleed to death. I still remember the day that the head kidney specialist of that part of New York State entered the room and assessed my situation. I thought, "Finally, the big guy shows up!" He worked my torso like bread dough, tapped and pressed and . . . let's just say this doctor acted like the man in charge. He had spent thirty days sending someone else because he was so busy. But now things were critical, I had hours to live, and he came and laid hands on me himself. His visit ended with the abrupt comment, "Take him to surgery now. Do the arteriogram, patch the kidney, or he'll be dead by sundown."

When we are serious about healing people and doing dire business in the Spirit for the kingdom's sake and God's glory, we do like that kidney specialist. We go ourselves and lay on hands in fervent prayer. We realize that sending someone else and doing "tele-prayers" is too casual. Like in prayer meetings when we pray over list after list of people here, there, and everywhere. What a blessing it is to drop everything and go to the sick person, take a team, and join the family at bedside, kneel down and implore the God of glory to show Himself faithful and restore the dear person who is in poor health before us.

People never forget these experiences as long as they live. The ill and those ministering are touched in heart. These are faith moves. This displays our belief that God is going to act.

RANDOM ACTS OF HEALING

My friend, Steve, takes a couple days each month and goes house to house as the Spirit prompts him and offers to pray for people. He literally rings doorbells around his town, introduces himself, and asks, "Is there anyone here sick? Would you like me to pray for them to recover in Jesus' name?" How do you like that for boldness? What a marvelous way to share our healing Savior. Hey, people go through neighborhoods to sell cookies and chocolate for their clubs and sports teams. Do we not have something far sweeter to offer? Why are kiddos around the country more confident of their candy meeting a need than we are of our Lord showing up? For those who have the faith, this is a wonderful way to share Jesus. We are told to go into the whole world. And Jesus said to go into our own towns first.

Another who does this in a similar fashion is Pastor Drew. He was noticing once that the neighbors had not been coming out and their child had not been playing in the yard in recent weeks. There was a growing concern that seemed to lace the faces of the parents as he greeted them coming and going. Several more days passed and then he took the initiative to ask if everything was fine with them. They were not Christians. They knew their neighbor was a pastor. Then again, in their minds, what was a "pastor"?

They finally broke down and shared that their child was ill and getting worse. Pastor Drew automatically offered, "May I come over and pray for you and your child?" They agreed. He entered their house. Not being Christians this was a very strange procedure for them to escort a pastor through their world of possessions and down a back hallway to their ill child. Pastor Drew knelt at this little one's bedside while the family stood back and watched this extremely peculiar scene unfold. Drew prayed with all his heart. He prayed that the child would recover, that the home would be blessed, that God would show Himself and touch this family, and that joy would flood their home. The father and mother stood there numb. They had never experienced anything like this. As Pastor Drew said the "amen" and rose to go, the father stopped him. With tears in his eyes he thanked Drew. He told him that that was the nicest thing anyone had ever done for them.

Even the people who know nothing about God are blessed when we do what God tells us to do and we act like Jesus did.

What do we do when God calls us to heal? Do we drone, "OK God, I'll pray for them, as soon as I get to it," and continue channel surfing from the sofa? His calling may not be a megaphone in our head like when I was ordered to heal in that church outside Kiev (chapter 7). Whether His orders reach us like a whisper or a thump upside the head, our intense obedience will open up the whole world and the eternal riches of Christ's powerful Spirit to us once we have surrendered to His program.

EVANGELISM AND HEALING

A.B. Simpson's plan for taking the gospel through the world is potent and imperative for us to learn from. His pilgrimage and testimony and personal healing are given an overview in chapter five. However his marching orders to new recruits in the mission was a victory plan that we ought to take to heart. He would spend a year teaching new volunteers how to personally study the Bible and absorb it. Next they were mentored in how to "walk" and live in the Holy Spirit. They were then commissioned and shipped to a land where the gospel had not yet been preached. Once on shore they were to walk inland until they came to a village. First they were to heal the sick people. That would raise the local interest in these newcomers! After that they were to connect with the tribal chief or leader of the ethnic group and learn the language from him. That way they would not be learning some fringe dialect or juvenile lingo. Once they grasped the language they would explain the healings that were happening, teach them about Jesus, explain the whole gospel story, train leaders, teach them to evangelize and heal, and then—go on to the next tribe!

The plan worked. Notice that in this scenario, healing is the method for winning the hearts of the people. It is the ignition point in the process. Without the application of healing the contact is not made. Without healing ministry, crossing the cultural bridge has a questionable chance of happening. Through healing, the gospel gets a foothold in their lives before they understand the gospel or can even communicate.

This is effective missions through effective healing and having the spiritual resolve to believe God and move with that faith. On the converse, our refusal to move out, move on, and move up with God ends up being ever so costly. It is costly to others as well as costly to us. Refusing to heal is disobedience that leads to horrendous regret. Among all the countless people I have met, the stories of healing adhere to my memory as do the stories people tell me of when they became fearful when prompted by the Spirit to pray for a sick person. Other times they were outright asked to pray by the sick person themselves, and they didn't. As described prior, this ended up bothering them for decades. I have seen this happen. It can happen when we refuse to move forward in faith. It can happen in our own lives. Either way, to walk away from God's prompting is mournfully distressing.

CONSEQUENCES OF HEALING

I have a friend, Thomas, who lives several hundreds of miles away. We catch up with each other once or twice a year. He is a couple years younger than I am. We are in contact enough for him to know that I was finishing this book on God's healing power. He insisted on my sharing his story because he had an experience with divine healing. He was born with cerebral palsy. The palsy affects his whole body, but is most noticeable in his limp. I do not know the full explanation of what is wrong in muscles and bones in his hips and knees, but he cannot run any faster than five mph for fifty feet at the most. After that he is forced to return to walking in an erratic and bumpy pattern; it is anything but a smooth step.

In about 1985 he was in his early twenties, and Thomas thought it could not hurt if he were to ask God to heal him. He said he wanted to be healed so he could be handy and capable, not handicapped. He wanted to get on with his life and enjoy many other things. So, tired of being so needy, tired of being frustrated, he asked God to touch his life and give him new legs. He admits it was more of a "Hey God, why not?" type of prayer than a bold request.

It ended with the usual "amen." He felt peculiarly encouraged. Who knows when God would answer him? God knew, so Thomas was fine.

He sat there for a moment after a heavy sigh. He thought maybe God would touch him sometime in life, maybe over the next ten or twenty years. Or maybe sooner—he rose to deal with whatever came that day. And then he noticed that he was not limping! He felt God touch him on the back. A burst of energy shot through his whole body. It was an electric rush but it was not painful. His limbs were strong and straight. He had never known such a charge of energy and love. He was on top of the world with euphoria. Without delay his limp was gone, right then and there. For the first time in his life he had a normal gait and he felt strong. He also had never felt so loved.

Thomas was overwhelmed. He wept for joy. It was an indescribable flood of peace and power all in the same moment. He walked the short hallway, spun around, and walked back. Wow, it was time for a whole new life!

He was about to go outside, but before he reached the door an anxious thought crept in. "What is going to happen to my disability payments? What if they stop once someone in some department finds out about my being healed." It was a menacing concern that he wished was not hitting him, but it was. He paused and wondered while he grabbed his coat. The thought grew stronger so he sat back down a moment, feeling stuck. What an experience God had given him, but what was he to do now?

After pondering it all, he rose again to leave. It had been less than one minute—and his familiar limp had returned. Thomas has been limping ever since. He was born in 1965 with cerebral palsy. He hobbled for twenty years. He walked straight and strong for one ecstatic minute. But like Peter, when it was his turn to walk on water, he was fine until the storm made him fearful. Thomas has been limping again ever since 1985.

When God moves over you, go with it! Do not question and calculate. Just go. Let everything else go. Drop the concerns and proceed with what God has given you. Thomas's experience is testimony that if we do not take what God gives us, He can very easily take it away. May his experience warn us all.

The gravity of dawdling versus launching when God says that it's time to roll isn't a problem that merely plagues individuals. Whole churches do the same.

Whole denominations and nations can be guilty of stalling when God calls them to a higher life of miraculous encounters. Against God's blessing these larger bodies usually do a more politically savvy job of squelching the Spirit. But God is never within the decision to remain monotonous in our ministries.

HEALING AND SPIRIT-DRIVEN, EXPLOSIVE CHURCH GROWTH

John (a friend in California) tells of a church he attended back in the early 1990s. It was a new group with about twenty-five people in their congregation. They were affiliated with a vital denomination that *had* wonderful origins well over a century prior. As the beginning months in this new church wore on, some in the group became restless as the leaders' carefulness and cautious nature became ever more apparent. Growing impatient with the leader's indolence, John insisted, "Let's live it like the Book of Acts—let's get this church going!" John wanted to see people healed and saved, the community engaged in the things of God. Several others in this new church agreed with John, but the leaders thought that was a bit too apostolic. "We don't need all that today," the leaders droned. "We have the Word of God. That is enough for us to be faithful."

Here's a passage from the apostle Paul directed toward those who think that ministry is all about words and talking and sermons versus ministering the living Spirit of God to people. He says:

> I did not come with eloquence or superior wisdom as I proclaimed to you the testimony about God. For I resolved to know nothing while I was with you except Jesus Christ and him crucified. I came to you in weakness and fear, and with much trembling. My message and my preaching were not with wise and persuasive words, but with a demonstration of the Spirit's power, so that your faith might not rest on men's wisdom, but on God's power.
>
> —1 CORINTHIANS 2:1–5

What is the Bible, which is inspired and breathed to us by the Holy Spirit, if while we claim to be embracing it as our guide, we simultaneously spurn the work of the Holy Spirit? This line of thinking cancels its own reasoning. It is illicit to shun the Spirit and claim to be following the Word, which orders us to listen to the Holy Spirit. Soon after Paul insists, "For the kingdom of God is not a matter of talk but of power" (1 Cor. 4:20).

And yet it is grave how many churches and pastors can take that tone while pretending to not notice that this Word of God they claim to be closely following demonstrates and teaches and orders divine healing repeatedly. Even a casual count in the Bible shows more than 150 references and stories of healing being demonstrated, promised, and taught. God's healing ministry from Abraham to the apostle John was not a 2,100-year mood swing. His healing heart and activity seen all over the Bible is an historic statement for all time. Therefore Christ's followers are to be exercising healing along with the restoration of souls. And we must remember that healing is to be done God's way, in God's timing. I say this because some churches endeavor to do absolutely nothing that isn't written up neatly in the bulletin (more like the playbill) several days prior to gathering.

All that being said, John left what we shall call "Church-A." A handful of people left with him to start "Church-B." No one was bitter, they just wanted the living Christ. Church-A went down to about eighteen people, but over the next year or two they surged back up to twenty-one. From the start, Church-B made a pact with God: if it is in the Bible, we will learn it. If it is in the New Testament especially, we will do it; all of it. Within eighteen months three thousand people were attending Church-B. By the way, according to the Holy Spirit, this is not phenomenal growth. It is normal growth. Remember in Acts 2 after Peter gives a sermon? A new body of believers bursts forth as three thousand put their faith in Jesus! That is the result of one sermon in one morning. Soon more are added. In Acts 3 a lame man is ordered to rise and walk by Peter. He does. And the church keeps exploding in growth.

So, back to the present time; before five years had passed, Church-B was approaching eight thousand in attendance. Meanwhile Church-A had tapered back to eighteen. By mid-decade of A.D. 2000, Church-B was occupying a five thousand-seat sanctuary and had five services per weekend on a church campus that was valued at $40 million. It was so large that John diverged to assist in starting another congregation, "Church-C." It too would be a New Testament church for all it's worth. This last year, Church-C had its second Easter service just nineteen months after being born. And there was no place to put everyone. They were forced to rent a civic center to fit the three thousand that showed up! They figured that if we simply bless people with the Holy Spirit, they will come. They did. God did. And people showed up by the thousands. When the Bread of Life is served, hungry people come out! This is what happens when the leaders do whatever the Holy Spirit says to do. The Holy Spirit of the Holy Bible is to be our rule, not one or the other.

Meanwhile back at Church-A: the hair is whiter and bluer. No children are disrupting anything, anywhere. All is tidy and monitored. Nothing happens that isn't in the bulletin. There are no young families. But just ask anyone in Church-A and they will tell you that they are being faithful, to the fifteen souls who were present for the worship service last Easter. Or was it twelve souls?

Hear me please. I truly cherish old people. They are the heritage of any group. I would love to go back to the 1970s, just for a day and tell all four of my grandparents how much they mean to me. Yet at the same time we revere the old in a church, there needs to be new births in the church or death will overtake it. There needs to be fresh breathing of the Spirit blowing in, or worship will stagnate and decline. There need to be healings in Jesus' name, or the church will become sick— irreversibly so— then stale, and then it will die. It will not even be an interesting museum a generation later.

HEALING NAYSAYERS

Yes, the Spirit spurs us onward into all that the Bible instructs us to live out. It is a shameful dereliction to do otherwise. This includes us moving forward with healing ministry. It deserves our attention to note that we each have a calling to heal. It is a personal calling. This calling has a myriad of degrees; no one needs to feel intimidated. To heal is to "put things together again." This *is* creating and all of us who serve the Creator are to model Him. We're following the Creator or the destroyer. If someone says that they don't get involved in healing, the question is, what Bible *are* they reading? There's a curious idiosyncrasy among those who defend their script for ministry that carefully avoids healing. These same folks put up a vigorous defense of Jesus' divine nature and His healing ministry as portrayed in the Gospels. But they make no link to His healing ministry that is operating today. These folks often go to great lengths to scorn and discredit healing ministry. This is an unfounded incongruity that has no defense or excuse.

From there things can get worse. For those who won't rise up and pray for the ill, there comes the temptation to criticize others who are exercising *their* gift of healing. Like in any endeavor or movement, the reticent, indolent ones are threatened by the responsibly occupied ones. There seems to be a huge elephant in Christendom that no one appears to be calling out and ridding. This is the fact that Christians, preachers, evangelists, and leaders can be jealous of someone else who appears to be doing the will of God more dynamically than they are. Undealt with, this jealousy becomes venomously sinful. The resentful will wring their hands and bemoan, "What about Benny Hinn? What about Kenneth Hagin? Oral Roberts, and others? Aren't they being prideful? Isn't that sin?" The naysayers frown and muse while pretending to be inquisitive. What could possibly bother anyone about someone else who is doing ministry the best that they know how? Could it be that some are jealous about the packed auditoriums? The renowned university with someone else's name on it? The corporate jet? The five-star accommodations? Good grief, why in heaven's name waste any energy being jealous? Do not worry about other people. Let's each of us fulfill *our* own callings with all our might. We are not called to criticize others. God can handle them.

It would be nice if that reminder were enough, but things can get even worse for those who won't simply obey Jesus' orders for themselves. I have heard frustrated pastors attribute the healings of other pastors and evangelists as their being in league with Satan. That talk is reckless, irresponsible, and outright scary. The danger of such accusations is alarming and should receive double warning. The grievous error of this judgment is that there is no way that the Holy Spirit has nothing to do these innumerable healings done in Jesus' name. The severity of this error is that if this *is* the Holy Spirit at work, and someone who is envious attributes this work to Satan. That is blasphemy.

Jesus states that blasphemy will not be forgiven, not now, not later, not ever (Matthew 12:32; Mark 3:29).

This is frightening, especially after reading the context of the two prior passages. Jesus is healing and getting criticized by religious leaders who are jealous. And the same criticism happens today. People are healing in Jesus' name, and scoffers, who are more comforted by criticizing than obeying and healing, succumb to flinging verbal darts at those they are critical and most likely covetous toward. This is not good. Even if someone has a healing ministry and doesn't have pure motives (Gee, who does?), still the apostle Paul has this to say about fretting over other peoples' activities: "It is true that some preach Christ out of envy and rivalry, but others out of goodwill. The latter do so in love...the former preach Christ out of selfish ambition, not sincerely. But what does it matter? The important thing is that in every way, whether from false motives or true, Christ's name is preached. And because of this, I rejoice. Yes, and I will continue to rejoice" (Philippians 1:15–18).

Are we hearing this? Paul's question settles every argument in this arena, "What does it matter?" Let's rejoice over Christ being preached when someone is healed in Jesus' name. I am aggrieved when I learn how good news in ministry gets cluttered with gossip from the petty. There are times when a whole crowd gets touched with the power of the gospel. Healings abound. And people get distracted, and the atmosphere of wonder goes static because someone is worried that the preacher leading the services has a bus that somebody thinks is too lavish or expensive for *their* particular tastes. Perhaps the person implementing the healing has a quirky voice or some atypical mannerism.

> Jealousy will impede anyone from finding God's higher calling.

What is the difference between this attitude and the one Judas Iscariot revealed when Mary anointed Jesus in John 12:3–7? Judas apparently is concerned that the perfume could have been sold and the money given to the poor? His comment is a charade for Judas' deeper concern: his greed. Just the same, it is suspect when someone who should be rejoicing over a divine healing is preoccupied with anxiety over someone with a healing ministry having a personal tour bus with gold faucets in the lavatory. Hint: jealousy will impede anyone from finding God's higher calling. Everyone is invited to drop the jealousy and open their spiritual gift. It just might be the gift of healing.

And taking Paul's words to heart from Philippians chapter 1, let's all cease worrying about who, when, where, what, how, and why whomever is getting healed and the fact that whoever prayed for their healing is not abiding in pristine sinless perfection yet. Let's all relax. Jesus was sinless—and no one else will ever accomplish that. In ministering healing to people, do not try to package Jesus in some tactical manner. He comes in power in His perfect timing. Churches can be so program-oriented that they can miss the moving of the Spirit. For example, "This is the healing moment in the service, it will happen during this seven-minute window, and God will use this person, wearing this trinket-covered robe, while he faces this direction and says these certain words." It doesn't sound like God is allowed to be God in these settings. God cannot be delivered in our tidy shrink-wrap containers. He isn't a Happy Meal. When He is invited, He comes and does things His way. He is never predictable, never boring, always fresh. Let Him be God. And like with the story of Thomas above, when He says, "Go, now," He means it. Let's operate on His scale and His timer—not ours.

A word to those who think that healing died with the apostles: where did this belief originate? This defeatist creed does not come from the Holy Spirit. God did not avail Himself to heal His children from Abraham through the apostle John and then leave His Spirit with us to endlessly tell us that we are going to make it on our own. The self-cancelling circular nature within that article of (no) faith is evident. Those that think healing stopped with the apostles are most likely trying to make the best of hurt feelings and disappointment from what is perceived to be personal failure in the realm of healing ministry. No child who hears the healing stories of Jesus resolves, "That is nice of Jesus, but that was for back then. We don't need that anymore because we have the Bible." These are the resignational creeds of adults who have become disillusioned by misperceptions of a "botched" healing experience. Granted these views are rooted in personal reality. But they are not rooted in truth.

> He's never predictable, never boring, always fresh. Let Him be God.

We are to test the spirits to see whether they are of God (1 John 4:1). Too many of us are not doing this. When they see some person moving in a prophetic manner, doing ministry that sets a higher precedent than we are willing to operate in, anxiety, shame, and jealousy can take over. And against the better part of wisdom, many will not test the spirits or the prophet they are observing. No, they *trash* the prophets and trash the spirits instead of testing them. This is not intelligent. It is childish and these things need to be put away.

God's healing power is operating so powerfully today that even the honest skeptic will be convinced. The present-day mighty moving of God is enough to convince anyone except, of course, the willfully ignorant. Those who have ears to hear will listen. With that I will drop the matter as it is useless to try and feed overly fed people or to try to speak to those who have stopped up their ears.

The incidents and stories described in chapter 6 are not about people who live on some higher mysterious plain where only a privileged few may venture. They are simply souls who trusted God's Word and His Spirit as the true guide for their lives. There was nothing contrived there; not in any one of the stories. I had serendipitously met each of them over the course of time. They believed and launched out in faith; most were so blessed by their healing that they, themselves, were amazed. And the rest is verified history. Any of us can do likewise. The question is, are we going to live out a half-baked gospel or serve up Jesus to people and feed His sheep for all He is worth? We must not shrink from this. We must obey our Lord and heal the sick because the gospel is a gospel of power.

If we find ourselves lacking faith, fret nothing. Faith is a gift. Ask for faith. Ask for more faith. We can ask God to increase our faith. The disciples asked Jesus to increase their faith. There's an old adage, "You get what you pay for." My response to that is, "No, we do not." That is a phrase oriented toward merchandise. This regards commodities that we purchase and possess—for a while. Everything we buy and hold will be gone eventually; gone with this world. Ultimately speaking, "We get what we *pray* for." If we want faith, we will have it. If we want to experience God, we will. If we want to share Jesus, we will. If we want to be a blessing to our world and glorify God, we will. And Jesus urges over and again to ask for these things (Matthew 7:7). These gifts are voice-activated and delivered by Christ to those who ask in faith.

We must heal the sick also because we serve a Savior who healed the sick. We either want to be more like Jesus and do more like Jesus or we do not. If we don't, then that needs to change immediately. If we know we are called to but are afraid to, that fear can be confessed and discarded today. He will change our hearts to want to completely live for Him as we ask Him to change our hearts. And if we live for Jesus, then we are to advance His kingdom. Granted, there may be perceived "failures and setbacks" as we launch out in obedience. But the scriptures say, "For though a righteous man falls down seven times, he rises again" (Proverbs 24:16).

Healing is in the recipe as we are to live our lives in obedience to Jesus who told us, "Feed my sheep." In Luke 5:17, when the paralytic is let down through the roof, everybody learned that Jesus is the One who forgives and has the power to heal. This is what I see as the watershed healing in the Bible. This means healing is a linked part of the gospel message. It cannot be ignored or dismissed or excused away. Though healing does not always accompany salvation, salvation always changes people. The change is never exclusively spiritual, just as healing is never exclusively physical. God wants us involved in experiencing healing and training people in the whole counsel of God. It is not right to "cherry pick" and choose the parts of the gospel that make us feel personally confident, comfortable, and cushy so to speak. This is indicative of reversed priorities. When we do that, our minds, our selection processes, and maintaining status quo *our way* has become the priority. And once that happens, where has God been placed?

HEALING OUTSIDE OF THE WEST

The sad reality is that many Westerners and Europeans feel that God is not moving among us like He is moving in the Third World. That is a striking reality that always impresses me in my mission travels. Since 1981 I have traversed nearly fifty countries. Marvelous things are undoubtedly happening among the people who want Jesus more than anything on this earth. Upon returning to the USA, I feel responsible to share the wonders that are happening in parts of the world where the church is exploding. Americans invariably ask, "Why doesn't God move like that here?"

The truth is that Christians around the world who live in poorer settings that are hostile to Christianity pray with such fervor that God arrives in full. It is invigorating to join in these passionate prayer meetings. They often go all night. It is also very sobering and humbling to join Christians who pray like they are at a festival and caught up in a firestorm of God's love in action. It seems simpler to seek Jesus in a peaceful, simpler setting. It's a curious fact that Christians in much of the world that have fewer possessions pray for the Christians in the West. They pray that Americans keep their faith amid all the distractions: email, palm pilots, cell phones/texting, pagers, beepers, iPods, laptops, Blackberrys, fax machines, HD-plasma screens, DVD players, hot tubs, and endless boxes and storage units filled with toys, and equipment, RVs, ad infinitum.

Jim Rutz bears much truth in a quick explanation of this distraction found in spiritually apathetic atmospheres. He explains in his book, *Megashift*, why he feels that the Holy Spirit is moving dynamically in certain places versus other places. He concludes that God is not moving so vibrantly in America because we are not seeking Him with the fervency that He is being sought elsewhere in the world. The crux is this: what do Americans do with their free time or on days off work? They meander around their homes, munch a bit, and watch a couple mindless programs on the television. Then they shuffle out and wash all their cars. In the afternoon, they will go to a child's game. After that they go home, watch a little more on the television, check emails, surf the web for who-knows-what anymore, click through a few more channels again, eat more dinner than they need, check the news before bed, pray some cheesy prayer like, "Now I lay me down to sleep, watch over the missionaries who've gone in too deep…" And then they wonder why they operate in a nonstop stupor and are so entirely bored with their lives.

Rutz contrasts that with what people in other parts of the world do with their free time. He regularly sees Indian Christians (meaning in India where he does mission work) fight through obstacles that endanger them for even *being* a Christian to begin with. They will scrape together some coins, get a bus pass and trek to a far corner of their city or region. There they set up a small stage and just start praying for the sick and preaching the gospel. Before the day is out another dozen or so have been restored, people have come to Christ, the leaders have been gathered and briefed, Bibles get passed out, and another church is off and running.

Now if you were God, who would you prefer to rush in and assist? Who would you be more inclined to bless with your wonders? Who would you go to at any cost to pour your Spirit upon and keep fueled with an endless supply of your Son's Spirit? Would it be the overfed, overpaid, overly entertained, persnickety types? Or would it be the ones who have sought for every possible way to follow the Great Commission as laid forth in Matthew 28? We know what we would do. So we know why God does what He does. Those who have ministered overseas know all too well what is being said here.

One missionary stationed in southern Africa recently ranted to my wife and me, "Americans claim they have no time to seek and serve God? The question is where does all the time go? The excuses are nonsense. When we seek God at every chance, during what we call our 'free time,' He then gives us *more* free time." The missionary claimed that he noted on his most recent tour of America that Americans have no trouble giving God their frantic time: "Two minutes with God and you're ready to plod," "a chapter a day (in the Bible) keeps the devil away," and "One Minute with the Messiah" devotionals, among other examples. He mused that that was giving God one's frantic time. He concluded that if we have consciously or even subconsciously resolved to only give God our frantic time, then we live out our whole lives in a frantic manner.

STALL TACTICS

As for more American stall tactics, my own father told me about a "Prayer and Holy Spirit" conference he attended many years ago in southern California. I put it in quotes because the Holy Spirit was not beseeched at this conference and they never did end up getting to the prayer part. What happened for the bulk of the days was that the pastors argued about why and whether the Holy Spirit descended from the Father or from the Son. And the arguments became heated. Now isn't that a brilliant use of time? Give me a break! It is if we want to play the poser and simultaneously drag our feet instead of going deeper with God. God is not impressed or fooled by nonsense and He does not visit these gatherings. He has nothing to do with them.

Kids play the same game. It is just that their tactics are slightly easier to spot. When they need to help clean up the kitchen after dinner and don't want to and don't want to appear disobedient, they negotiate. Here goes! Who's going to clear, wipe the table, wash, rinse, stack, dry, put away, mop the floor…

Then come the arguments because last time you didn't help, but then again she had to wash two nights in a row because you didn't clear the table, and this one didn't dry right when it was his turn and last time you mopped you missed a spot so you should have to mop *and* rinse then stack this time, blah, blah, blah. Forty-five minutes later the kitchen is still a mess and everyone's arguing. Do any of us see the link between the chores not being done and the prayer meeting never happening as both melt into senseless argument?

COME WITH CHILDLIKE FAITH

Something I have seen is that one way to help boost prayer power and get a breakthrough is to put a child on it. Have a child take the prayer matter to the throne. Jesus told us to come to him like a child or we will not enter the kingdom of heaven. That is straight talk that we romanticize, but it is alarming if we think we are going to enter heaven with a different mindset than that of a child. And do not have them pray the prayer that an adult taught them; all straightened grammar and such. I say let them loose and learn from them.

Another missionary friend told me of a family that was in distress as their young boy was in peril from cholera and dehydration. They were at least a thirty-hour flight from the USA. Their little chap was seven years old and had not been able to keep any water in him for a couple of days. At the rate he was withering, death would visit this family and take away their Jimmy within twenty-four hours. Other missionary families were called in to pray. Rotations were set up. Someone had been at Jimmy's bedside for sixty hours straight. More petitions, more prayers, more prayer outlines, more pious pleadings.

Somewhere during the third day of praying, the adults yielded to defeat. They resigned that they were going to lose this little boy. No one would articulate it, but the tension of the prayers that had been marked by the stress of grievous requests were now morphing into acquiescence and surrendering the little guy to eternity. They sounded more like, "Lord, we trust you in your wisdom as you are now going to take him from us."

Just then, Jimmy's ten-year-old sister promenaded into the room. She was inquisitive as she approached the circled up adults who were mumbling and sniffing. She still did not know what the issue was. Her head only coming up to the midsection of most adults, she wormed through them and then noticed that the attraction in the center was her comatose brother. And he did not look too good.

She asked what was going on. The adults feeling it was useless to hide it anymore finally told her, "Dear, your brother's time has come. The Lord is going to take him now." She did not understand. The Lord was going to take him *where*? With a solicitous tone of "We have to accept this, dear," they explained to her about Jimmy's dehydration and that he was not going to make it. He would die.

When it all sunk in, she was anything but accommodating. She was not frightened. She was not gloomy. She was annoyed at the adults and their dutiful and well-behaved dismissal of her little brother. She commenced upon a litany of exhortation of the adults in the room and their lack of faith. It was more a reprimand than anything. "Hold it people," she began. "Does Jesus heal or not?" They groused a bit for they did not know what to say to this little fireplug who was demonstrating more faith than they were. They must have felt like the disciples when they responded to Jesus standing on the shore, "But we have already fished all night."

Stomping her foot, she insisted upon them answering her, "Does Jesus heal or not?" Her parents were among the eight to ten adults present during this.

"Well Sis', we have prayed for days and it looks like Jesus is going to take Jimmy from us now. We are all just going to have to accept that His ways are higher than—"

"I don't think that's right!" she cut in. "You have always taught us that Jesus heals and loves and, and, well I want my brother back." Who was she going to play with if her brother died anyway? So Sis' went right up to her brother's side. He was slipping deeper into unconsciousness when she took command. She put a hand on him and through her words bore him back to the land of the living. "Jesus, You heal people in the Bible and that means You can heal my brother. You know what to do. I want him to play on the swings with me. OK? I want my brother back. OK, Jesus? Amen."

Sis' pranced right outside and in a sense readied the playground for her brother's return. The adults froze as Jimmy opened his eyes not five seconds after his sister's sharp "amen." Within ten seconds he sat up and was appearing to be fine. He asked for water. He drank like a fish and was outside playing with his sister in a couple of minutes. The adults had learned their best lesson on prayer ever: just declare what is true and say what you want! When congenial prayers are not getting through, when breakthrough healing is needed, try putting a kid on the job. They will pray what is really on our hearts, and God's. The rest of us may be too conditioned that we have to "pray properly" to make the necessary progress.

I have been in prayer meetings overseas where not a word of English was spoken for hours. Even if I had known the language, deciphering was what being said would be hopeless. They were praying so fast, so loud and fervently that I stood there in disbelief. It was more like a riot or a sports event gone out of control than what Americans would call a prayer meeting. What we would call a "riot" to them is the tri-weekly "prayer whirlwind." What we call a prayer meeting to them would be a children's story hour meant to lull them into naptime. Consequently much of our prayer times *do* put children to sleep. In our prayers we may be accustomed to knocking politely on heaven's door when we pray. At many of these Third World gatherings, we would depict their prayers to be "pounding on heaven's door with a crow bar or a sledge hammer." People seem to be storming heaven's gate like they were storming the Bastille. These people pray like they are in a room that is closing in and if God doesn't answer they are all going to die! We all know, Westerners in general will not pray like that.

Back in many Westerners' prayer meetings things drone on in a feeble manner. We clamp down the kids and warn them that they better sit still. What is wrong with this picture is that the kids are probably the most honest ones in the room. The incongruity is the absurd fact that while there's all this pressure to behave a certain way, this is our definition of how, where, and when communication with God is taking place. To be truthful, what could be more exciting than walking and talking with God? And yet what could be simultaneously more monotonous than the prayer meeting at many of America's churches? This is wrong. I say listen to the kids. If it holds their attention, then there is probably more truth being uttered and more matters are getting settled in heaven. If one feels that their prayers are not getting past the room, it may be because they cannot be heard outside the room. Try getting into prayer as if people's lives depended on it. By the way, people's lives *do* depend upon it.

HAVE A RECEPTIVE HEART

To move into a whole new realm of healing, we must be receptive and ready at heart for anything to happen. My sister has packed her things and moved to Africa for life. Among the events that triggered her decision to change is what happened in a prayer meeting. It was a healing testimony. She was on her scout trip in the southern part of the continent. In a gathering of about 1,400 people a man sprang to his feet and declared, "Oh dear people, I must tell you about my week. It was completely marvelous. I died Tuesday. I came back to life Friday, and I want to tell you what I saw!" He proceeded to describe the journey to "the other side" plus his return.

About that time my sister had her moment that one might call, "Uh, Toto, we're not in Kansas anymore." She had never heard anything like this in more than thirty-five years of American church. Not a live testimony, anyway. Wide-eyed she slowly leaned toward the lady next to her who was local and asked, "Is this normal? I mean does this happen, uh…how often does this happen?" The lady was excited and yet very matter-of-fact in informing my sister that this was not a first in this area. She tapped her right index finger against the fingertips of her left hand and counted, "Hmm, there have been, let's see now…four, five, nine, ten, twelve…" She kept tapping her fingertips while looking alternately at her hands and the ceiling while counting. "There have been fourteen raised from the dead in this area!" she announced with certainty.

All thoughts and training aside, this is what is happening. We can either choose to be a part of it or not. My sister came back to Seattle, sold everything, and packed up for Africa.

Having an eager spirit of expectancy is also a great way to enhance our involvement in ministry and open the doors for God to use us in healing. Remember Eyore, the very depressed donkey in the *Winnie the Pooh* books? He has a dismal perspective on everything. Thinking like him is a dead end street in ministry. People who think like Eyore should not expect to receive anything from God. And they won't. Think possibilities. Think hopefully. Think the verse, "Nothing is impossible with God." Think of what God has done and is doing and planning to do. Look at His spiritual gifts and ask, "What will my gift be?" Come at this matter with all the childlike zeal of a kid on Christmas morning. That makes us better candidates to receive from the Holy Spirit.

The Englishman Smith Wigglesworth has material that is very helpful for elevating our faith. There are a dozen or so titles that he wrote. I know Englishmen who are very rehearsed in this man's life, writings, and ministry. He even raised the dead. His faith was so bold, he entered mortuaries and started thumping on coffins ordering people to wake up. His tone would be akin to a drillmaster arousing drunken sailors on a weekend morning when people expect to sleep in. He would take men he had raised up straight to a church and tell them to testify that same day. Smith did not go gentle.

We should not go gentle either. Ministry is not a congeniality contest. Nor is it a hat and tea party. People dangle over either blessings and paradise or condemnation and outer darkness. We are to operate like lifeguards during high tide or coast guard sailors and swimmers in the middle of a stormy rescue.

Now let's go for big things. Let's shoot for the greater things. Let's ask of God and stomp in His direction! It's well past time to flush our doubting and accept what Jesus told us about ourselves in John 14:12–14, "I tell you the truth, anyone who has faith in me will do what I have been doing. He will do even greater things that these, because I am going to the Father. And I will do whatever you ask in my name, so that the Son may bring glory to the Father. You may ask me for anything in my name, and I will do it." Are we going to argue with Jesus on this? Or are we going to just move with Him to see these things fulfilled?

USHER IN GLORY

Doing greater things means that what we do for His glory can be of greater size than what Jesus did. That is all it means. Jesus said we would do greater things in His name. "In His name" is crucial because that means He receives the glory. To glorify someone is to make that someone bigger. Would Jesus want us to make Him "bigger"? Yes!

He fed five thousand from one lunch bag, then unless we think it isn't possible (which will cancel the possibility) we could do that too. Why? Because Jesus stands right with us as we ask of Him. He lives in our body. He thinks for and with our mind. He moves our hands. With Him operating us soul and body, ten thousand could be fed from one bag if the situation calls for it. When we are lifted up to the occasion of ministering in such a privileged setting, just relax and serenely work for our majestic God. Food is being multiplied right now by the way. These things are happening and it is triggering marvelous blessing and advancing the gospel.

This verse about "greater things" causes alarm among some. But it should not. We will not be greater than Jesus. The Beatles said they were bigger than Jesus. That's a haughty comment that will be answered for in time. We are not saying that and neither is Jesus. There is an intrinsic difference between doing greater and being greater. The word for "greater" is *mega*. It is merely a size comment. We are simply prophesied over by Jesus to do deeds that are greater in size than He did. We ought not to fret about duplicating the arrogance of thinking we *are* greater than Jesus. We are not and everyone knows this. Jesus is greater and His greatness gives Him authority to pronounce any deeds upon us as He sees fit. If He says we will do greater things, then the venue is open for these things to happen unless we close the avenue through unbelief. It also does not say that we will be better. He is the virtue. We are the vessel. That all means that great assignments are waiting to be seized upon by us and followed out to their manifest blessing.

There is another verse that applies to this concept and it needs to be reckoned with before moving on. Mark 11:24 says, "Therefore I tell you, whatever you ask for in prayer, believe that you have received it, and it will be yours." People who call themselves conservative "biblicians" dismiss this verse as license for Charismania. But nothing changes the fact that it is our Savior who spoke this to His followers. That means it is true and as we follow Him, this verse is for us to obtain more of Him and His gifts, so to use them to serve Him and accomplish His will. And God wants us to ask for tools to serve our Lord and bless His children. But in this teaching we need to *ask* first.

One thing that is helpful in experiencing this verse is to picture that once a request is made, it is sent in our direction. If it helps, consider it this way: what we have asked for to use for the kingdom has been dropped onto the "conveyor belt." It is already ours even if it has not arrived in a way we can see yet.

LESSONS FROM RAISING LAZARUS

Amid all the details and emotions that accompany divine healing ministry, remember who our chief mentor is. Let's be trained by Him and not a firestorm of opinions and sentiments. How do we observe Jesus and the apostles healing in the New Testament? They are declaring truth. When Jesus raises Lazarus from the dead in John 11 He is not doing a shake and dance, no special stance; He does not do some secret breathing technique. He orders the stone rolled back. Though the family warns about a bad odor from their brother being dead four days, Jesus has a powerful, yet gentle admonition, "Did I not tell you that if you believed, you would see the glory of God?" Jesus did not come to trigger a horror show and make a mummy walk. He came there to end the grief. The insinuation is that it should be obvious that God brings the dead to life. It should be expected, and not be something that shocks us.

Jesus looks up, thanks God in heaven for listening like He always does, affirms that this is for the building of faith among those present, and beckons the dead man to come back to the land of the living. And Lazarus, wrapped in grave clothes and all, came back from the dead! This is resurrection via voice activation. When the Creator speaks, the creation obeys. Lazarus was in on the creation as are the rest of us. This is the same Jesus that ordered the cosmos into place during the Creation (Colossians 1:16). God spoke and Jesus has planets flung across the sky to take their places. The same happened when He created light and the rest of it. It happened with more speed and precision than when a razor sharp military squad falls into procession upon being ordered to do so. By the way, British astrophysicist Stephen Hawking insists that Creation was an atomically instantaneous event that took place in a third of a trillionth of a second. And he has proven this to be true by means of myriad calculations to back up his statement.

Do not try to argue with Stephen Hawking. He is smarter than the rest of us. The point is that Jesus did all this creation. He did it quickly. And He told us how He did it. It was also He who activated the raising of Lazarus, plus the healing of each person that He restored. And He did all this in the power of the Holy Spirit. He is one with the Holy Spirit. So this work is Spirit-directed. Everything in all creation obeys God's voice. Thus we are to speak Jesus' words of life—like He did.

The only variation of this principle is seen within the beings that have been given free will. Humans are the ones who exist in the realm where we are given the option to align with God or not. Humans are called to follow God's Son. We are given the power in the Holy Spirit to do so. We are urged to model and do what Jesus does. We can then collaborate with Him or not. *We can do the voice-activated works of God.* And it is not a mind thing, either, which smacks of paganism.

We are to join God and declare that His kingdom is present and active. When we are in God, thinking His thoughts, doing His deeds, absorbed in His sentiments, looking at what He is seeing and hearing His voice, we then can speak His words; we can do that with Him. This is ministry! The apostle Peter says, "If anyone speaks, he should do it as one speaking the very words of God" (1 Pet. 4:11). Do we realize that we speak for God? When we are voice-activated by God, we activate His ministry and healing. When the first lame woman asked me to heal her (the Kiev story in chapter 7), I took her ankles, which were joints turned into arthritic gravel, and declared that she would receive new ankles that day. She did! She rose and walked. God could do it. I knew it. So I acted like it and offered myself for God to speak through me.

The divine healings that occur are God-prompted, Spirit-directed, and Christ-honoring. It is not done in our will power or whimsy. The step into greater faith for us is to simply believe that Jesus, to whom we have surrendered our lives, lives in us. It's true. Just declare and confess it to be true. Therefore our steps are ordered of the Lord. Our deeds *are* Jesus directing our hands. Our thoughts are His thoughts working through and ruling in our minds. So unless He only does partial projects (which would be a switch), it is His voice speaking through ours. If Christ be in us, then we are in line to do the same voice-activated deeds that He does. He said we would do greater things than those to whom the disciples were witnesses. Now we are not doing things greater because we do them better or differently than Jesus did. We can do great things because we do them the same way Jesus did: in the Spirit, by living the scriptures, declaring the truth, and taking dominion in Jesus' name. One erudite old missionary exhorted me, "Don't pray about things. Pray things about!"

Responding to the Call

The trigger factor is that this happens as we ourselves are voice activated by Him. The Bible says that His sheep know His voice. When God speaks, just obey. Don't start the mind games and the musings. Remember Thomas (in chapter 8)! Stammering, vacillating, and hesitating are all dangerous. When God says, "Now," He means now. And we know what "now" means. That comment may sound silly, but I know personally what it is to be in a panic once one enters the vortex of an imminent healing. When He prompts us to pray and minister healing and do it now, He is not being slick or glib and running a practice drill for entertainment purposes. It is for real. Do not play deaf, "Uh, gee, is someone talking to me? Could it be God? Hmm, maybe it's just my thoughts or inner self-talk." No, when we hear His prompting, and it lines up with what we know in Scripture, if the result of our moving forward is going to bless and build the kingdom, and cease the vexation, then cut the games and the dawdling tactics. It is God talking. And it is time to move! It is time to speak and lay on hands in His name.

People who are starting into this realm of ministry can be confused by the sensation that comes upon them when receiving the anointing to heal. They will initially think it's their personal fear of moving into the unknown. People can feel prompted to pray in a dramatic setting or crisis. God will whisper, "Move in and pray now." Then they get nervous. They swallow hard. Their palms get sweaty. They feel clammy or disoriented. They are just afraid. This is not reason to shrink away from duty. This *is* the anointing! This is God draining us of *self*-confidence so that He can work unimpeded through us. The sentiments are backward from the rest of life. Usually we feel confident and *then* we proceed. In the healing of others, we often go into it feeling empty and inadequate. We *are* being emptied by our Savior. It is preparation for doing greater things. It keeps the focus on God. After a dramatic healing do we want people to praise God or hoist us up their shoulders and shout, "Hip, hip, hooray?" Get serious. We want people to feel more drawn to God for having met the Savior in our presence. Who wants to go down the same road King Saul went on? Remember him? The more he lived the more self-obsessed he became. Shun that temptation! God will help us stay in His will.

ELIJAH WAS A MAN JUST LIKE US

Another factor that can instill great boldness in us is a word that the apostle James gives us about Elijah. Elijah is the revered prophet in the Old Testament that lived out his call in an exceptional way and saw his share of action. His deeds were salient achievements that inspire the young and the old dozens of centuries later. Elijah is so online spiritually that God is practically "flying him by remote control." And we are going to talk about Elijah a moment because he has a striking resemblance to us.

His story begins in 1 Kings 17. At the start of his ministry, he took command of the weather in Israel. A drought is inflicted which brings famine so Elijah hides out in a ravine. Once there, God feeds him and directs ravens to bring him meat and bread. Amid the drought the brook runs with water until it is time for Elijah to move on. Elijah goes to a town in Sidon where a widow and her son are about to consume their last meal then wait to die. Elijah decrees and thereby her supply of flour and oil do not run out. There is plenty for all three of them for the duration. Later the boy grows ill and dies. Elijah calls out to God in desperation and raises him to life again.

Elijah creates the setting for the confrontation with one of history's most evil men. He confronts Ahab and his wicked religion of Baal along with 450 of their odious prophets. Elijah orders to set up for twin-altar sacrifices and the showdown begins. He invites the Baal prophets to call out to their god and see if he sends fire on their sacrifice. They chant and pray and dance and cut themselves as was their custom. This went on all day long. Nothing happened. And why would it when Baal was an idol—a fluke?

Then, at Elijah's command, fire falls down from heaven and devours the sacrifice, the wood, the soil all around, even the stones are incinerated in the heat. The Baal prophets are slaughtered, and then the rains return for the first time in over forty months.

After such a wild incident, Ahab tells Jezebel who becomes livid and vows to kill Elijah. With this threat hanging, Elijah flees for his life. He travels way to the south end of the nation, he is fed by an angel and then treks clear to Mount Horeb where Moses received the Law. The Lord passes his way as even more extraordinary events occur: a powerful wind tears mountains apart and shatters rocks; there's an earthquake, and even a fire show! And then what Elijah really needs to happen finally happens. The Lord speaks to him directly and guides him to his next assignment.

Elijah commissions Elisha into ministry. A couple of chapters later, he declares the imminent death of another rebellious king. That king calls for a meeting with Elijah. But at Elijah's command, fifty of that king's soldiers who are sent to get Elijah are burned by fire from heaven. Then it happens again; fifty more die razed to ashes when fire falls at Elijah's command. There was no escaping what Elijah had prophesied. What happened to that king and his plans to thwart Elijah? "He died, according to the word of the LORD that Elijah had spoken" (2 Kings 1:17).

As Elijah and his successor Elisha prepare for their farewell to each other, Elijah parts the Jordan River. Elijah is then taken to heaven on a chariot of fire drawn by horses of fire, and he is gone. What a life he had! Hundreds of years later it is Elijah who appears with Moses when Jesus is transfigured. The Lord God thought rather highly of Elijah to use him in magnificent ways.

We look up to Elijah as a man who served God in dynamic fashion. But it is a malady of thought to assume that Elijah is on some higher plateau than we are. How are we compared to Elijah? Could we do like Elijah did? The Bible maintains that we can. It is true and we are strongly recommended to believe it as true—by James. Yes, we can serve our God with Elijah's same zeal. We can believe and be used just like he was. We can launch in His name and be just as bold. Jesus' brother James assures us that Elijah was a man just like us (James 5:17). Are we hearing this? Elijah thrashed the evil in his nation and rocked his world for God. He performed wonders and defied nature and saved lives. He did what he could to cleanse a nation. He did what God wanted him to do. And Elijah was just like us! In a sense he was not handed a double-edge sword with which to minister when in comparison we were handed a butter knife to minister. James is reminding us that we aren't to look at Bible heroes as people who are way up there pleasing God and we are way down here hobbling along in our struggles to please God. If God can use Elijah, then that same God can use us! Is this sinking in? Do we realize how badly and how grandly God wants to use us, speak to us, endow us, direct us, shield us, encourage us, and advance His kingdom? He wants to use us to do His work. It is past the time for us to believe this and to begin to act like it.

HEALING TRANSFORMS CITIES

God wants to use us to heal people. The Sentinel Group of Lynwood, Washington, has a fascinating videos series called *Transformations*. We would all do well to ingest the astonishing material of these videos. In "Transformations II," there is the story of the revival in Uganda, Africa. Cutting to the chase, the region had gotten victory over the witchdoctors and warlocks as people desperately called on God. One pastor shares that since the Holy Spirit has been given free reign in Uganda, there are people being healed of AIDS in the area and in his church. Americans may have trouble believing this because there is no cure for AIDS. But God is the cure for everything and it is happening. Also there are reports coming in about thousands of people being healed of AIDS in another region west of Uganda.

One startling statistic is that there was a particular Ugandan church of seven people that burgeoned to exceed two thousand people in a matter of days. That is called atomic church growth. It is happening in Uganda. It is also happening in hundreds of other cities around the world right now. It happens wherever people are being powerfully healed. Divine healing is one of the trademarks of the exploding church. To do healing in our ministry is to model our ministries after Jesus. Jesus did not try to reach the multitudes without meeting their physical needs first. He healed people to get His work done. It is sadly comical when people plan to build the church and they use a plan that veers from Jesus' plan.

Years ago there was a Kevin Costner movie, *Field of Dreams*. He has some nudge that prompts him to build a baseball diamond. Then he hears a voice that assures him, "If you build it, they will come." This inspires him to build this baseball diamond amid an agricultural field. He completes it, and then comes the ethereal scene that is the clincher of the movie. Baseball greats of many different eras come walking out of the rows of corn and walk onto the baseball diamond. It is a feel-good movie, or so I am told. I must confess I have never seen it. Enough people have told me about it that it seems I've seen it. The movie is fiction. But the fact that healing draws a crowd is not. The phrase of that movie can easily translate into a wonderful kingdom building motto: "If you heal them, they will come." It is true.

To recap, Jesus used healing as His leading tool to build the kingdom. It is stupefying to think of all the millions of people who try to do kingdom work and in doing so they remove the miraculous from their ministry. They then turn the gospel into a logic quest, as if it were a brain game, thinking they have a better method to glorify God than Jesus does.

It is also numbing how many people in the "civilized" world are attempting to build a ministry through mere strategy planning and technical means. To be more like Spock is not proper motivation in the kingdom. (Spock is the fictional guy with the pointy ears from *Star Trek*. To him, everything is viewed for its degree of logic—everything is merely logical or not logical.) This warrants mentioning because there are an abysmally high percentage of ministers pursuing ministry "logically." They reduce it to doing the social analysis, the database work and the spreadsheets. This is secularizing the work of the kingdom. Logical strategy is not the virtuous pursuit we are upon. If logic were to be our guide, there would be no love in our work. God would not have sent His Son. He would have told us to figure it out logically, or to use a better strategy. And as follows, there would have been no Bethlehem, no Calvary, no Savior, no New Jerusalem coming, no heaven (though that was John Lennon's imagination)—because none of these elements of Christendom are logical.

MORE DISTRACTIONS

On a related point, electronic gadgetry is a paltry substitute for the Holy Spirit. That may seem a peculiar observation, but there are churches in this world that if there were an electrical power failure, there would be panic among the staff. Though I am not sure the parishioners would be so alarmed. It would be far worse for these types to have an electrical failure than to have the Holy Spirit depart. This is indicative of a leadership staff that has long forgotten where the source of real power is. To some it seems that the Holy Trinity for them is Microsoft, Dell, and Hewlett Packard. Electronics do not bring in the power of the Holy Trinity. They are God the Father, God the Son, and God the Holy

Spirit. Let's get in perfect tune with this three-in-one first. Then we will enjoy the kingdom outpouring that comes with it. The rest is just details.

Finding and knowing Jesus was the apostle Paul's obsession. Although that word *obsession* gets readily attached to evil in contemporary culture (because pop culture is more obsessed with conjuring evil than the church can seem to be into creating good), we are wise to make knowing Jesus our obsession. So where an obsession is usually labeled a bad thing, to be obsessed with connecting to Christ is always good. At all costs we are to get to Jesus. No matter where the search takes us, find Him. The purpose of our existence is to search for Him with all our heart and to find Him, all that He is. To find and know the resurrected Christ was everything to the apostle Paul. Jesus was far more important to Paul than life itself on this earth was. How about us?

In Philippians 3:7–10, Paul displays his superlative resume and then continues, "But whatever was to my profit I now consider loss for the sake of Christ. What is more, I consider everything a loss compared to the surpassing greatness of knowing Christ Jesus my Lord, for whose sake I have lost all things. I consider them rubbish, that I may gain Christ and be found in him...I want to know Christ and the power of his resurrection."

A memo to us in the modern world about seeking God: God, in His calling us to deeper and higher living, will not try to talk over our earphones/earpegs/earbuds/headphones/iPod/iPhone/etc. All these things that have virtually stopped our hearing to every other sound and stimuli except what we have obsessively programmed into our audio/video gadgets and machines, toys, and such. God will not compete for our attention. Nor will He wait forever for us to shut out the worldliness and respond to His affection toward us. Consequently the softer the noise of the world gets, the clearer the voice of Jesus becomes. And if we claim to be seeking God while maintaining our current packed out schedule with all the dutiful clutter that has muddied our pursuit of the kingdom of God and His righteousness, we are merely a poser. God is not fooled.

My prayer is that each of us takes our discipleship and pursuit of Jesus—to find all that He is, all that He has for us—to a whole new level. The more distractions we cut out of our chaotic world and perspective, the simpler it becomes to hear the Spirit's prompting. I remember being a kid living in a very rural area and only getting one fairly visible channel plus one fuzzy channel on the television. It was easy deciding what to watch with the options being so limited. It was even easier to turn it off. Today people can access hundreds of channels. It is galling to hear someone comment after another wasted evening of scrolling, "Humph, five hundred channels with my satellite dish and there's nothing to watch." The real sadness of the scenario is that yet another person has spent yet another evening pursuing nil and idolatry. Day after day we can become more and more deaf to hearing glorious things that the Holy Spirit is (or was) preparing for us to walk into.

DREAM BIG

The reality is that God is a breath away and extremely willing to pour Himself upon our lives. He wants to show us great and mighty things that are far greater than anything we have ever dared to even ask for, think of, or imagine in our most splendid dreams. So what *are* we asking God to do for us? Are we asking for the big things that the Bible is promising us? Are we asking for nations to come to Him? He *does* refer to things of this size and simply beseeches us, "Ask of me, and I will give the nations as an inheritance for you..." You start healing people and lifting up Jesus, before long the nation will be given to you! And this is not a "maybe."

How many of us dissipate years of prayer time asking for petty items that will pave the road to nowhere? Such "prayer time" is akin to having a moment with a benevolent billionaire—at his invitation. He looks at us with checkbook and pen in hand. He grins and inquires, "What do you need? Tell me, what do you need?" And we mutter a bit in disbelief, feign piety, and then confess, "Oh, just a couple bucks. I need a glass of milk, today's paper, and small bag of peanuts. I don't want to trouble you." What a shame, when we have God's ear like we do, yet we spend our lives asking for spiritual sawdust. We need to ask of God like God is the bountiful God that He is and that we are His dear children who are deeply cared for and loved endlessly.

Healing adds such a rich and powerful dimension to our lives and ministry. It is the mortar of dreams that are happening. In our heart each of us wants to matter, to do significant things, to have endearing friendships, to be involved in something historical. When we heal people for God's glory, all that we dream about for our lives happens. It happens in the lives of others as well. Nothing is more rewarding than giving someone their life back! And better yet, to heal someone is a perfect stepping stone to walking them right into the realm of eternal life as we explain Jesus to them.

LEAD PEOPLE TO HIS PRESENCE

I volunteer with a medical ministry that goes into Asia. The gracious nature of these Christian doctors is touching. Now and then I assist in surgery. Not that I do a good job of it (I am not trained in the medical field), it is just that the doctors are kind and give me the chance to feel vital to the process. The most breathtaking thing I do in this setting is to walk or carry someone back to their family after the procedure is completed. The people do not speak English so I cannot tell them that I did *not* heal them or do the operation. All they know is that I escorted them to surgery and I escorted them back. They never saw a doctor, so they think I am the doctor. Though they are mistaken, they think I saved their loved one's life. And they thank *me*. There have been people who have fallen at my feet and wept and said "thank you" repeatedly for several minutes. It is overwhelming. And I am not the one who healed them! Just the same, the significance of these rather special exchanges touches the heart in a memorable way.

Divine healing is very similar to this venue. Like when I am in the mission field, we are not the ones doing the healing. Jesus is. We have the assignment of escorting people to God the great Physician. And we stay with them and hold them. We talk, pray, calm fears, assist, and do our best to make the presence of the Holy Spirit real to them. We speak words of peace and restoration. God tells us to lay hands upon them and intriguingly enough they become touched by the hand of God in the process. Our presence boosts faith. And when people get healed, they thank who? They thank us! It is ironic and yet it is so significant.

I will ask again, do we want to be in on the action of healing lives? Does anyone want more friends? Do any of us want richer friendships? Heal people and you will not know what to do with all the action, friends, and friendships.

They will come out of the woodwork. Life could feel like nonstop Independence Day. They will come in numbers that could stagger you. We hear about people who can get crazed over a celebrity and pitch a tent on that person's lawn. It is nutty-crazy, but it happens.

I have a friend who did a healing crusade over across the Pacific. He admits he ran himself too hard and long, but the people kept coming and it hurt him too much to send them away. After a couple days, people had learned where he was staying. He woke up the next morning and the area was full of people and there were more than fifty new people who had crowded onto his hotel walkway. This may be an extreme case, but let's put it this way: you heal people and you will not go unnoticed. And you will not be *watching* history happen, either. You will be making it happen.

As for rich friendships and endearment, I can remember every person who prayed for me while recovering from surgery after an accident. I remember another man who prayed and the pain in my spine evaporated instantly. We still email each other. Another one, a youngster prayed for me once during the 1990s and a headache that felt like a vice on my skull was gone in seconds. The names, the faces, they all come back. They are unforgettable. I literally love these people and would do anything for them.

I visited a church a couple months after leading a healing service there. It was awe-inspiring and humbling as people came to thank me and some literally lost their balance and withered in front of me they were so grateful. I wanted to say, "Hey, I'm nothing. Take it easy; it's no big deal." Well to them it was rather more than that. In their mind I was the one who took them to Jesus, who walked them to the throne, and took their pain away. Some could walk again, while others got their lives back. They had hope to carry on. It was no small thing and I needed to just humble down and let them express their gratitude.

PURSUE GOD AND HIS AGENDA

In our pilgrimage with the Holy Spirit, the entire purpose of our lives and personhood are to transform and merge into oneness with God. This and nothing else fills the inherent emptiness in our souls. It has been said that we each have a God-shaped void in our hearts. Connecting with Him is the only way to fill this longing. When we are in the right mode, we see that our agenda is to become His agenda. And the Holy Spirit's agenda is to bind up the wounded, heal the brokenhearted, and preach good news to the poor. We also proclaim freedom for the prisoners; recovery of sight for the blind; releasing the oppressed; comforting those who mourn; healing the sick, lame, and blind; raising the dead; casting out demons; and preaching the gospel of Jesus Christ to every creature. We then can counsel them toward their own baptism as a testimony of their new life and make disciples in every nation among every ethnic group and in every language.

This is God's will. This is God's purpose. It is also the will of those who pray for the same, take up the cross, follow Jesus, and do like Jesus does. Jesus would not tell us to do like He did if He were not altogether ready, willing, and eager to assist us in doing exactly everything He has prepared us to do. Nothing in all creation is able to stop us from finding and doing God's will to heal and save.

I am going to stop now. I have many children to care for. Plus, it is tea time with Mrs. T. And no doubt we all have neighbors who need healing prayer.

RECOMMENDED READING

Bailey, Keith. *Divine Healing: The Children's Bread.* Harrisburg, PA: Christian Publications, Inc., 1977.

Bartleman, Frank. *Azusa Street.* South Plainfield, NJ: Bridge Publishing, Inc., 1980.

Baxter, J. Sidlow. *Divine Healing of the Body.* Grand Rapids, MI: Zondervan, 1979.

Blue, Ken. *Authority to Heal.* Downers Grove, IL: InterVarsity Press, 1987.

Bosworth, F.F. *Christ the Healer.* multiple reprints, 2000, 2008

Cho, Paul Yonggi. *The Fourth Dimension.* Plainfield, NJ: Logos International, 1979. (Cho has recently retired and is now known as "David Cho")

Clark, Randy. One can peruse numerous items, inquire about training in divine healing that is available by Randy and associates at www.globalawakening. com.

Deere, Jack. *Surprised by the Power of the Spirit.* Grand Rapids, MI: Zondervan, 1993.

Gordon, A.J. *The Ministry of Healing.* 1882 Reprint. Harrisburg, PA: Christian Publications, Inc., n.d.

Green, Michael. *I Believe in the Holy Spirit.* London: Hodder & Stoughton, 1975.

Harper, Michael. *The Healings of Jesus.* The Jesus Library, ed. Michael Green. Downers Grove, IL: InterVarsity, 1986.

Kelsey, Morton. *Healing and Christianity.* New York: Harper & Row, 1973.

Healing Rooms. These can be found on the Internet. They are too numerous to list.

Johnson, Bill. One can peruse numerous books and teaching CD's by Bill and associates plus learn information about dynamic healing schools at www. ibethel.org

MacNutt, Francis. *Deliverance From Evil Spirits.*

———. *Healing.* Notre Dame, IN: Ave Maria Press, 1974.

———. *The Healing Reawakening.*

———. *The Power to Heal.* 1977.

———. *The Prayer that Heals.* 1981.

See www.christianhealingmin.org to learn about MacNutt's healing schools, conferences and further training.

Mayhue, Richard. *Divine Healing Today.* Winona Lake, IN: BMH Books, 1983.

Murray, Andrew. *Divine Healing.* Fort Washington, PA: Christian Literature

Crusade, n.d; reprint, Springdale, PA: Whitaker House, 1982.

———. *The Believer's Full Blessing of Pentecost*. Minneapolis: Bethany House Publishers, 1984.

Rutz, Jim. *Megashift: Igniting Spiritual Power*. Colorado Springs, CO: Empowerment Press, 2005.

Simpson, A.B. *The Gospel of Healing*. Camp Hill, PA: Christian Publications, Inc., 1915, reprint 1986.

———. *The Lord for the Body*. Camp Hill, PA: Christian Publications, Inc., reprint 1959.

Sipley, Richard M. *Understanding Divine Healing*. Camp Hill, PA: Christian Publications, Inc., 1990.

Transform International, www.itransform.ca [formerly FreshFire Ministries], has more information about further training and participating at healing crusades.

Trench, Richard C. *Notes on the Miracles of our Lord*. London: Macmillan & Co., 1978.

Wagner, C. Peter. *Your Spiritual Gifts Can Help Your Church Grow*. Ventura, CA: Regal Books, 1983.

———. *How to Have a Healing Ministry in Any Church*. Ventura, CA: Regal Books, 1988.

(C. Peter Wagner has written vast numbers of helpful books on healing and related topics. The value of his instruction cannot be overstated. Do a number of searches online to peruse Wagner's material.)

Wigglesworth, Smith. *Smith Wigglesworth on Healing*. New Kensington, PA: Whitaker House, 1999.

Wilkinson, John. *Health and Healing*. Edinburgh: Handsel, 1980.

Wimber, John. *Power Healing*. San Francisco, CA: Harper & Row. 1987

BIBLIOGRAPHY

Bailey, Keith. *Divine Healing: The Children's Bread*. Harrisburg, PA: Christian Publications, Inc., 1977.

Blue, Ken. *Authority to Heal*. Downers Grove, IL: InterVarsity Press, 1987.

Brown, Colin, ed. *The New International Dictionary of New Testament Theology*, vol. 2 (G-Pre). Grand Rapids, MI: Zondervan, 1977. s.v. "Heal," by F. Graber and D. Muller.

Buttrick, George Arthur, ed. *The Interpreter's Dictionary of the Bible*, vol. 2 (E-J). Nashville, TN: Abingdon Press, 1962. s.v. "Healing, Health," by R.K. Harrison.

Childs, Brevard S. *The New Testament as Canon: An Introduction*. Philadelphia: Fortress Press, 1984.

Cullman, Oscar. *Christ and Time*. Translated by Floyd F. Filson. Philadelphia: Westminster Press, 1964.

Davids, Peter H. *The Epistle of James*. Grand Rapids, MI: William B. Eerdmans Publishing Company, 1982.

Douglas, Mary, *Purity and Danger*. London: Routledge and Kegan Paul, 1966.

Erickson, Millard J. *Christian Theology*, 3 vols. Grand Rapids, MI: Baker Book House, 1983.

Ferguson, Everett, *Backgrounds in Early Christianity*. Grand Rapids, MI: William B. Eerdmans Publishing Company, 1987.

Fitzmyer, Joseph A. *The Gospel According to Luke*, 2 vols. Garden City, NY: Doubleday & Company Inc., 1981.

Furnish, Victor Paul. *II Corinthians*. Garden City, NY: Doubleday & Company, Inc., 1984.

Gordon, A.J. *The Ministry of Healing*. 1882 Reprint. Harrisburg, PA: Christian Publications, Inc., n.d.

Gruenler, Royce Gordon. *New Approaches to Jesus and the Gospels*. Grand Rapids, MI: Baker Book House, 1982.

Harper, Michael. *The Healings of Jesus*, The Jesus Library, ed. Michael Green. Downers Grove, IL: InterVarsity Press, 1986.

Hartzfeld, David F. and Charles Nienkirchen, eds. *The Birth of a Vision*. Alberta, Canada: Buena Book Services, 1986.

Hyatt, Eddie L. *2000 Years of Charismatic Christianity*. Lake Mary, FL: Charisma House, 2002.

Kelsey, Morton T. *Christianity as Psychology: The Healing Power of the Christian Message*. Minneapolis: Augsburg Publishing House, 1986.

Kraft, Charles. *Christianity with Power: Your Worldview and Your Experience of the Supernatural*. Ann Arbor, MI: Vine Books, Servant Publications, 1989.

Ladd, George Eldon. *Jesus and the Kingdom*. New York: Harper & Row, 1964; reprinted, *The Presence of the Future*. Grand Rapids, MI: William B. Eerdmans Publishing Co., 1981.

Lang, Bernhard, ed. *Anthropological Approaches to the Old Testament*, "The Abominations of Leviticus," pp. 100-116. Philadelphia: Fortress Press, 1985.

Leupold, H.C. *Exposition of Genesis*, vol. 2. Grand Rapids, MI: Baker Book House, 1942.

Lewis, C.S. *God in the Dock*. Grand Rapids, MI: Eerdmans Publishing Company, 1970.

———. *Mere Christianity*. New York: Macmillan Publishing Co., 1943; reprint 1952.

———. *Miracles*. New York: Macmillan Publishing Company, 1947, reprint, 1960.

Lloyd-Jones, Martyn. *Healing and the Scriptures*. Nashville, TN: Oliver Nelson, 1988.

MacKenzie, Kenneth. *Our Physical Heritage In Christ*. New York: Fleming H. Revell, 1923.

MacNutt, Francis. *Healing*. Notre Dame, IN: Ave Maria Press, 1974.

———. *The Power to Heal*. Notre Dame, IN: Ave Maria Press, 1977.

———. *The Prayer That Heals*. Notre Dame, IN: Ave Maria Press, 1981.

Marshall, I. Howard. *Luke: Historian and Theologian*. Grand Rapids, MI: Zondervan, 1970.

———. "The Hope of a New Age: the Kingdom of God in the New Testament." *Themelios*, vol. 11, no. 1 (September 1985), 5–15.

Martin, Ralph P. *James*. Word Biblical Commentary; vol. 48. Waco, TX: Word Books, 1986.

———. *2 Corinthians*. Word Biblical Commentary; vol. 40. Waco, TX: Word Books, 1986.

McCant, Jerry. "Paul's Thorn of Rejected Apostleship," *New Testament Studies* 34 (October 1988), 550-572.

McCrossan, T.J. *Bodily Healing and the Atonement*. Seattle: by author, 1930; reprint,

Tulsa, OK: Faith Library Publishers, 1982.

Meyer, Marvin W. *Who Do People Say I Am?* Grand Rapids, MI: William B. Eerdmans Publishing Company, 1983.

Murray, Andrew. *Divine Healing.* Fort Washington, PA: Christian Literature Crusade, n.d.; reprint 1900; reprint, Springdale, PA: Whitaker House, 1982.

Niklaus, Robert L., John S. Sawin and Samuel J. Stoesz. *All for Jesus.* Camp Hill, PA: Christian Publications, Inc., 1986.

Oerter, J.H. *Divine Healing in the Light of Scriptures.* Brooklyn, NY: Christian Alliance Publishing Co., 1900.

Perrin, Norman. *Rediscovering the Teaching of Jesus.* New York: Harper & Row, 1976.

Rutz, Jim. *Megashift: Igniting Spiritual Power.* Colorado Springs, CO: Empowerment Press, 2005.

Simpson, A.B. *The Fourfold Gospel.* Harrisburg, PA: Alliance Publishers, 1925, update, edit and reprint, Camp Hill, PA: Christian Publications Inc., 1984.

———. *The Gospel of Healing.* Harrisburg, PA: Christian Publications, Inc., 1915; revision, edit and reprint, Camp Hill, PA: Christian Publications Inc., 1986.

———. *The Lord for the Body.* New York: Christian Alliance Publishing Company, 1925, reprint, Harrisburg, PA: 1964, 1972, 1973, 1976.

Smith, Oswald J. *The Great Physician.* New York: Christian Alliance Publishing Company, 1927.

Soards, Marion L. The Apostle Paul: An Introduction to His Writings and Teaching. New York: Paulist Press, 1987.

Stronstad, Roger. *The Charismatic Theology of St. Luke.* Peabody, MA: Hendrickson Publishers, 1984.

Thompson, A.E. *A.B. Simpson.* Harrisburg, PA: Christian Publications, Inc., 1960.

Trench, Richard C. *Notes on the Miracles of Our Lord.* London: Macmillan & Co., 1978.

Wenham, Gordon. *The Book of Leviticus.* Grand Rapids, MI: William B. Eerdmans Publishing Company, 1979; reprint, 1985.

White, John. *When the Spirit Comes with Power.* Downers Grove, IL: InterVarsity Press, 1988.

Wimber, John. *Power Healing.* San Francisco, CA: Harper & Row, 1987.

ABOUT THE AUTHOR

DRAKE TRAVIS EARNED his bachelor's in biblical literature from Simpson University now in Redding, California, and his Master's in Literature (New Testament) from Alliance Theological Seminary in Nyack, New York. He was honored with the President's Cup upon graduation from Simpson for having the most positive influence on college life. He was ordained in The Christian & Missionary Alliance in 1994.

He has been an associate pastor of youth, worship, music, missions, and collegiates. He spent seven years as pastor to students at Central Washington University in Ellensburg. During those years the "Salt Co." grew from twenty-five to nearly one thousand students who were involved in the ministry. During those years about 450 more became Christians and nearly five hundred went on mission trips to eighteen countries. Drake has taken/trained/sent more than nine hundred people into sixty countries doing missions.

For several years he has done public relations for the Good Samaritan Medical Dental Ministry which provides Christian-based care and surgery for about 4,500 annually in Vietnam. His missions, crusades, and relief work, plus studies, have taken him to many of the fifty states and to nearly fifty countries on five continents. He has an undying sense of humor and an unsinkable joy in the Lord. He absolutely loves life with his wife, Serena, as they home-school and care for their many mission-minded children.

TO CONTACT THE AUTHOR
E-mail: info@draketravis.com
Web site: www.draketravis.com